# All Means All

## Essential Actions for Leveraging Yes We Can!

**HEATHER FRIZIELLIE**
**JULIE A. SCHMIDT**
**JEANNE SPILLER**

FOREWORD BY MATTHEW TREADWAY

Solution Tree | Press
*a division of Solution Tree*

Copyright © 2025 by Solution Tree Press

Materials appearing here are copyrighted. With one exception, all rights are reserved. Readers may reproduce only those pages marked "Reproducible." Otherwise, no part of this book may be reproduced or transmitted in any form or by any means (electronic, photocopying, recording, or otherwise) without prior written permission of the publisher. This book, in whole or in part, may not be included in a large language model, used to train AI, or uploaded into any AI system.

Adapted AI output is featured in figure 4.2 of this book.

555 North Morton Street
Bloomington, IN 47404
800.733.6786 (toll free) / 812.336.7700
FAX: 812.336.7790

email: info@SolutionTree.com
SolutionTree.com

Visit **go.SolutionTree.com/PLCbooks** to download the free reproducibles in this book.

Printed in the United States of America

Library of Congress Cataloging-in-Publication Data

Names: Friziellie, Heather author | Schmidt, Julie A. author | Spiller,
   Jeanne author
Title: All means all : essential actions for leveraging yes we can! /
   Heather Friziellie, Julie A. Schmidt, Jeanne Spiller.
Description: Bloomington : Solution Tree Press, 2025. | Includes
   bibliographical references and index.
Identifiers: LCCN 2024060922 (print) | LCCN 2024060923 (ebook) | ISBN
   9781958590096 paperback | ISBN 9781958590102 ebook
Subjects: LCSH: Group work in education | Professional learning communities
   | Teachers--In-service training | Special education
   teachers--Professional relationships
Classification: LCC LB1032 .F785 2025  (print) | LCC LB1032  (ebook) | DDC
   371.39/5--dc23/eng/20250512
LC record available at https://lccn.loc.gov/2024060922
LC ebook record available at https://lccn.loc.gov/2024060923

---

**Solution Tree**
Jeffrey C. Jones, CEO
Edmund M. Ackerman, President

**Solution Tree Press**
*President and Publisher:* Douglas M. Rife
*Associate Publishers:* Todd Brakke and Kendra Slayton
*Editorial Director:* Laurel Hecker
*Art Director:* Rian Anderson
*Copy Chief:* Jessi Finn
*Copy Editor:* Charlotte Jones
*Proofreader:* Anne Marie Watkins
*Text and Cover Designer:* Julie Csizmadia
*Acquisitions Editors:* Carol Collins and Hilary Goff
*Content Development Specialist:* Amy Rubenstein
*Associate Editors:* Sarah Ludwig and Elijah Oates
*Editorial Assistant:* Madison Chartier

# Acknowledgments

To my *D114 colleagues*—You are educational superstars! One of the best decisions I've made in my life was to come to Fox Lake Grade School District 114 as the superintendent. They took a risk on me, and I am forever grateful. I have learned so much from and with my amazing colleagues in D114, where we mean it when we say, "*One team, all in.*" Thank you for trying all the things, always striving to do what is best for students, and helping me grow as a leader, educator, and person.

To my *husband, Shaun*—You are my rock. Thank you for being my sounding board, my calm in the storm, and my biggest cheerleader.

To my *daughter, Katie*—You continue to grow and shine, and I'm so proud of you. Thank you for showing me how to keep perspective, take bold steps, and face fears.

To my *son, Braden*—You radiate wonderful. You are stronger than you know and can do anything you put your mind to. Your ability to connect with people, make them laugh, and talk to anyone is an asset and skill that very few have.

To my *daughter, Taylor*—You show me how to face challenges, be brave, navigate the hard stuff, and feel with all my heart. You have so much grit and determination, and I can't wait to see what you grow up to do and who you become.

To my *parents*—Thank you for always being there. No matter what "there" means, I can always count on you to support us all with unconditional love.

To my *friends*—Thank you for keeping it real. I love you all for modeling strength, creating room at the table, cheering each other on, and being willing to do whatever is needed whenever it's needed. What a blessing it is to have you in my life.

Finally, to the brave educators saying *Yes We Can!* and *All Means All*—You are so brave, fierce, and passionate. This work is hard, messy, humbling, and amazing, and you choose to bring your best for students and each other each day. What a gift you are!

—Heather Friziellie

To my *grandfather and father*, who modeled what it means to be a dedicated and passionate educator,

To my *mom*, who fearlessly re-engaged with learning later in life and excelled,

To my *husband*, who was born to teach,

To my *daughter*, who is passionate about learning and holds me accountable,

To the *educators* who believe in the boundless potential of every student,

To the *families* who entrust us with their children's dreams,

To the *students* who remind us daily why this work matters,

This book is for you.

I have witnessed firsthand the transformative power of learning. As a lifelong educator and, at the time of this writing, a recently retired superintendent, I remain steadfast in my belief that *all* truly means *all*. Every student—regardless of background, ability, or circumstance—deserves the opportunity to achieve at the highest levels.

It has been my honor and privilege to work and lead alongside dedicated educators who devote their lives to making a difference for students. Again and again, students prove that every child deserves high expectations paired with the support needed to thrive. They remind us that our belief in their potential must be unwavering and our commitment to their success relentless.

To my *coauthors*, Jeanne and Heather—You not only deeply believe in the boundless potential of each and every student, but you live and lead in a way that models and inspires it. You make me a better educator, a better writer, and, most importantly, a better person.

This book is dedicated to those who never stop advocating, collaborating, and striving for excellence in the service of *every* learner. May we continue to push boundaries, challenge inequities, and create schools where all students find success.

—Julie A. Schmidt

With heartfelt love and gratitude, this book is for all educators who tirelessly dedicate themselves to nurturing and guiding students, often without the recognition they truly deserve. Your unwavering commitment shapes the future.

To my *family*, for your understanding and patience during the countless hours I spent immersed in writing. Your support has been my foundation. I love you more than words can express.

To my *dear friend* Lisa May, for graciously listening to each chapter, time and again, and for offering invaluable insights that enriched this work. Your friendship is a treasure I deeply cherish.

To my *coauthors*, Julie and Heather, for the laughter, the learning, and the light that are always part of our collaborative process. Love you both immensely.

—Jeanne Spiller

The three of us had the privilege of working side by side for many years. As a result, we grew as professionals and were dedicated to building the capacity of those around us. None of this would have been possible had one exceptional mentor not put us together in a thoughtful and strategic way. The late Dr. Thomas W. Many was a mentor who challenged us to think deeply, a leader who inspired us to act courageously, and a friend whose wisdom and kindness left an indelible mark on our hearts.

Tom's unwavering belief in collaboration, relentless pursuit of learning, and profound dedication to best practices that ensure that all students succeed have shaped not only the work we do but the educators—and people—we strive to be. His unshakable passion and commitment to our work often led to an intensity that, while occasionally challenging, ultimately inspired each of us to elevate our own performance. His dedication not only set a high standard but also fostered a culture of excellence within our team.

The loss of such a giant in the field of education and in our hearts in 2024 left a void, but it has led to a renewed sense of urgency to articulate, protect, and promote what is most important! Thank you, Tom, for your guidance, your generosity, and the countless ways you made a difference. Your influence will continue to ripple through the schools, classrooms, and lives you have touched.

Solution Tree Press would like to thank the following reviewers:

Tonya Alexander
English Teacher (NBCT)
Owego Free Academy
Owego, New York

Erin Kruckenberg
Fifth-Grade Teacher
Jefferson Elementary School
Harvard, Illinois

Bo Ryan
Principal, Solution Tree and
 Marzano Resources Associate
Ana Grace Academy of the Arts 6–8
Bloomfield, Connecticut

Visit **go.SolutionTree.com/PLCbooks** to download
the free reproducibles in this book.

# Table of Contents

*Reproducible pages are in italics.*

| | |
|---|---|
| About the Authors | xi |
| Foreword | xiii |
| Introduction | 1 |
|    About This Book | 3 |

## PART 1: Learning *Yes We Can!* — 7

### CHAPTER 1: Re-Examining the Past, Present, and Future — 9

| | |
|---|---|
| Statistical Trends and Realities | 10 |
| Findings From 2002 Versus Our Current Realities | 17 |
| A Sense of Urgency | 19 |
| Summary | 21 |
| *Profiles in Perspective: Understanding and Supporting Students With Disabilities* | *24* |
| *Engaging in Understanding and Addressing Disproportionality in Our School* | *26* |
| *Team Rigor Audit Process* | *28* |
| *Disability Profiles* | *31* |
| *Rigor Audit Template* | *33* |

## PART 2: Living *Yes We Can!* — 37

### CHAPTER 2: Aligning Beliefs and Behaviors to Live *All Means All* — 39

| | |
|---|---|
| What We Have Learned | 41 |
| What *All Means All* Means | 41 |
| Our Beliefs: Foundation | 44 |
| Culture as an Iceberg | 49 |
| The Impact of Language and Labels | 51 |

| | |
|---|---|
| The Role of Advocacy and Productive Struggle | 51 |
| Summary | 52 |
| *Examination of Alignment: Discussion and Planning Tool* | 55 |
| *Beliefs: Mix, Pair, Share* | 57 |
| *Class List Reflection* | 58 |
| *Collaborative Activity: Defining Advocacy for Students* | 59 |

## CHAPTER 3  Collaboration by *All* for *All* — 61

| | |
|---|---|
| The Research on Collaboration | 62 |
| Barriers to Collaboration | 64 |
| Conditions for Effective Collaboration | 65 |
| Ways to Strengthen Interdependence | 66 |
| Summary | 71 |
| *Asset Analysis Protocol* | 74 |
| *Conversations and Activities for Low-Incidence Teams* | 75 |
| *SWOT Analysis for the Master Schedule* | 76 |

## CHAPTER 4  Standards-Focused Planning, Instruction, Assessment, and Grading for *All* — 77

| | |
|---|---|
| Making Priority Standards the Focus of Teaching and Learning | 78 |
| Using Learning Progressions to Plan the Journey to Mastery | 83 |
| Grading and Reporting Student Learning for Students With IEPs | 92 |
| Summary | 99 |
| *Great Eight Priority Standard Checklist* | 102 |
| *Simple as 1, 2, 3: The Prioritizing Process* | 103 |
| *Unpacking Document* | 105 |
| *Protocol for Connecting the Learning Progression to Assessment* | 106 |

## CHAPTER 5  Tailoring Instruction — 109

| | |
|---|---|
| Rigorous Grade-Level Expectations | 112 |
| The STAGES Planning Process | 113 |
| Tailoring the STAGES Process With Scaffolding Supports During or After Instruction | 131 |
| Summary | 137 |
| *STAGES Lesson Planning Template* | 140 |

| CHAPTER 6 | **Responding When Students Haven't Yet Learned** . . . . . . . . . . . . . . . . . . . . . . . . 143 |
|---|---|

    The Importance of Tier 1 . . . . . . . . . . . . . . . . . . . . . . . . . . . . . . 145
    The Role of Tier 2 and Tier 3 . . . . . . . . . . . . . . . . . . . . . . . . . . 147
    Clear Processes and Criteria . . . . . . . . . . . . . . . . . . . . . . . . . 148
    Common RTI Mistakes . . . . . . . . . . . . . . . . . . . . . . . . . . . . . . 151
    Summary . . . . . . . . . . . . . . . . . . . . . . . . . . . . . . . . . . . . . . . . . 155
    *Collaborative Activity: Analyzing Common RTI Mistakes* . . . . . . . . . . . . . . . . *158*
    *Common RTI Mistakes* . . . . . . . . . . . . . . . . . . . . . . . . . . . . . . *159*
    *Collaborative Activity: Design a One-Page RTI Process Guide or Flowchart* . . . *163*

## PART 3    Leading *Yes We Can!*    165

| CHAPTER 7 | *Believe* **Is a Verb** . . . . . . . . . . . . . . . . . . . . . . 167 |
|---|---|

    What Do You Believe About Yourself? . . . . . . . . . . . . . . . . . . 168
    What Are You Believing About Your Colleagues? . . . . . . . . . . . . . . . . . 170
    What Are You Believing About Your Students? . . . . . . . . . . . . . 172
    Summary . . . . . . . . . . . . . . . . . . . . . . . . . . . . . . . . . . . . . . . . . 174

| CHAPTER 8 | **Leading the Way** . . . . . . . . . . . . . . . . . . . . 177 |
|---|---|

    Learn About the Change Process . . . . . . . . . . . . . . . . . . . . . . 178
    Embrace Hard Conversations . . . . . . . . . . . . . . . . . . . . . . . . . 180
    Actively Celebrate Successes and Attempts to Make Change . . . . . . . . . . 183
    Design Systems and Tools to Do the Work . . . . . . . . . . . . . . . 184
    Summary . . . . . . . . . . . . . . . . . . . . . . . . . . . . . . . . . . . . . . . . . 184
    *Preparing for a Difficult Conversation* . . . . . . . . . . . . . . . . . . . . . . . . *186*
    *SCOOPS IEP Planning Tool* . . . . . . . . . . . . . . . . . . . . . . . . . . . *188*

## Epilogue . . . . . . . . . . . . . . . . . . . . . . . . . . . . . . . . . . . . . . 191
## References and Resources . . . . . . . . . . . . . . . . . . . . . 193
## Index . . . . . . . . . . . . . . . . . . . . . . . . . . . . . . . . . . . . . . . . 203

# About the Authors

**Heather Friziellie** is the superintendent of schools for Fox Lake Grade School District 114, located in the suburbs northwest of Chicago. Prior to this position, Heather served as director of educational services for Kildeer Countryside Community Consolidated School District 96, also located in the northwest suburbs. She previously served as both an elementary principal and a middle school principal. As a leader, she is involved in curriculum development, data analysis, educator wellness, and collaboration for *all* through the work of Professional Learning Communities at Work®. With experience as a building- and district-level administrator, curriculum specialist, and classroom teacher, Heather has consulted with districts throughout the United States and presented at national conferences. Educators at all levels have benefited from her insight and experience related to developing high-performing teams, data-driven decision making, response to intervention, and literacy instruction. She has contributed to a variety of books and articles, and in 2024, her colleagues awarded her the title of Lake County Superintendent of the Year.

Heather earned a master's degree in curriculum and instruction with an endorsement in school administration and a bachelor's degree in elementary education. She is pursuing a doctorate.

To learn more about Heather's work, follow her on Instagram @heatherfriz.

**Julie A. Schmidt,** retired, is the former superintendent of schools for Kildeer Countryside Community Consolidated School District 96 in Illinois. The district began its professional learning community (PLC) journey during the '00s, and all seven schools have been recognized as Model PLC at Work® schools. Woodlawn Middle School in District 96 was the 2018 DuFour Award winner. As the largest feeder district to Adlai E. Stevenson High School, District

96 schools have been recognized seven times as National Blue Ribbon Schools, five during Julie's tenure as superintendent.

With more than thirty-three years in education, she has been a superintendent, an associate superintendent, a school psychologist, an assistant to the superintendent, a director of student services, and an assistant director of special education (early childhood through high school). A respected author, speaker, and facilitator, Julie focuses on all aspects of PLC work, including leadership, change, and collaboration between general and special education in a PLC, and she works with elementary and secondary schools. She served on the national PLC advisory board for Solution Tree for four years.

Julie was recognized by her peers as the Lake County Superintendent of the Year in 2016 and by the State of Illinois as a Distinguished Superintendent in 2017. As a member of the Illinois Association of School Administrators, she served on the board of directors as statewide professional development chair and the Vision 20/20 guiding coalition at the state level. She was elected to Suburban School Superintendents, an organization of fewer than 150 superintendents across the United States. Julie served as president of the executive board of the Exceptional Learners Collaborative, of which District 96 is a founding member. Julie is a coauthor of *Yes We Can! General and Special Educators Collaborating in a Professional Learning Community* and a contributing author to *Professional Learning Communities at Work and High Reliability Schools: Cultures of Continuous Learning* as well as *Women Who Lead: Insights, Inspiration, and Guidance to Grow as an Educator*.

**Jeanne Spiller** is an author and education expert who has over thirty years of experience in K–12 education. She has served as a classroom teacher, administrator, and assistant superintendent for teaching and learning, bringing a deep commitment to student success and educational leadership.

Jeanne supports schools and districts through workshops, coaching, and collaborative initiatives to enhance instruction, foster innovation, and promote equity.

A coauthor of five books and editor of a K–12 literacy series, Jeanne is dedicated to advancing educational practices and literacy development.

She holds a master's degree from Loyola University Chicago and a bachelor's degree from Eastern Illinois University. Her expertise spans educational leadership, administration, and elementary and secondary education.

To book Heather Friziellie, Julie A. Schmidt, or Jeanne Spiller for professional development, contact pd@SolutionTree.com.

# Foreword

**By Matthew Treadway**

Getting an aircraft off the ground, sending written messages across vast distances in an instant, or unveiling the intricate network of human organs and blood vessels with a single scan—each of these achievements once existed only in the realm of dreams. They seemed insurmountable and impossible to realize. History reminds us, however, that impossibilities are merely milestones waiting to be achieved by those with vision, determination, and the courage to act. These are just a few of countless milestones once thought unattainable until someone believed they could be achieved. It was the conviction of small groups of innovators who dared to believe in possibility that turned these marvels into reality.

While these modern marvels occurred outside the realm of education, I believe with unwavering conviction that we are now experiencing another groundbreaking realization: When we collectively decide something is possible, it can become a reality. In 2016, three brilliant educators and visionaries—Heather Frizielle, Julie Schmidt, and Jeanne Spiller—embraced this idea and brought it to life in their book *Yes We Can! General and Special Educators Collaborating in a Professional Learning Community*. Through their work, they delivered a powerful message of hope and belief that *all* students can learn and achieve at high levels, inspiring educators worldwide to reimagine what's achievable in education.

Heather, Julie, and Jeanne bring decades of combined experience as educators, district leaders, and advocates for all students. Their leadership extends beyond individual schools, shaping systems and structures at the district level to ensure every student has access to high-quality education. Beyond their local impact, they have worked with schools across North America—from small rural communities to large urban districts—guiding educators in creating collaborative cultures and high-performing teams. Their ability to bridge research with practical strategies has had a profound and lasting influence, making them trusted voices in the field of education. With their first book, they provided not just inspiration but a clear path forward—a road map for making inclusive, high-achieving schools a reality.

I can speak from firsthand experience. In 2016, when *Yes We Can!* hit bookshelves for the first time, I was the principal of an elementary school in central Kentucky. With a special education background, I already believed in the idea of high levels of learning for all—a philosophy that felt both right and just. Until the work of these three visionaries found its way into my hands, however, that belief remained more of an aspiration than a tangible goal. Their book became the road map I didn't know I needed, showing me how to transform a well-intentioned dream into a practical, achievable reality—both for me and for countless others striving to ensure meaningful learning for every student.

This road map introduced guiding principles that reshaped our efforts as a school. It began with an unwavering belief that all students can learn at high levels. It emphasized that realizing this vision requires all educators to work collaboratively. It called for high expectations driven by standards-focused instruction and assessment. It advocated for thoughtful planning tailored to individual learning needs, captured in collaboratively developed and implemented individualized education plans. Finally, it highlighted the importance of creating systems of support to catch students when they struggle. These principles became the foundation of our work, transforming the way we approached learning, teaching, and student success.

As our beliefs translated into action, the impact became evident in our student data. Achievement levels rose, gaps began to close, and more students experienced success. This shift in both mindset and practice confirmed what *Yes We Can!* champions: When educators believe in possibility and act with purpose, extraordinary outcomes follow.

Now, in 2025, Heather, Julie, and Jeanne return with a powerful complement to *Yes We Can!* that stems from the heart of that original work. With six core concepts and their supporting essential actions, *All Means All: Essential Actions for Leveraging Yes We Can!* provides deeper tools and resources to operationalize these principles with even greater precision. The authors offer reproducible templates, reflection opportunities, and actionable strategies that make implementing this framework more accessible than ever before. With this new work, educators are equipped not only to sustain their efforts but to elevate their practice and transform schools into thriving, inclusive environments where every student can succeed.

What sets this new book apart is its ability to inspire educators while providing concrete steps to bring these principles to life. It builds on the strong foundation of *Yes We Can!*, offering practical guidance to tackle the complexities of today's classrooms and address the diverse needs of all students. With this update, the impossible becomes possible—not a distant dream but a reality within reach for every educator and every school that dares to believe in what's possible.

Just as small groups of visionaries once turned the impossible into reality in science and technology, today's educators have the tools to do the same in their schools. The opportunity before us is one that demands both our attention and our action. Armed with the insights and tools in this book, you can transform dreams into reality for every student who walks through your doors. It's time to believe in the impossible, collaborate with purpose, and take bold steps that will shape the future of education—for *all* students.

# Introduction

In 2016, we published a book titled *Yes We Can! General and Special Educators Collaborating in a Professional Learning Community* (Friziellie, Schmidt, & Spiller, 2016). Our "why" was multifaceted, but suffice it to say, we were struck at the time by the absence of clear expectations around how special educators and special education in general "fit" into Professional Learning Communities (PLCs) at Work® processes. A common question posed to us as we worked with schools across the United States was, "What does special education have to do with PLC work?"

We had experienced significant improvement in outcomes for students who qualified for special education services over a span of six years as a result of our focused PLC work and felt a sense of urgency around memorializing the PLC practices that resulted in higher levels of learning for *all* of our students.

The good news is that, by 2025, some schools have made progress in recognizing how critically important it is for *all* educators to take collective responsibility for the learning of *all* students, including those eligible for special education services. While we cannot say that we believe a majority of schools across the United States have a sense of urgency regarding this, we can say that schools who are deeply engaged in the work of a PLC recognize this is essential to their continuous improvement journey. We see an increase in the number of schools that recognize collaboration between general and special educators is essential. Some of those schools have continued to work to ensure there is time identified for that collaboration to happen. For those schools, the question has shifted from answering why they should collaborate to what, exactly, they should be collaborating about.

This book takes a deep dive into examining this very challenge! A key lesson we have had since we wrote *Yes We Can!* is that schools that are doing the work of a PLC at a deep level consistently focus on essential actions aligned to six core concepts.

1. **Aligning beliefs and behaviors to live *all means all*:** All educators articulate a mindset and demonstrate through behaviors their belief that *all*

students can learn and demonstrate proficiency on grade-level standards. Policies, procedures, practices, and routine behaviors align with what we say we believe in.

2. **Collaboration by *all* for *all*:** All professionals in the school collaborate around meeting the needs of each and every student. Time in the daily and weekly schedule is dedicated to team collaboration. Regardless of the identified structure, these teams include both the general and special educators responsible for student learning.

3. **Standards-focused planning, instruction, assessment, and grading for *all*:** Priority standards and learning progressions are identified and used to guide instruction and assessment at each grade level in each course for *all* students. Teachers collaboratively determine the criteria for assessment so they more deeply understand the criteria for success and can design instruction so students succeed.

4. **Tailoring instruction:** It is critical to design initial grade-level instruction to keep expectations high for *all* students and use scaffolds for support to specially frame instruction for students who struggle or have special needs, without lowering expectations. This requires teams to develop strategies for all students to access grade-level material.

5. **Planning goals and monitoring progress:** Individualized education plan (IEP) goals are measurable, achievable within the annual review timeline, aligned to grade-level standards, collaboratively developed, and reflective of the individual abilities and needs of the student.

6. **Responding when students haven't yet learned:** Systems are in place to support *all* students who struggle to learn essential content above, beyond, and before special education is considered.

You have likely noticed how often we have already put emphasis on the word *all*. This is purposeful. Through this book, we strive to dig deeper into the core concepts we have seen teams, schools, districts, cooperatives, and even states take to truly bring *all means all* to life. This book is designed around the following three big ideas.

1. Learning about the roots of *Yes We Can!* (Friziellie et al., 2016) and what has developed since its publication

2. Living the *Yes We Can!* way, clarifying five of the six essential core concepts of the work and providing action steps and tools you can use to improve your reality

3. Leveraging *Yes We Can!*, digging into how one must believe and lead to have an even greater impact on making sure all students learn at high levels and that teams of educators collaborate to make this happen

You will notice that core concept 5, planning goals and monitoring progress, is not expanded on in this text. The heart of this core concept is about the importance of committing to, collaboratively developing, and consistently implementing IEPs that are aligned to standards and to identified student needs. This requires in-depth exploration and learning and, as such, an entire book has been written to provide guidance in this work: *The Collaborative IEP: Working Together for Life-Changing Special Education* by Kristen M. Bordonaro and Megan Clarke (2025) delves deeply into this concept, providing practical strategies for educators to develop effective individualized education plans through a collaborative approach.

It is also important to clarify that core concept 6, responding when students haven't learned yet, is not meant to be a step-by-step guide on developing and implementing response to intervention (RTI). Rather, it is designed to reflect on systems of intervention through the lens of access for students with identified disabilities. Several robust resources already exist to support the identification and implementation of RTI and, if you prefer, multitiered systems of support (MTSS), and we strongly encourage you to consider those as you begin that work or continually refine those systems.

## About This Book

This book is intended to take its readers more deeply into the practices initially discussed in *Yes We Can!* (Friziellie et al., 2016) with an even greater focus on *how* to do the work. Since its publication, we have been lucky enough to learn with and from many caring educators trying to answer the same question: How can we ensure all students learn at high levels and reach grade-level proficiency? While the original book builds the rationale for *why* doing this work is essential, begins to explore *what* the work looks like, and provides strategies for *how* to do the work, this book builds more knowledge while giving readers much more explicit support in doing the work, with built-in opportunities to reflect and put the core concepts into a current context.

To get the most from this book and improve the lives of students who are struggling with school, we ask that you approach reading it with a commitment to embrace a *Yes We Can!* mindset and the following aligned actions. Simply put, we must:

- Make decisions as if we are making them about or for the number one child in our lives
- Be open-minded

- Bring all ideas and thoughts forward, with no idea or thought going unturned
- Think and act differently to get different results
- Show grace to one another as we consider changing mindsets

To help you embrace these ideals, each chapter follows a similar structure, allowing readers to reflect before, during, and after they read. To begin each chapter, we ask readers to envision a school where the core concept is fully implemented, as in the following example.

**Envision What's Possible**

| Picture a school where... | ...A visionary point to consider when thinking about a school or system bringing the focus of that chapter to life |
|---|---|

At the end of each chapter, we ask readers to reflect on their connections, learning, and plans. Figure I.1 is an example.

| Picture a school where... | ...A visionary point to consider when thinking about a school or system bringing the focus of that chapter to life |
|---|---|
| Consider your role in making this vision a reality in your context. How would you contribute? | A reflection opportunity to consider your own role in helping your context move closer to the vision |
| Identify some challenges you may face in achieving this possibility. | A chance to truly focus on the current reality and what may be inhibiting progress toward that desired reality |
| Consider ways to overcome these challenges (over, around, and through). | A space to apply your thinking, background experiences, and learning from your reading to identify potential strategies for innovation |
| Anticipate the impact on students. How would bringing this possibility to life impact students academically and personally? | A note-making opportunity to weigh how the next steps you consider will impact the most important people in your context—students |

**Figure I.1:** Example of this book's chapter-ending reflections.

We encourage you to take notes as you read to make connections and capture moments that resonate with your experiences. This book aims to equip you with knowledge, clarity, and tools to bring all means all to life in your reality. To support this outcome, each chapter ends with a reflection rubric, a tool we created to help you assess your current reality, identify areas for growth, and build your strategic plan. Paired with the Envision What's Possible frameworks that open each chapter, these reflection rubrics will enhance your purposeful progress.

While enhancing academic achievement is central, we also recognize that student behavior and executive function are critical to learning. Skills like organization, time management, task initiation, and emotional regulation are foundational to success. Many students with IEPs have goals targeting behavioral and executive function deficits. Addressing these skills is essential for these students' growth across domains. If you want to learn more about specific strategies to support students who struggle with communicating their wants and needs, regulating their behavior, or demonstrating executive function skills, we suggest starting with the following resources.

- *Behavior Solutions: Teaching Academic and Social Skills Through RTI at Work* by John Hannigan, Jessica Djabrayan Hannigan, Mike Mattos, and Austin Buffum (2021)
- *Behavior Academies: Targeted Interventions That Work!* by Jessica Djabrayan Hannigan and John Hannigan (2024)

Creating supportive, responsive environments requires understanding students' strengths, challenges, and experiences. By applying the strategies in these resources with a holistic perspective and pairing them with the knowledge and best practices found in this book, you can better meet the diverse needs of all learners and promote lasting success.

We believe that through this book and its organization around the principles of learning, living, and leading, you will find new tools to use, new research to consider, and new and renewed motivation to be a champion for all learners. We hope that, after finishing this book, you feel empowered to say, *"Yes we can!"* and make a profound impact on students.

# PART 1

# Learning *Yes We Can!*

They always say time
changes things,
but you actually have to
change them
yourself.

**—Andy Warhol**

# CHAPTER 1

# RE-EXAMINING THE PAST, PRESENT, AND FUTURE

| **Envision What's Possible** ||
|---|---|
| Picture a school where . . . | . . . Educators are constantly examining national, state, and local data in order to narrow the knowing-doing gap |
| At the end of this chapter, you will have the opportunity to further reflect on this vision by considering your role in its achievement, potential challenges along the way, ways to address those challenges, and the positive impact achieving this vision will have on students. ||

The Individuals with Disabilities Education Act (IDEA; 2004) was initially passed as the Education for All Handicapped Children Act (EHA), Public Law 94-142, on November 29, 1975. It was later renamed the Individuals with Disabilities Education Act in 1990 during a series of amendments aimed at enhancing and expanding its provisions. In an effort to ensure access to a free and appropriate education for all, it has been reauthorized four times: in 1986, 1990, 1997, and 2004. The 2004 reauthorization came on the heels of the release of the President's Commission on Excellence in Special Education (2002). Each iteration has expanded the scope and quality of services to be provided for students who qualify for special education services. The key question about these is: Have the scope and quality of services and supports actually led to better outcomes for students?

An exploration of what the data tell us about the answer to this question is the focus of this chapter. And while we focus on trends across the United States, we do not mean to make sweeping generalizations. We recognize that there are outliers to these trends and that our readers may fall into those categories. Nevertheless, being aware of the national realities and understanding which services our students are entitled to are responsibilities we all bear.

## Statistical Trends and Realities

Since 2016, we have seen some movement in eligibility statistics across the United States. Unfortunately, post-pandemic, the number of students who have been made eligible for special education services has increased from 6.7 million (13 percent of the total student population) in 2016 to 7.5 million (15 percent of the total student population) in 2023 (National Center for Education Statistics [NCES], 2024). With more widespread implementation of systemic intervention strategies such as RTI and MTSS ensuring schools have robust support available between what individual teachers are providing in a classroom and special education, there has been a steady decline in the percentage of students eligible for services in the category of a specific learning disability. While the percentage of eligible students who qualify for services based on a specific learning disability has declined from 42 percent to 32 percent since 2012, the percentage of students qualifying under the autism category continues to tick up from 7 percent in 2012 to 13 percent in 2023 (NCES, 2024).

When we ask ourselves whether special education has been effective in providing specialized instruction and closing the gaps, thus leading to students no longer being eligible for services, the data become less clear. According to the 42nd Annual Report to Congress on the Implementation of the Individuals with Disabilities Education Act, 2020 (U.S. Department of Education et al., 2021), 5–10 percent of eligible students exited special education each year for various reasons. One would expect, and it is the case, that the highest percentage *of those who exit* (aged fourteen to twenty-one) do so by graduating from high school, with approximately 52.9 percent of that 5–10 percent earning a regular high school diploma. The report goes on to say that 6.7 percent of those who exited earned a certificate and that 10.3 percent dropped out. It is enlightening to note that of the existing categories identified, "transferring to regular education" accounts for 7.6 percent of those students who exited, *but* that category includes students whose parents withdrew permission for services. Thus, there are no data that specifically identify what percentage of our students was dismissed from services because we were successful in actually closing the gap. We can infer from the data available, however, that it continues to be approximately 1.8–2.4 percent each year—a chilling note! The stark reality is that *a significantly higher percentage of eligible students exit services each year due to dropping out of school than from actually becoming ineligible.*

Given these statistics, it is unfortunately clear that while we have seen some movement, some things have not changed at all.

In 2022–2023, the number of students aged three to twenty-one who received special education or related services under IDEA (2004) was 7.5 million, or the equivalent of 15 percent of all public school students (NCES, 2024). This number has risen since 2012, when approximately 6.4 million students were eligible. When it comes to the disability category of eligibility, we have seen some movement since 2012, specifically in two categories.

1. Students with specific learning disabilities have seen a decline of 10 percent over ten years, from 42 percent of identified students in 2012 to 32 percent in 2023. Historically, this is the largest category, and the reason for the decline may, in part, be attributed to the implementation of tiered intervention frameworks like RTI and MTSS (which we treat synonymously going forward) in schools across the United States. Built to provide early and targeted intervention for students who experience difficulty, RTI implementation, when done well, prevents the widening of skill gaps, reducing the need for special education services.

2. Most educators working in schools, regardless of location, will tell you that the number of students diagnosed with autism has increased and continues to do so. Of all students eligible for special education across the United States, those diagnosed with autism have increased by 6 percent over ten years (NCES, 2024). The Centers for Disease Control and Prevention (CDC; 2025b) reports a prevalence rate of approximately one in forty-four children diagnosed with autism spectrum disorder (ASD). At the time of this writing, we were unable to obtain valid data regarding future prevalence rates.

These data are a starting point for discussions around effectively supporting students in special education, but success for these students requires more than numbers. We must know who our students are and understand the impact of disproportionality.

## Who Our Students With Disabilities Are

We know the number of students identified as eligible for special education services across the United States has risen and continues to rise (see table 1.1). While overall enrollment in public schools has increased by 12.73 percent, the percentage of students receiving special education services has increased by over 50 percent. Several factors contribute to the rise, including a shift in awareness, diagnostic criteria, and policy. The trend continues, however, despite the fact that schools across the United States have been moving toward deeper levels of RTI implementation and have higher awareness of the flaws in identification and service delivery models.

**Table 1.1:** Students Eligible for Special Education Services

| 1976–1977 | 1990–1991 | 2000–2001 | 2010–2011 | 2017–2018 | 2020–2021 | 2022–2023 |
|---|---|---|---|---|---|---|
| 3,694,000 | 4,710,000 | 6,296,000 | 6,436,000 | 6,964,000 | 7,183,000 | 7,526,000 |

*Source: NCES, 2022.*

Here's a summary of the thirteen disability categories IDEA (2004) recognizes.

1. **Specific learning disability (SLD):** This is a disorder in one or more basic psychological processes involved in understanding or using language, which may affect reading, writing, listening, speaking, or mathematics. Dyslexia, dyscalculia, and other processing disorders fall under this category.
2. **Speech or language impairment (SLI):** This is a communication disorder, such as stuttering, impaired articulation, language impairment, or voice impairment, that affects a student's educational performance.
3. **Other health impairment (OHI):** This is a category that covers a variety of health and medical issues (such as ADHD and epilepsy) that affect a student's strength, vitality, or alertness, impacting their educational performance.
4. **Autism spectrum disorder:** This is a developmental disability significantly affecting communication, behavior, and social interaction. ASD typically manifests before age three, though it can be diagnosed later. Characteristics include repetitive behaviors, difficulties with social interactions, and challenges in understanding nonverbal communication.
5. **Developmental delay:** This is a delay in physical, cognitive, communicative, social, or emotional development, typically recognized in children aged three to nine. States may choose to use this category as an alternative for young children with developmental delays who may not yet meet the criteria for other disability categories.
6. **Intellectual disability (ID):** This is a disability characterized by significantly below-average intellectual functioning and adaptive behavior. It affects cognitive skills, social behaviors, and practical skills necessary for daily life.
7. **Emotional disturbance (ED):** This is a disability that affects a student's educational performance due to issues like an inability to build or maintain interpersonal relationships, inappropriate behaviors, persistent feelings of unhappiness, or physical symptoms related to personal or school problems.
8. **Multiple disabilities:** This is the simultaneous presence of two or more disabilities (such as intellectual disability and physical impairment) that require complex accommodations and specialized education, excluding deaf-blindness.
9. **Hearing impairment:** This is a permanent or fluctuating hearing loss that adversely affects a student's educational performance but is not classified as "deafness."
10. **Orthopedic impairment:** This is a severe physical disability that impacts a student's educational performance, physical functioning, or motor control, such as cerebral palsy.

11. **Traumatic brain injury:** This is an acquired injury to the brain caused by external physical force, leading to functional disabilities or psychosocial impairments that affect educational performance. This category does not include congenital or degenerative brain injuries.

12. **Visual impairment:** This is vision loss that, even with correction, adversely affects a student's educational performance. This includes partial sight and blindness.

13. **Deafness:** This is a severe hearing impairment that affects a student's ability to process linguistic information, often impacting spoken communication and resulting in significant educational challenges.

These categories provide a framework for identifying and supporting diverse student needs. Table 1.2 illustrates the distribution of special education students who fall into each disability category and some of the most recent shifts. (Deafness was not included as its own category in these data.)

**Table 1.2:** Distribution of Special Education Students by Category

| Disability Category | National Percentage in 2012 | National Percentage From 2019–2020 | National Percentage From 2022–2023 |
|---|---|---|---|
| Specific learning disability | 42 | 33 | 32 |
| Speech or language impairment | 19 | 19 | 19 |
| Other health impairment | 13 | 15 | 15 |
| Autism spectrum disorder | 7 | 11 | 13 |
| Developmental delay | - | 7 | 7 |
| Intellectual disability | 8 | 6 | 6 |
| Emotional disturbance | 6 | 5 | 4 |
| Multiple disabilities | - | 2 | 2 |
| Hearing impairment | - | 1 | 1 |
| Orthopedic impairment | 5 | 1 | - |
| Traumatic brain injury | 0.4 | 0.4 | 0.3 |
| Visual impairment | 0.4 | 0.4 | 0.3 |

*Source: NCES, 2024.*

The following websites provide excellent resources to further support an in-depth understanding of each disability, associated adverse effects, and detailed suggestions and recommendations for supporting students and families.

- **Center for Parent Information and Resources (CPIR):**
  www.parentcenterhub.org

- **National Center for Learning Disabilities (NCLD):** https://ncld.org
- **Understood:** www.understood.org
- **American Speech-Language-Hearing Association (ASHA):** www.asha.org
- **Council for Exceptional Children (CEC):** https://exceptionalchildren.org/about-us
- **IDEA (U.S. Department of Education):** https://sites.ed.gov/idea/about-idea
- Local and state departments of education

As we consider the percentage of students who receive services in each of the disability categories, we have to ask ourselves: Given what we know about the potential adverse effects of each of these disabilities, what percentage of students should we assume exposure to and mastery of grade-level expectations is inappropriate?

When we ask this question of educators, responses range from 0 percent to as high as 10 percent. However, the purpose of the question is not to determine a correct answer. If, for argument's sake, based on responses, we settle on 3 percent, the question becomes: "What do the data tell us about the 97 percent for whom exposure and expectations are appropriate? Are we anywhere near 97 percent of our students with disabilities reaching proficiency in mathematics and literacy?"

According to the National Center for Education Statistics (2022), only 6 percent of students entitled to special education services demonstrated proficiency in mathematics, which is down from 8 percent in previous years, and 6 percent in reading, which is a decline from a previous 9 percent.

We can and must do better as a profession. To support this effort toward higher levels of awareness and a deeper understanding of who our students with disabilities are and to ignite a sense of urgency around collective ownership of their learning, we recommend engaging staff in "Profiles in Perspective: Understanding and Supporting Students With Disabilities," found at the end of this chapter (page 24). While these statistics are startling, as we dig deeper, an even greater sense of urgency emerges.

## Disproportionality

*Disproportionality* in special education refers to the overrepresentation or underrepresentation of certain student groups in special education programs relative to their presence in the general student population. This typically involves students from specific racial, ethnic, or linguistic backgrounds being identified for special education services at rates that are higher or lower than expected. For example, African American students have historically been overrepresented in categories such as intellectual disabilities or emotional disturbances, while some Hispanic or English learners may be underrepresented in receiving necessary supports (National Center for Learning Disabilities, 2020). This disproportionality can arise from various factors, including cultural biases in assessment practices, lack of access to early interventions, and varying educational resources. Our ongoing alarm around disproportionality in special education continues to escalate, as education reflects systemic biases that can impact equitable access to appropriate supports and services for all students.

Our concerns are underscored and substantiated by research indicating that all students have a lack of consistent access to grade-level materials and expectations and that students of color, students who come from low-income households, and students who start a school year behind grade level have even less access (The New Teacher Project [TNTP], 2018). This continues to be the reality across the United States despite the overwhelming evidence indicating that access to appropriate grade-level rigor is critical (Cushman, 2003; Darling-Hammond, 2010; Duckworth, 2016; Dweck, 2010, 2016; Hattie, 2012, 2023a, 2023b; Ladson-Billings, 2006; Marzano & Pickering, 2011). In his research, Robert J. Marzano has consistently emphasized the importance of rigorous instruction and aligning standards and objectives with high expectations (Marzano & Pickering, 2011; Marzano, Pickering, & Pollock, 2001; Marzano, Warrick, & Simms, 2014). His research supports the idea that all students, including those with learning challenges, benefit from rigorous and structured learning opportunities.

IDEA (2004) mandates that school districts monitor and address disproportionality to ensure all students have equitable access to appropriate educational supports. Addressing disproportionality involves using culturally responsive assessments, utilizing diverse instructional practices, providing access to grade-level rigor, and fostering inclusive environments that meet students' unique needs.

Further, there are three separate but related trends that impact a student's educational experience and fall under the category of "significant disproportionality."

1. **Identification (also called eligibility):** In this trend, Black students, for instance, make up about 15 percent of the overall student population but represent 27 percent of those identified as having intellectual disabilities and 19 percent in emotional disturbance categories (U.S. Department of Education et al., 2021). Similarly, Hispanic and Native American students are often overrepresented in certain special education categories but tend to be underserved in others, such as gifted programs (Office for Civil Rights, U.S. Department of Education, n.d.).

2. **Placement (once identified as eligible for special education):** This trend is compounded by differences in placement. Once identified, students of color are more likely to be placed in restrictive settings that separate them from their general education peers, affecting academic performance and social outcomes (Office for Civil Rights, U.S. Department of Education, n.d.).

3. **Discipline:** Students of color with disabilities face harsher disciplinary measures, including higher rates of suspension and restraint, compared to their White counterparts (Office for Civil Rights, U.S. Department of Education, n.d.).

Based on a few federal reports (Cortiella & Horowitz, 2014; National Center for Education Statistics, 2022; U.S. Department of Education et al., 2021), the following are additional stark examples of disproportionality.

- American Indian and Alaska Native students receive special education at twice the rate of the general student population. This means that if the general student population receiving special education is 5 percent, for example, then 10 percent of American Indian and Alaska Native students would be receiving special education.
- Black students are 40 percent more likely to be identified with a disability than all other students. If 10 percent of all students are identified with a disability, for example, then 14 percent of Black students would be identified.
- Fifty-five percent of White students with disabilities spend more than 80 percent of their school day in a general education classroom, compared to only a third of Black students with disabilities.
- Among Black, Native Hawaiian and Pacific Islander, American Indian and Alaska Native, and multiracial students with disabilities, one in four boys and nearly one in five girls receive an out-of-school suspension. This translates to 25 percent of boys and nearly 20 percent of girls in these racial and ethnic groups receiving out-of-school suspensions.
- Black students with disabilities make up only 19 percent of students with disabilities served by IDEA (2004) but account for 36 percent of students who are restrained at school by equipment meant to limit their movement.

We strongly contend that public education in the United States must act as the "great equalizer" ensuring that, regardless of background, *every* student has access to a quality education that helps to ensure access to opportunity, as championed by Horace Mann (1849). These current examples of disproportionate percentages are a cause for alarm and a heightened sense of urgency. The issue of disproportionality underscores broader inequities that lead to an even more profound lack of access to the benefits of public education.

The shifts in mindset, practices, and access outlined in this book are meant to create a greater sense of urgency around righting the ship and finally accelerating the dismantling of the silos that have been in place since the 20th century. Utilizing the "Engaging in Understanding and Addressing Disproportionality in Our School" reproducible (page 26) requires the examination of disproportionality trends locally that may be negatively impacting the future of students in your own school community.

## Findings From 2002 Versus Our Current Realities

In *Yes We Can!* (Friziellie et al., 2016), we summarized the findings of a report titled *A New Era: Revitalizing Special Education for Children and Their Families* (President's Commission on Excellence in Special Education, 2002). The findings and recommendations focused on the need for significant reform in the way that education and services are delivered for students with identified disabilities in the United States. Major recommendations fell into six different categories, and while progress has been made in some areas, minimal progress has been made in others.

1. **Focus on prevention and early intervention:** The commission emphasized that the special education system should prioritize *early identification and intervention* for students at risk of disabilities. The discrepancy model often requires students to demonstrate a significant gap between their intellectual ability (typically measured by IQ tests) and academic achievement before they are eligible for services. This delay means students might struggle for years without receiving the necessary support, causing emotional and academic setbacks. By establishing a goal of preventing the need for special education services, education soon saw a shift toward early intervention services (EIS) through the reauthorization of IDEA (2004), where 15 percent of federal special education funds were allocated specifically for EIS. Recognizing that there needed to be a system of support available in all schools between what an individual teacher was doing in the classroom and special education services, federal law incorporated RTI through the reauthorization of IDEA (2004).

2. **Accountability for results:** If there is one thing that *traditional* special education has taught us, it's that staying compliant does not necessarily lead to improved student learning—in fact, the opposite is more often the case (Mattos et al., 2025). To shift away from a focus on compliance and procedural safeguards, a more outcome-based approach was recommended. This came in the form of accountability for the learning of students with disabilities. And while there have been much clearer accountability measures put in place, we would argue that those measures have not resulted in *widespread* improvement in learning outcomes.

3. **Use of scientifically based instruction:** The commission recognized that the focus on compliance had led to a lack of focus on good instruction. The report called for the use of evidence-based practices and instruction. Unfortunately, teacher preparation programs for special educators rarely require or provide robust coursework on instructional practices, leaving this learning to be done "on the job" or "by the district." In our experience, when districts have provided professional learning focused on

instructional practices, special educators have not been invited to the table. Instead, they have been given time to—you guessed it—work on all of the procedural and compliance requirements associated with being a special education professional.

4. **Reform of funding structures:** Funding for special education has historically been tied to the number of students identified as being eligible for services. The report advocated for funding to align with student outcomes, and the goal was to incentivize positive educational results. While we believe that funding the education of students with disabilities should be a given and not tied to a financial incentive, this recommendation never materialized. Federal funding for special education services is specified in IDEA (2004), and the federal government aims to fund 40 percent of the cost of providing services based on the number of those eligible. However, the current funding rate is between 13–16 percent of the actual cost.

    Conceptually, states are then primarily responsible for funding each service using their own formula to do so. But the reality is that local districts must cover the gap, which, in most states, is substantial. For instance, in the state of Illinois, local school districts shoulder approximately 60 percent of the cost of providing services to students who are eligible; in Florida, local districts pay 49.1 percent of the costs; and in New Mexico, 90 percent of the costs come from local sources (Kaput & O'Neal Schiess, 2024; National Education Association, 2021). To say that there has been minimal reform when it comes to funding services for our most complex students is putting it mildly.

5. **Teacher quality and professional development:** This recommendation emphasizes the need to improve the professional learning opportunities for special education teachers as well as general education teachers working with students with disabilities. In *Yes We Can!* (Frizielle et al., 2016), we highlight the lack of ongoing professional learning aligned with instructional practices for special educators. What we did not address explicitly is the ongoing need to also provide deep learning for general educators on understanding and meeting the needs of students with disabilities. When educators do this learning together, collaboratively, it is powerful and can be immediately impactful. The recognition of the need for ongoing adult learning is prevalent. The commitment to general and special educators learning together in service of high levels of learning for *all* students is less so.

6. **Parent involvement:** The commission stressed the importance of involving parents more actively in decision-making processes regarding their children's education, ensuring that parents are fully informed and able to participate in shaping their child's educational programming. In *The Collaborative IEP*,

Bordonaro and Clarke (2025) stress that when we embrace the requirements of IDEA (2004), we are building a partnership that is in the best interest of the student. Parent participation rates vary widely across the United States, but simply attending the IEP meeting does not necessarily mean that parents are engaged in and participate in the process. In a collaborative culture where we embrace mutual accountability for student learning, we must also embrace that parents are critical collaborative partners in designing, implementing, and supporting the IEP.

While we, the authors, tend to be optimistic, "glass half full" kinds of people, we are disheartened at the excruciatingly slow pace at which change and "reform" are happening in the world of special education. After all, the President's Commission on Excellence in Special Education report was published in 2002! After twenty-three years, it is hard to say that "a new era" actually came to fruition for our most complex learners and their families.

That lack of progress means our students with disabilities continue to have a lack of access to what they need in order to ensure they will have opportunities when they leave us. Whether it be the opportunity to continue their education at a two- or four-year college or university, enroll and be successful in a vocational program, or have the skills needed to be a contributing employee, a lack of access and the absence of high expectations continue to lead to windows of opportunity closing.

It is our hope that this new work will be an important part of lighting a fire under our collective practices across the United States and igniting the momentum of progress for our students.

## A Sense of Urgency

*The Opportunity Myth*, a 2018 report by TNTP, reveals the significant gap between students' educational experiences and their potential to succeed. The report is based on extensive research involving over four thousand students across five diverse school systems. The TNTP (2018) report analyzes data from over twenty thousand student work samples, nearly one thousand lessons, and over five thousand teacher assignments and evaluations.

Key findings highlight that while students were generally meeting expectations, *the expectations themselves were often too low*. The report concludes that students were not given consistent access to grade-appropriate assignments, strong instruction, deep levels of engagement, or high expectations. These students spent most of their time on assignments that *did not challenge them academically*, creating a gap between their goals (such as attending college) and the preparation they received in school. The reality for students from marginalized backgrounds, including those who qualify for special education services, is even more stark.

The report identifies four critical resources to which all students need consistent access in order to be adequately prepared to meet their post-high school goals (TNTP, 2018).

1. **Grade-appropriate assignments:** Many students spend the majority of their time on work *below their grade level*, which fails to build the skills needed for future success. In fact, students succeeded on 71 percent of their assignments yet only met grade-level standards on 17 percent of those exact same assignments. Of the 180 classroom hours in each core subject during the school year, students spent 133 hours on assignments that were not grade level and only 47 hours on assignments that were actually grade appropriate.

2. **Strong instruction:** Effective teaching, characterized by deep content knowledge and pedagogical skills, is essential for student growth. However, this quality of instruction is inconsistently delivered. According to the report, even when the content was of high quality and suited to students' grade level, many students did not get the chance to actively participate in the work. The report observes that teachers made decisions that either shielded students from engaging in the critical thinking required for the lesson or hindered their ability to do so.

3. **Deep engagement:** Students learn best when they are intellectually engaged. The report defines *engagement* as a deeper emotional and cognitive investment in learning that goes beyond compliance. The report reveals that many students feel bored or unchallenged in class. Middle and high school students in this report found their lessons engaging or worthwhile less than half of the time.

4. **High expectations:** Students rise to the level of expectations set for them, but teachers often underestimate students' abilities, particularly for students of color, low-income students, English learners, and students with disabilities. In the article "John Hattie on the Factors That Influence Learning in Schools," John Hattie (2023a) makes clear that the key responsibility for teachers is to maintain high expectations for all students. This involves refraining from labeling students—such as calling them *bright*, *strugglers*, *ADHD*, or *autistic*—which can inadvertently lower expectations from both teachers and students. Instead, Hattie (2023a) stresses that educators should view every student as a learner capable of significant growth in their academic journey.

TNTP (2018) also points out that the opportunity gap is not inevitable. When students receive access to rigorous, grade-level work, they are able to meet the challenge, regardless of their starting point. The report calls for urgent action to provide all students—especially those from underserved populations—with consistent access to grade-level content and high-quality teaching. We recommend that all teams in all schools implement a rigor audit as an ongoing part of a school's and team's continuous cycle of improvement. This represents a vital action for ensuring *all* students, including those entitled to special education services, have access to tasks, activities, and assessments aligned to the rigor level being asked of grade-level standards. At the end of this chapter, we have provided reproducibles for the "Team Rigor Audit Process" (page 28) and "Rigor Audit Template" (page 33) to support this ongoing examination.

Ultimately, *The Opportunity Myth* (TNTP, 2018) challenges schools, educators, and policymakers to reimagine what's possible for all students and to take deliberate steps to close the gap between what students experience and what they need to succeed. Reflecting on where we've come from and where we need to head, it's crucial to understand that progress depends on our involvement. The realization of "a new era" for our most complex learners hinges on our commitment to *act*.

## Summary

The call to action in this chapter centers on *all* educators—general and special educators alike—raising collective awareness around and learning deeply together about who our students with disabilities are, both locally and across the United States. When we do so, the collective sense of urgency that results ensures we are all not only in the same boat but also rowing in the same direction in pursuit of high levels of learning—not for most but for *all*. We know that thinking about it and talking about it may be valuable, but we also know that engaging in learning leading to action together will make the difference!

Use the rubric featured in figure 1.1 to assess your progress toward these goals.

| Criteria | 4—Highly Effective | 3—Effective | 2—Developing | 1—Beginning |
| --- | --- | --- | --- | --- |
| Statistical Trends and Realities | Trends and realities are examined on an ongoing basis, and action steps are implemented to address them. | Trends and realities have been discussed, and there is a high level of awareness. | There is awareness that trends and realities exist, but they have never been discussed. | Trends and realities have never been examined or discussed. |
| Disproportionality | There is widespread awareness of local disproportionality data, and annual action steps have been created to address disproportionality. | There is ongoing discussion regarding local disproportionality data. | There is some awareness regarding local disproportionality data. | There is a general lack of awareness regarding local disproportionality data. |

**Figure 1.1:** Reflection rubric for raising collective awareness about who our students with disabilities are.

*continued →*

| | | | | |
|---|---|---|---|---|
| Accountability for Results | Special educators are always included in professional learning opportunities provided for general education teachers focused on student learning. | Special educators are frequently included in professional learning opportunities provided for general education teachers focused on student learning. | Special educators are periodically included in professional learning opportunities provided for general education teachers focused on student learning. | Most of special educators' time outside of instruction is spent on compliance tasks. |
| Access to Rigor | Students entitled to special education have consistent access to grade-level rigor and teachers who consistently hold high expectations of them. | Students entitled to special education have consistent access to grade-level rigor. | Students entitled to special education have access to grade-level rigor in limited circumstances. | Students entitled to special education do not have access to grade-level rigor. |

*Visit **go.SolutionTree.com/PLCbooks** for a free reproducible version of this figure.*

Through the lens of a school where educators regularly examine data to narrow the knowing-doing gap, use figure 1.2 to reflect on your role, potential challenges, ways to overcome these challenges, and the impact on students both academically and personally.

| Picture a school where . . . | . . . Educators are constantly examining national, state, and local data in order to narrow the knowing-doing gap |
|---|---|
| Consider your role in making this vision a reality in your context. How would you contribute? | |
| Identify some challenges you may face in achieving this possibility. | |
| Consider ways to overcome these challenges (over, around, and through). | |

**Figure 1.2:** Envision What's Possible reflection tool for planning action to support raising collective awareness about who our students with disabilities are.

*Visit **go.SolutionTree.com/PLCbooks** for a free reproducible version of this figure.*

Use the following aligned activities included at the end of this chapter to support your work around this chapter's core concept.

- **"Profiles in Perspective: Understanding and Supporting Students With Disabilities" (page 24):** Use this reproducible tool to raise awareness and collectively engage in learning about who our students with disabilities are.

- **"Engaging in Understanding and Addressing Disproportionality in Our School" (page 26):** Use this reproducible tool to understand the barrier disproportionality creates and to examine current local realities.

- **"Team Rigor Audit Process" (page 28):** Use this reproducible tool to assess the rigor level of tasks and assessments to ensure you are maintaining high expectations aligned to grade-level standards.

- **"Disability Profiles" (page 31):** Use this reproducible to support your implementation of "Profiles in Perspective: Understanding and Supporting Students With Disabilities."

- **"Rigor Audit Template" (page 33):** Use this reproducible to support your implementation of the "Team Rigor Audit Process" reproducible.

# Profiles in Perspective: Understanding and Supporting Students With Disabilities

**Objective:** Participants will gain insights into the challenges and adverse effects associated with various disabilities recognized by the Individuals with Disabilities Education Act (2004) to better inform their instructional approaches.

**Time:** Approximately 1.5 hours *(can be adapted for a shorter time frame)*

**Materials:**

- Printed or digital "Disability Profiles" (page 31) for each IDEA-recognized disability, distributed to each group
- Reflection and discussion worksheet (see part 2, step 3)
- Chart paper and markers (optional for group brainstorming)

This activity breaks down into the following parts, each with its own set of steps.

### Part 1: Introduction and Grouping (15 minutes)

Introduce the activity and form participants into groups as follows.

1. Begin with an overview of IDEA's (2004) disability categories, emphasizing that each disability has unique characteristics and potential adverse effects and requires tailored support to meet students' needs.
2. Divide teachers into small groups, assigning each group one IDEA-recognized disability (autism, specific learning disability, visual impairment, and so on). Ensure a balanced group size for each category.

### Part 2: Profile Reading and Reflection (15 minutes)

Participants explore their assigned disability category and associated adverse effects and educational needs.

1. Provide each group with a disability profile for their assigned category. The "Disability Profiles" reproducible lists, by disability, potential adverse effects and best practice accommodations and supports.
2. Instruct each group to read through the profile together and discuss how this disability might affect a student's academic, social, and behavioral experiences. Ask teachers to consider the following questions.
    - → What are the primary challenges associated with this disability?
    - → How might these challenges manifest in a typical classroom setting?
    - → What aspects of the student's experience might be impacted by these challenges (such as engagement, behavior, and peer relationships)?
3. Each group member then completes a reflection worksheet with questions like the following.
    - → What stood out to you about this disability's impact on students?
    - → How might this change the way you view student behavior and learning needs?
    - → What initial ideas do you have for adapting your classroom practices to support a student with this disability?

**All Means All** © 2025 Solution Tree Press • SolutionTree.com
Visit **go.SolutionTree.com/PLCbooks** to download this free reproducible.

**Part 3: Group Strategy Development (15 minutes)**

Participants draw on their experiences to apply the information to students in their classrooms.

1. Continuing in their assigned groups, teachers discuss their reflections and share insights gained from the profile. Encourage groups to think beyond the profile and imagine specific scenarios where a student with their assigned disability might struggle in the classroom.
2. Ask each group to brainstorm potential accommodations, modifications, or strategies to support students with the assigned disability. They can refer to suggestions within the profile as well as their own ideas, focusing on the following.
   - → Instructional strategies (such as visual aids, simplified language, and frequent check-ins)
   - → Classroom environment modifications (such as seating arrangements and minimizing sensory distractions)
   - → Social-emotional support strategies (such as structured peer interactions and behavior management tools)
3. Groups record their accommodation ideas on chart paper or a shared document for easy reference later. When brainstorming accommodations, groups should ensure each identified accommodation addresses a specific adverse effect of the disability.

**Part 4: Sharing and Cross-Group Learning (25 minutes)**

Participants share their learning and applications across the groups.

1. Have each group present a summary of its disability profile along with their suggested accommodations and strategies to the whole group. Presentations should address the following.
   - → Key challenges of the disability
   - → Insights on how it might impact a student's school experience
   - → Recommended accommodations or supports directly aligned to the identified adverse effects of that disability
2. Encourage all participants to ask questions, share additional strategies, and discuss how each disability may affect students differently, even within the same category.

**Part 5: Whole-Group Reflection and Wrap-Up (10 minutes)**

Participants reflect on their learning and sharing.

1. Facilitate a group discussion to reflect on the following.
   - → What new insights did you gain about how disabilities impact learning and behavior?
   - → How can understanding these profiles help you better meet the needs of all students?
   - → Are there common strategies or universal accommodations that could benefit students across multiple disability categories?
2. Conclude by encouraging teachers to continue reflecting on how they can create an inclusive classroom environment that supports students with a wide range of needs. Optionally, provide a summary document of all strategies discussed for future reference.

References

Individuals with Disabilities Education Act, 20 U.S.C. § 1400 (2004).

# Engaging in Understanding and Addressing Disproportionality in Our School

**Objective:** Teachers will collaboratively examine data to identify patterns of disproportionality in their school or district, discuss potential causes, and brainstorm actionable steps toward equity.

**Time:** 30 minutes

**Materials:**

- *Disaggregated school or district data (for example, enrollment in special education, disciplinary actions, or gifted programs) broken down by demographics (for example, race, ethnicity, language, or socioeconomic status)*
- *Chart paper, markers, and sticky notes*
- *Handout on key terms and concepts (disproportionality, equity, overrepresentation, underrepresentation, and so on*

This activity breaks down into the following parts, each with its own set of steps.

### Part 1: Introduction (5 minutes)

Lay the groundwork through local data.

1. Begin by introducing the term *disproportionality* and its significance in education. Emphasize how disproportionality in areas like special education, discipline, and academic programs can indicate potential inequities in the system.
2. Provide a quick overview of the data set teachers will be examining (such as percentages of students from different demographic groups in special education, disciplinary records, and gifted programs).

### Part 2: Data Review in Small Groups (10 minutes)

Participants examine data and apply questions of disproportionality.

1. Divide teachers into small groups of four to six and assign each group a specific data set (such as special education enrollment, disciplinary actions, and gifted and talented enrollment).
2. Ask each group to review the data and identify any patterns of disproportionality. Groups should seek to answer the following key questions.
    → Which student groups are over- or underrepresented?
    → Are there notable differences in outcomes between demographic groups?
3. Encourage teachers to jot down observations on chart paper, using sticky notes to mark any questions or areas needing further investigation.

### Part 3: Discussion and Reflection (10 minutes)

Participants reflect and share across groups.

1. Have each group share its findings with the larger group.
2. Facilitate a discussion around the following reflection questions.

→ What factors might contribute to these patterns of disproportionality?

→ How might implicit biases, structural inequities, or a lack of resources play a role?

→ Are there existing practices or policies in place that may inadvertently contribute to these disparities?

**Part 4: Action Planning (5 minutes)**

Participants engage in brainstorming aligned to the following action steps.

1. Ask each group to brainstorm one actionable step the school or team can take to address disproportionality and record its observations, patterns noted, potential contributing factors, and proposed action steps in the chart provided. Examples could include the following.

   → Conducting further research into referral practices for special education

   → Implementing culturally responsive teaching practices

   → Increasing teacher training on implicit bias and equitable discipline practices

2. Have each group share its action step with the larger team, creating a collective list of next steps.

| Data Set | Observations | Patterns of Disproportionality | Potential Contributing Factors | Action Steps |
|---|---|---|---|---|
| Special Education | *Example:* Fifteen percent of students identified as needing special education are from a specific demographic group, despite representing 10 percent of the student body. | *Example:* There is overrepresentation of certain demographic groups in special education. | *Example:* Possible factors include referral process, assessment criteria, implicit biases, and lack of interventions. | *Example:* Review referral practices, provide teacher training on bias, and review system of interventions, ensuring a multitiered approach. |
| Discipline Referrals | | | | |
| Gifted and Enrichment Participation | | | | |
| Academic Performance | | | | |

# Team Rigor Audit Process

**Team discussion protocol:** Analyzing the assignment, task, or assessment rigor and alignment with standards

**Objective:** The purpose of this team process, which is designed to support the "Rigor Audit Template" (page 33), is to collaboratively analyze assignments, tasks, and assessments to *evaluate their rigor level and alignment with grade-level standards*. The discussion aims to gather diverse perspectives and insights and to ensure students have consistent access to grade-level rigor and learning.

By incorporating preparation steps for each team member, the protocol ensures the collaborative discussion is informed by thoughtful individual assessments of selected assignments. This approach enhances the depth and effectiveness of the analysis during the team meeting. Adjust the time allocations based on *the complexity of the assignments* and *the depth of analysis required.*

**Preparation steps for each team member:**

1. *Individual* audit artifact selection (before audit meeting):
    - → Each team member is tasked with selecting one assignment, task, or assessment that they believe is representative of the grade-level standards *that they individually use* during a unit of instruction.
    - → Consider diversity in content, formats, and skills addressed within the chosen assignments.
    - → Identify the grade-level standards with which the assignment, task, or assessment aligns.

2. *Collective* audit artifact selection (before audit meeting):
    - → As a team, select one to two assignments, tasks, or assessments that are common to all team members during a unit of study.
    - → Identify the grade-level standards with which the assignment, task, or assessment aligns.
    - → Review the grade-level standards and ensure a clear understanding of the expectations.
    - → Verify the selected assignments align with the specified grade-level standards.

**Materials:**

- *Grade-level priority standards*
- *Depth of Knowledge (DOK) chart (see the following resources)*
    - → For reading—*www.webbalign.org/dok-definitions-for-reading*
    - → For mathematics—*www.webbalign.org/dok-definitions-for-math*
    - → For social studies—*www.webbalign.org/dok-definitions-for-social-studies*
    - → For science—*www.webbalign.org/dok-definitions-for-science*
- *Bloom's Taxonomy graphic (search online)*
- *Chosen team and individual artifacts*
- *Any rubrics that align with chosen artifacts*

**Part 1: Rigor Audit Process**

The following lists the steps necessary to complete the rigor audit process. Steps 1–3 cover introduction and standards identification. Steps 4–5 detail task or assessment analysis.

1. **Introduction (2–3 minutes):**
    a. Briefly review the purpose of the analysis and the importance of collaborative input.
2. **Review of grade-level priority standards (3–4 minutes):**
    a. Identify the specific grade-level priority standards with which the *team-chosen* assignments, tasks, or assessments should align.
    b. Discuss any nuances or points of emphasis within the standards.
3. **Brief review of the DOK chart for the appropriate content area (mathematics, reading, and so on) and the Bloom's taxonomy graphic (3–4 minutes):**
    a. Have a brief conversation reviewing the DOK framework and Bloom's taxonomy. The DOK purpose is to evaluate task complexity and depth. Use Bloom's taxonomy to assess thinking processes.
4. **Audit of team-chosen artifact (25 minutes):**
    a. Apply the "Rigor Audit Template" (page 33) to each artifact individually, beginning with the artifacts the entire team uses.
5. **Individual reflection (5 minutes):**
    a. Using the "Rigor Audit Template," team members individually reflect on the selected artifact, making an individual determination regarding alignment with priority standards.
    b. Team members individually reflect on the selected artifact, considering the cognitive complexity using the DOK chart and thinking processes using Bloom's taxonomy graphic.
    c. Team members individually note the DOK and Bloom's levels associated with different aspects of the assignments.
    d. Team members individually determine whether the rigor level they identified is aligned with the *rigor level the priority standards require*.

**Part 2: Task Revision**

During this part of the process, individual team members share their thinking, and the team comes to consensus on revisions.

1. Initiate the discussion by asking each team member to share their reflections, focusing on the DOK levels and Bloom's taxonomy observed in the selected artifact and alignment to the rigor level of the priority standards.
2. Encourage specific examples and evidence supporting the alignment or misalignment and the identified thinking processes required (Bloom's) and level of task complexity (DOK). Use the following questions for consideration (Anderson & Karthwohl, 2001; Hess, n.d.).
    → How many of the questions within the text are at high levels of Bloom's taxonomy and DOK? Do students move beyond basic recall for analysis and synthesis?
    → Consider projects or extended response questions. Are they at the higher levels of DOK or Bloom's taxonomy, or do they only require basic thinking?
    → What percentage of the material is review? Although some review is needed, students must move beyond review to new material to work at rigorous levels.

3. Identify strengths and items that need recalibration. Use the following actions to guide this step.
   a. Facilitate a discussion on the strengths observed in the assignments, considering the cognitive complexity based on DOK levels and cognitive complexity based on Bloom's taxonomy.
   b. Identify areas that may need improvement, focusing on elevating DOK and Bloom's taxonomy levels where necessary.
   c. Explore how adjustments can enhance both rigor and alignment with standards.

**Part 3: Accessibility and Equity Check**

During this step, participants consider the principles for Universal Design for Learning (UDL) and closely evaluate accessibility.

1. Using the "Rigor Audit Template" (page 33), consider the four UDL checkpoints, including language and vocabulary support, visuals and graphic organizers, scaffolding and supports, and opportunities for student choice.

**Part 4: Evidence and Reflection**

Last, participants consider any evidence or student performance data they may have and how adjustments will be made where appropriate.

1. If students have already engaged in the task or assessment being audited, consider student performance data as they relate to rigor alignment.
2. Identify standards.

Once the team has applied the process to all team-chosen artifacts individually, it can be applied to artifacts chosen by individual team members.

References

Anderson, L. W., & Krathwohl, D. (Eds.). (2001). *A taxonomy for learning, teaching, and assessing: A revision of Bloom's taxonomy of educational objectives.* Allyn & Bacon.

Hess, K. (n.d.). *The Hess Cognitive Rigor Matrices (Hess CRMs) integrating DOK and Bloom.* Accessed at www.karin-hess.com/free-resources on January 9, 2025.

# Disability Profiles

This table contains a brief summary of information from section 300.8 of the Individuals with Disabilities Education Act (2004), the website for the Center for Parent Information and Resources (CPIR; https://parentcenterhub.org), and the website for the Council for Exceptional Children (CEC; https://exceptionalchildren.org).

| Disability Profile | Potential Adverse Effects | Best Practice Accommodations and Supports |
|---|---|---|
| Autism Spectrum Disorder (ASD) | • Difficulty with communication, social interaction, and repetitive behaviors<br>• Sensory sensitivities, executive function challenges, and anxiety<br>• Difficulty with transitions and changes in routine | • Visual schedules, social stories, and task analysis<br>• Structured, predictable environments with clear routines<br>• Communication supports (such as Augmentative and Alternative Communication [AAC] system, Picture Exchange Communication System [PECS], and speech therapy)<br>• Sensory breaks and noise-reducing tools<br>• Explicit social skills instruction |
| Deaf-Blindness | • Severe communication and developmental delays<br>• Limited access to information, leading to isolation<br>• Challenges with mobility and orientation | • Tactile communication systems (such as Braille and tactile sign language)<br>• Assistive technology (like hearing aids and refreshable Braille displays)<br>• Orientation and mobility training<br>• Highly individualized instructional approaches |
| Deafness | • Delays in language development and literacy<br>• Limited access to auditory-based learning activities<br>• Social isolation in mainstream environments | • Sign language interpretation or captioning<br>• Hearing assistive technology (such as FM systems and cochlear implants)<br>• Visual supports and direct instruction in language<br>• Accessible learning materials (captions, written transcripts) |
| Emotional Disturbance (ED) | • Challenges with behavior regulation, social interactions, and academics<br>• Anxiety, depression, or conduct disorders may impact school performance<br>• Increased suspensions or exclusionary discipline | • Positive Behavioral Interventions and Supports (PBIS)<br>• Access to counseling or mental health support<br>• Clear behavior intervention plans (BIPs) with structured supports<br>• Check-in and checkout systems and emotional regulation strategies |
| Hearing Impairment | • Difficulty following spoken instructions or group discussions<br>• Speech and language delays<br>• Social challenges due to communication barriers | • Hearing assistive devices and amplification systems<br>• Preferential seating and visual cues<br>• Written instructions and note-taking assistance<br>• Speech-language pathology (SLP) services |

| Category | Characteristics | Supports and Strategies |
|---|---|---|
| Intellectual Disability (ID) | • Delays in cognitive functioning, problem-solving, and adaptive skills<br>• Difficulty generalizing learned skills to new settings<br>• Limited independence in life and academic skills | • Task analysis and scaffolded instruction<br>• Life skills and functional academics<br>• Repetition, visuals, and hands-on activities<br>• Individualized pacing and prompting (verbal and visual) |
| Multiple Disabilities | • Significant limitations in mobility, communication, and self-care<br>• Difficulty accessing general education curriculum<br>• Complex medical needs impacting attendance and stamina | • AAC systems<br>• Adaptive equipment for mobility and positioning<br>• Functional life skills instruction<br>• Collaboration with specialists (occupational therapy [OT], physical therapy [PT], SLP, medical team) |
| Orthopedic Impairment | • Physical limitations impacting mobility, access to materials, and participation<br>• Fatigue and coordination challenges | • Assistive technology for writing, mobility, and positioning<br>• Adaptive physical education and modified physical activities<br>• Accessible classroom environments<br>• Extended time for tasks |
| Other Health Impairment (OHI) | • Fatigue, inattention, and inconsistent school attendance<br>• Chronic health conditions (such as ADHD, asthma, and epilepsy)<br>• Impact on focus and stamina in learning | • Scheduled breaks and modified workload<br>• Health care plans with staff training for medical needs<br>• Preferential seating and visual supports<br>• Organizational supports (timers, checklists) |
| Specific Learning Disability (SLD) | • Difficulty with reading, writing, mathematics, or processing information<br>• Challenges with organization and memory<br>• Frustration leading to avoidance of learning tasks | • Structured, explicit instruction (such as Orton-Gillingham for dyslexia)<br>• Graphic organizers, audiobooks, and speech-to-text tools<br>• Extended time and small-group testing<br>• Multisensory learning approaches |
| Speech or Language Impairment (SLI) | • Difficulty with articulation, fluency, or expressive or receptive language<br>• Social communication barriers and low self-esteem | • SLP services<br>• Visual aids and preteaching vocabulary<br>• Simplified or chunked instructions<br>• Communication supports (visuals, AAC, and so on) |
| Traumatic Brain Injury (TBI) | • Cognitive challenges (memory, attention, processing speed)<br>• Fatigue, behavior changes, and executive function deficits<br>• Physical impairments or speech challenges | • Individualized supports and gradual workload increases<br>• Cognitive supports (timers, checklists, reminders)<br>• Health care and behavior plans<br>• Collaboration with specialists (OT, SLP, PT) |
| Visual Impairment (Including Blindness) | • Limited access to print materials and visual media<br>• Mobility challenges in navigating environments<br>• Delays in literacy and social development | • Braille instruction, tactile materials, and assistive technology (screen readers)<br>• Orientation and mobility training<br>• Enlarged print, high-contrast visuals, and audio supports<br>• Preferential seating and accessible learning materials |

References

Individuals with Disabilities Education Act, 20 U.S.C. § 1400 (2004).

# Rigor Audit Template

Use this template to support your implementation of the "Team Rigor Audit Process" reproducible (page 28). See the sources at the end of this reproducible for access to resources for Depth of Knowledge (DOK; Hess, n.d.) and Bloom's taxonomy (Anderson & Karthwohl, 2001).

**Part 1: Standard Identification**

What are the **standards addressed**?

- Insert the full text of the priority standard here.

  _____
  _____
  _____
  _____
  _____

- What are the key skills and concepts required for mastery?

  _____
  _____
  _____
  _____
  _____

Using the resources provided, **identify the DOK level**. (Circle one.)

- *Level 1: Recall/Reproduction*
- *Level 2: Skill/Concept*
- *Level 3: Strategic Thinking/Reasoning*
- *Level 4: Extended Thinking*

Using the resources provided, **identify the appropriate level for cognitive process in Bloom's taxonomy**. (Circle one.)

- *Remember*
- *Understand*
- *Apply*
- *Analyze*
- *Evaluate*
- *Create*

**Part 2: Task or Assessment Analysis**

Briefly **describe** the task, activity, or assessment.

_____
_____
_____
_____
_____

Using the table provided at the end of this section, **answer the following questions about the current cognitive demand**.

- *With which DOK level does the task align?*
- *What Bloom's taxonomy level does it reflect?*

**Analyze task alignment**. Is the task aligned with the standard's expected rigor? If not, what is missing?

_____
_____
_____
_____
_____

| Alignment Element | Current Task or Assessment | Expected Standard | Notes |
|---|---|---|---|
| Cognitive Skill (Bloom's Taxonomy) | | | |
| Complexity (DOK) | | | |
| Depth of Understanding | | | |

**Part 3: Task Revisions**

**Make recommended adjustments.** How can the task be revised to meet the expected rigor?

_____
_____
_____
_____
_____

**Revise the task.** Based on your answer to the previous question, fill in the following prompts.

- *Revised description:*
  _____
  _____

- *Revised DOK level:*
  _____

- *Revised Bloom's taxonomy level:*
  _____

The following is an example of a revised task.

| Original Task | Revised Task |
| --- | --- |
| List three causes of the U.S. Civil War. | Analyze three causes of the U.S. Civil War, and explain how each contributed to the conflict. |

**Part 4: Accessibility and Equity Check**

**Consider the Universal Design for Learning (UDL; CAST, 2024) principles (checkpoints)** shown in the following table. Are there multiple means of engagement, representation, and action or expression?

_____
_____
_____
_____
_____
_____

| UDL Checkpoints | Notes on Accessibility |
| --- | --- |
| Language and vocabulary support | |
| Visuals, graphic organizers, and so on | |
| Scaffolding or supports provided | |
| Opportunities for student choice | |

**Review access considerations.** Does the task ensure access for all learners (such as multilingual learners, students with disabilities, and students with varying abilities)?

_____
_____
_____
_____
_____

**Part 5: Evidence and Reflection**

**Conduct a student work analysis** (if student performance data are available) by answering the following questions.

- *What is the evidence of alignment with the expected rigor?*

  _____
  _____
  _____
  _____
  _____

- *What does student performance reveal about the rigor of the task?*

  _____
  _____
  _____
  _____
  _____

**Determine next steps.** How will instruction or tasks be adjusted moving forward?

_____
_____
_____
_____
_____

**References**

Anderson, L. W., & Krathwohl, D. (Eds.). (2001). *A taxonomy for learning, teaching, and assessing: A revision of Bloom's taxonomy of educational objectives.* Allyn & Bacon.

CAST. (2024). *Universal Design for Learning guidelines version 3.0.* Accessed at http://udlguidelines.cast.org on January 17, 2025.

Hess, K. (n.d.). *The Hess Cognitive Rigor Matrices (Hess CRMs) integrating DOK and Bloom.* Accessed at www.karin-hess.com/free-resources on January 9, 2025.

# PART 2

# Living *Yes We Can!*

# CHAPTER 2

# ALIGNING BELIEFS AND BEHAVIORS TO LIVE *ALL MEANS ALL*

| Envision What's Possible | |
|---|---|
| Picture a school where . . . | . . . Ongoing examination of espoused beliefs and day-to-day policies, practices, and behaviors ensures alignment and leads to high levels of learning for all |
| At the end of this chapter, you will have the opportunity to further reflect on this vision by considering your role in its achievement, potential challenges along the way, ways to address those challenges, and the positive impact achieving this vision will have on students. ||

In *Dare to Lead*, Brené Brown (2018) asserts:

> **Living into our values means that we do more than profess our values, we practice them. We walk our talk—we are clear about what we believe and hold important, and we take care that our intentions, words, thoughts, and behaviors align with those beliefs. (p. 186)**

The continual examination of whether our behaviors are aligned with what we say we believe in is not unique to individuals.

All organizations, including schools and school districts, must also participate in this ongoing reflection. Organizations develop and publicize a mission statement that makes clear to stakeholders the reason for their existence and what the organization prioritizes. Mission and vision statements make clear what an organization believes in. Schools and districts highlight and celebrate publicly those things that are aligned with what they want their stakeholders to know about them. In schools, these things might be high student achievement, performing and visual arts, athletic accomplishments, or students participating in service projects. Oftentimes, the resources dedicated to these priorities are very visible in the hallways of your facilities, on the local website, and on social media.

When a school is dedicated to building and sustaining an *all means all* culture, structures and systems are in place to ensure *all* students have access to rigorous instruction, and there is a universal commitment to keeping *all* students on grade-level standards, with very few exceptions. You hear language that is asset based, and the organization's vocabulary consistently demonstrates a strong belief that *all* students can reach grade-level proficiency. Advocacy focuses on ensuring access to rigor, not rescuing students from struggle, and when teams are presented with a challenge or barrier, they focus on those things in the school they control. In order to make this culture a reality, schools must be connected to the foundational principles of a PLC.

A PLC, as envisioned in *Learning by Doing* (DuFour et al., 2024), is built on four pillars: (1) mission, (2) vision, (3) values, and (4) goals. These four pillars act as the foundation for the examination of and interconnections between espoused beliefs and behaviors. In addition, the work is driven by three big ideas: a (1) focus on learning in a (2) collaborative culture with a (3) results orientation. Teams in these schools live up to these three big ideas by continually working to answer four critical questions: (1) What do we want all students to know and be able to do? (2) How will we know if they have learned it? (3) How will we respond when some students have not learned? and (4) What will we do when they have already learned it?

However, as schools and teams dig in and commit to a cycle of continuous improvement, they must also examine two *core beliefs* that drive the work in a school culture where *all* truly means *all*. These beliefs are as follows.

1. We believe that *all* students can learn at high levels.
2. We must take collective responsibility to *ensure* that *all* students learn at high levels (Mattos et al., 2025).

As we have facilitated learning around best practices in ensuring high levels of learning for *all*, we have challenged educators to peel back the layers of their PLC work and specifically apply the practices to students entitled to services. When they do so, a stark reality tends to settle in. Even when schools are making exceptional growth year after year when it comes to most students, their data regarding outcomes for special education–entitled students continues to stall. One of the reasons we believe this to be true is that while teams may be working to answer the four critical questions of a PLC on an ongoing basis, if they are not *also* continually examining the evolution of core beliefs and the alignment of practices, it will act as the proverbial elephant in the room. This chapter addresses this challenge by demonstrating the reasons educators must *believe* in the reason education as an institution exists *and* take action to align practices where they identify misalignment. This is particularly crucial when it comes to the beliefs and aligned practices as they relate to students with disabilities.

At the end of this chapter, we have included some suggested activities that facilitate examination of the current reality regarding these beliefs and associated practices.

We find that the reflection and conversation that occur between professionals as they engage in these learning activities can be a catalyst for meaningful progress. If left unexamined, a lack of commitment to your mission, vision, values, and essential beliefs will likely act as a barrier to ongoing improvement for *all*. And once schools commit to transparently examining these beliefs, they must also commit to the ongoing examination of whether the day-to-day behaviors of those in the organization are consistent with what they espouse to believe.

## What We Have Learned

Since the publication of *Yes We Can!* (Frizielle et al., 2016), we have been encouraged by the continued rise in the number of schools and school districts that have amplified their commitment to all students learning at high levels. The commitment to the idea is becoming more widespread. However, there is a persistent disconnect between espousing to hold the belief and the day-to-day behaviors, policies, and practices that translate the belief into reality.

Thus, we have learned the following.

- We must explicitly define the vocabulary we use over and over again, with tedious redundancy.
- We cannot gloss over the importance of returning to and acknowledging the foundational concepts and beliefs of this work and expect progress to be made.
- If the foundational concepts and beliefs are not attended to on a regular basis, the misalignment between the beliefs and behaviors of those in the system will act as a barrier to high levels of learning.
- The examination of alignment is an ongoing process and not something to be addressed only at the beginning of the PLC journey.
- In order to gain multiple perspectives, *all* adult members of the school community must examine and discuss beliefs and behaviors together with professionals in the system, including those with whom they may not work on a day-to-day basis, just as they do with their collaborative teams.
- It is not uncommon for some educators to have the perception that spending time on cultivating the foundational and cultural realities in their school is not time well spent.

## What *All Means All* Means

In a PLC, the fundamental purpose and the reason for collaboration, as expressed through the three big ideas, are to ensure *all students learn at high levels* (DuFour et al., 2024). As Richard DuFour and colleagues (2021) write in *Revisiting Professional Learning Communities at Work*, "Not most students. Not all the regular education students.

Not all students who come to school ready to learn, or who show proper effort and self-responsibility. *All students*" (p. 230).

**All students.**

There it is. It seems crystal clear on its face. Unfortunately, we continue to have to clarify and define what high levels of learning mean and what they look like. Schools and districts that live *all means all* identify areas of misalignment and create action steps to address those areas.

Invariably, when we deliver keynote addresses, conduct workshops, or facilitate sessions that dedicate time and attention to examining our beliefs as educators, some participants perceive the topic to be "fluff" or not as important as other sessions focusing on priority standards, assessment practices, or systems of intervention. We would contend that nothing could be further from the truth. In fact, as we work with schools and districts across the United States, we continue to find that not nearly enough time and attention are paid to explicitly examining beliefs. The failure to do so on an ongoing basis is often the missing link between best practices and better outcomes for students. You see, our beliefs influence how we act and the decisions that we make about everything, ultimately impacting our behavior on an ongoing basis (Argyris, 1990).

Over a decade ago, Julie Schmidt was in the midst of delivering an opening address during a statewide conference for special education leaders. As she laid the foundation for the upcoming content, she addressed the mission of schools across the United States and two core beliefs: (1) that all students *can* learn at high levels and (2) that we must take collective ownership of the learning of *all* students in order to make progress.

Suddenly, one brave audience member raised her hand. Deciding that the participant's apparent level of discomfort was too high to redirect until later in the session, Julie acknowledged the now very anxious audience member, who asked, "Before we move on, can you please define *all*?"

Momentarily speechless, Julie finally replied, "All."

"Yes, I understand, but who exactly are you including in the all?"

It was then that it became clear that when working side by side with educators, we could not make any assumptions about our mission or how we define it. After all, the first step, or pillar, of the PLC at Work process, according to DuFour and colleagues (2024), is building consensus around this shared mission.

Richard DuFour, Rebecca DuFour, Robert Eaker, Mike Mattos, Anthony Muhammad, or any other educator whose work is deeply rooted in PLC practices, define *high levels of learning* as grade-level proficiency or higher, and educational research supports this assertion. For example, in *Focus: Elevating the Essentials to Radically Improve Student Learning*, Mike Schmoker (2018) emphasizes that success comes from a strong, deliberate focus on high-quality, grade-level instruction in every classroom and that high levels of learning are inherently tied to achieving grade-level proficiency or higher. That leads us back to our anxious audience member from Julie's conference address. Given that high levels are defined as grade-level proficiency or higher, in that context, what is the definition of *all*? Is it realistic and appropriate to expect grade-level learning for all of our students, regardless of their individual characteristics?

In *Yes We Can!* (Friziellie et al., 2016), we addressed this question by noting that unless significant shifts are made to dismantle the pervasive assumptions that most students with identified disabilities cannot learn, we are unlikely to make progress toward closing the gap across the United States. As underscored by *The Opportunity Myth* (TNTP, 2018), *all* students have a lack of access to not only grade-appropriate assignments but also to teachers who consistently hold high expectations. Lack of access to both is even more significant for students of color and for students with identified disabilities. So, high levels of learning for all truly means *all*.

The key for students entitled to special education services is to pair consistent high expectations with scaffolds and accommodations directly aligned to the adverse effects of an individual student's disability. Note the use of modifications, intended or unintended, is absent from this statement. That is intentional. Modifications, by definition, change the playing field by altering the level of rigor being asked of the student. Providing such modifications does not address the gap; it compounds it.

When a full team is considering if modifying grade-level expectations is appropriate, we use the following questions to guide us: Will this student be expected to function independently once they leave the school system? Will the student leave high school, potentially transition services, and be expected to live on their own? Get a job? Pay bills? Will they need to remain dependent at some level on services and supports?

If the answer is *yes*, then it is our moral, ethical, and professional obligation to provide the road map to get them to grade-level proficiency. If the answer is *no*, a second layer of discussion should take place. The second layer includes identifying whether the adverse effects of the disability are cognitive in nature. Students with some disabilities (vision impairment, mobility impairment, and so on) may need to access supports and services, but there may be nothing diagnostically that would indicate that we should alter our expectations related to high levels of learning while providing appropriate scaffolds, accommodations, and supports.

For these most complex learners, collaborative teams responsible for their learning should answer the same four critical questions that all collaborative teams work to continually answer, with one adjustment. For each of these learners, teams should ask the following questions.

1. What do we want *this* individual student to know and be able to do?
2. How are we going to know that *this* individual student is learning?
3. What will we do when *this* student is not learning?

4. How will we respond when *this* individual student's data indicate they will exceed their goals? How will we inject more rigor?

In summary, high levels of learning mean grade-level expectations or higher, and for our most complex learners, an additional layer of questioning must take place in order to ensure high expectations are maintained while individualizing the four critical questions.

## Our Beliefs: Foundation

When we assert that continually examining the alignment between beliefs and behaviors is a core concept that needs ongoing attention in inclusive practices to work, we are often asked, "What do you mean by 'what we believe in' or 'espoused beliefs'?" In order to clearly examine this alignment, we need to be clear on *what, exactly, we are aligning to*.

As a reminder, in a PLC, the work is framed by three big ideas (DuFour et al., 2024).

1. A focus on learning
2. A collaborative culture
3. A results orientation

And collaborative teams work in recurring cycles to continually answer four critical questions (DuFour et al., 2024).

1. What do we want *all* students to know and be able to do?
2. How will we know that they are learning?
3. What will we do if they are not learning?
4. What will we do if they have already learned it?

All of this ongoing work is supported by four pillars that act as the supporting foundation (DuFour et al., 2024).

1. Mission
2. Vision
3. Values (collective commitments)
4. Goals

The pillars prevent any structure from collapsing under its own weight or from external forces. In our context, these pillars very publicly declare what a school and district believe in. Thus, this is where your alignment efforts begin.

### Mission

There is a reason that mission statements for schools across the United States all sound similar. It is because a *mission statement* simply makes clear why an organization exists. It is your fundamental purpose. Below are some examples of mission statements publicly displayed on school and school district websites (emphasis is ours).

- "Ensure **every child** achieves his or her maximum potential" (Kildeer Countryside Community Consolidated School District 96 [Illinois], 2021).
- "Ensure high levels of learning for **each student** preparing them for successes beyond high school" (White River School District 416 [Washington], n.d.).
- "The purpose of Mason Crest is to ensure high levels of learning for **all**—students and adults" (Mason Crest Elementary School [Virginia], n.d.).

You will be hard-pressed to find a school mission statement that claims that their fundamental purpose is to ensure high levels of learning for *most* or *some* of their students. It is a very public and a very clear declaration of purpose . . . *all*. But we know that there is a big difference between writing or creating a mission and living one (DuFour et al., 2024).

For instance, it is not uncommon for a school's or district's mission statement to include the declaration that their purpose includes ensuring students reach their potential or their maximum potential. It sounds logical. But if you were to closely examine the practices of some of these schools, you might discover some misaligned practices that, in fact, demonstrate a tendency toward *predetermining what the potential of any given student actually is*. Some examples of such practices are as follows.

- Tracking and the rigid grouping of students by perceived ability levels
- Lowering expectation levels when students struggle or have had a history of struggling
- Differentiating instruction based on deficits and not on what students can do
- Maintaining criteria that result in a lack of access to rigorous coursework
- Relying heavily on past performance data to justify low expectations and a lack of access to rigorous coursework
- Modifying assignments, activities, projects, and assessments to alter the playing field, thus ensuring students with disabilities will not close the gap
- Meeting students where they are and staying there

Schools that live their mission do not leave any practice unexamined and consider alignment on an ongoing and continuous basis.

## Vision

A vision statement is something different. A *vision statement* describes your aspirations or what you are working to become. A powerful vision results in inspiration, aspiration, and perspiration and inspires people to rally around a greater purpose (Williams & Hierck, 2015). Note the bold verbs and descriptors used in the following vision statements, which are representative of publicly displayed messaging on many successful school and school district websites from across the United States.

- We envision that every district school will be a **thriving, dynamic, and inspiring** educational environment that produces self-directed learners and stimulates citizens of all ages to **trust in, invest in, and benefit from** public education.

- The City School District strives to be a **top-performing district,** as measured by student growth, engagement, safety, and fiscal responsibility.

- This district seeks to become the **premier** elementary school district in the United States.

The question becomes, How does a school or district use its vision statement to inspire and guide decision making on an ongoing basis? In the Kildeer Countryside Community Consolidated School District 96 (2021) in Illinois, their vision statement is to "become the premier elementary school district in the nation." As superintendent of schools during the global COVID-19 pandemic, Julie experienced firsthand how an organization's commitment to using its vision to drive decision making can be tested.

When schools were forced to close their doors for a period of time and to reimagine how high-quality instruction could be delivered given the circumstances, the district, at times, found itself nearly paralyzed by the rapidly changing information and direction and by differing input. The one constant question that supported their decision making was, "What would a premier school district do?" The constant consideration of how "premier" deviated from easy, efficient, or adequate drove the decision-making process for what became a two-to-three-year journey. They used their vision as a beacon to inspire and guide their actions during a critical time.

## Values (Collective Commitments)

While not every school or district has come to consensus on publicly shared value statements or collective commitments, many have. A school's or district's stated values, also identified as collective commitments in some organizations, are the specific attitudes, behaviors, and commitments that must be demonstrated in order to advance the organization's vision (DuFour et al., 2024). Values turn our beliefs into behaviors and our thinking into doing. The following are some representative examples derived from schools and districts that have worked with stakeholders to clearly identify values or collective commitments.

- Modeled expectations
- Every child, every school, every day
- Best practice, not first practice
- Learning without boundaries
- Every student
- Caring schools
- Collective responsibility

- Resource optimization
- **Excellence** by challenging our students and ourselves to meet the highest expectations of our community

    **Trust** by building relationships based on integrity, mutual respect, and open communication

    **Inclusiveness** by valuing individual differences and the contributions of a diverse student body and staff

    **Innovation** by encouraging ideas and practices that foster adaptability

    **Accountability** by aligning our actions and resources with our stated objectives and taking responsibility for the outcomes

By addressing how we will live our mission and make progress toward our vision, these commitments give us a concrete path to success. As articulated by Adam Bryant (2014) in "Management Be Nimble," the key to values having a positive impact is for the organization to "live by its values, reinforce them every day and not tolerate behavior that's at odds with them."

## Goals

Finally, we know goals are the glue that ensures we are identifying action steps and monitoring our progress toward living our mission, pursuing our vision, and staying true to our values or collective commitments. For example, if a school district's mission is to ensure high levels of learning for all students, but its annual goals consistently overlook improved student learning, it undermines the district's commitment to that mission.

Effective goals that anchor PLC work have two essential components: (1) they reflect the organization's highest priorities, and (2) they are aligned across all levels to ensure coherence, consistency, and feasibility.

In a high-functioning data-driven culture, a system is acutely aware of areas of greatest need. Those needs might include addressing achievement gaps among subgroups like special education–entitled students or those who are economically disadvantaged, reducing disproportionality in special education or in disciplinary practices, or addressing chronic absenteeism. Whatever a school district's greatest needs are, as identified by data, their district-adopted goals must make it clear that, as a system, action steps have been developed to address those needs.

Once those district-level goals are adopted, goals at all levels of the organization should be aligned with those established priorities. While district-level goals may look broader, they cascade into more specific, actionable objectives at the school and team levels, maintaining a shared focus while addressing unique contexts and needs. Figure 2.1 (page 48) illustrates how an aligned goal-setting process might look.

### District Goals
*These are developed by the superintendent in collaboration with staff and administrators.*

| Development, purpose, and use: | Goal-monitoring process: |
|---|---|
| • Developed by the administrative team using feedback from staff and stakeholder groups<br>• Focused on continuous improvement and improved student learning<br>• Used to guide district decision making | • Reviewed at district leadership meetings following fall, winter, and spring data updates<br>• Reviewed with full faculty two times per year<br>• Updates brought to the board of education in the fall, winter, and spring |

### School Improvement Goals
*These are completed by the principal with staff input.*

| Development, purpose, and use: | Goal-monitoring process: |
|---|---|
| • Aligned to district- or board-adopted goals<br>• Developed by the principal using local data<br>• Focused on student growth and proficiency<br>• Developed for the purpose of school improvement and to identify students projected not to meet grade-level expectations<br>• Used to determine an action plan for school improvement and to meet the needs of identified students<br>• Used to guide school decision making | • Discussed and adjusted by the principal and superintendent at goal meetings three times per year<br>• Discussed at administrative leadership meetings and collaborative team-level meetings |

### School Team Action Steps and Commitments | Team SMART Goals and Data Conversations

*These are accomplished through collective efficacy and shared ownership of school improvement.*

| Development, purpose, and use: | Goal-monitoring process: | Development, purpose, and use: | Goal-monitoring process: |
|---|---|---|---|
| • Aligned to district- or board-adopted goals<br>• Developed by the principal and school teams to outline specific actions of school teams<br>• Developed for the purpose of school, grade-level, and individual student improvement<br>• Used to guide team decision making<br>• Used to guide Tier 1 interventions | • Discussed and adjusted by teams regularly at team meetings using fall, winter, and spring data | • Aligned to district- or board-adopted goals<br>• Developed by teams using data from common formative and end-of-unit assessments<br>• Designed for the purposes of tailoring and differentiating instruction<br>• Used to guide instructional decision making at a student level | • Discussed and adjusted by teams at scheduled meetings that align with assessment windows using data from ongoing common formative and end-of-unit assessments |

### Personal Professional Goals
*These goals are individual goals for personal and professional growth.*

| Development, purpose, and use: | Goal-monitoring process: |
|---|---|
| • Aligned to district- or board-adopted goals<br>• Developed by individual teachers in the goal-setting cycle with guidance from school principals or assistant principals based on the evaluation rubric<br>• Developed for the purpose of continued personal professional growth<br>• Used to guide individual decision making and improvement | • Discussed and adjusted by the staff member and principals or assistant principals at the beginning, middle, and end of the school year |

**Figure 2.1:** Example of an aligned goal-setting process.

Some questions to guide goal setting are as follows.

- Are our goals clearly aligned with the needs of our students and our school vision?
- How do we ensure all team members are invested in achieving our goals?
- What data are we using to set and evaluate our goals?
- How often do we revisit and refine our goals to ensure they remain relevant and impactful?
- Is it clear how goals will align with each other at each level of the organization?

If we are to make progress toward ensuring higher levels of learning for all of our students and in closing the gap for those students who need the most, then districts and schools must be diligent in identifying priorities based on data and ensuring system alignment. If such diligence is lacking, you may end up with an overwhelming number of goals, with a low probability that many will be reached.

## Culture as an Iceberg

In 1976, Edward T. Hall described the culture of any given organization as an iceberg consisting of two distinct components. He explained that external or surface components make up 10 percent of the culture. These are explicitly learned and conscious components such as traditions and customs and are very publicly celebrated and, therefore, more easily impacted or changed. One can typically identify these indicators fairly easily on websites, on the walls of a school, or during a public celebration. However, Hall also argued that 90 percent of an organization's culture is made up of those things that lie below the surface or below the waterline. These are internal and deeply embedded components that are implicitly learned and are unconscious, making them much more difficult to impact or change. These include assumptions, nonverbal behaviors, and perceptions. These indicators are more challenging to identify and may be more subtle during a staff meeting or in the teacher's lounge as members of the school community communicate what they are thinking and feeling through nonverbal body language and the use of vocabulary (see figure 2.2, page 50).

When a teacher or staff member is new to a school community, they immediately begin to learn about the most visible components of the culture. They receive the employee handbook, perhaps scroll through the school's website, and attend any orientation sessions, where the school or district communicates the things they most want the new members of their community to know, most of which live above the waterline. Then, school begins, employees return, parents attend curriculum nights, and students flood the hallways. This is when anyone new to the school begins to listen and observe the behaviors that live below the waterline and, thus, learn how "things are done around here."

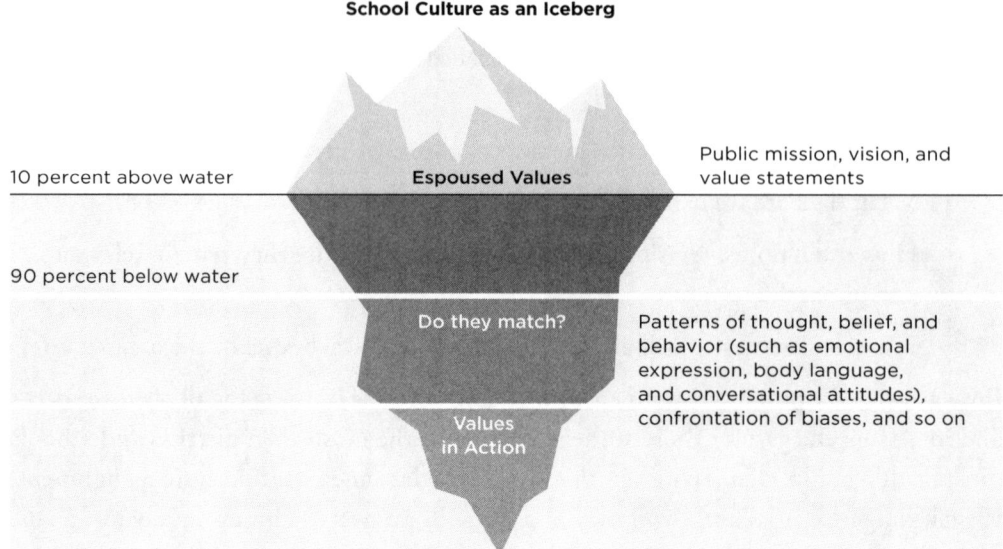

**Figure 2.2:** Components of school culture.

As Rebecca DuFour so powerfully pointed out time and time again, if culture reflects "the way we do things around here," we face the challenge of making conscious that which typically is unconscious. This can only be done through an unrelenting commitment to examine those indicators that live below the waterline on an ongoing basis to ensure they match the values and beliefs we so publicly espouse and to begin to influence those things that live below the waterline by forcing them to the surface for transparent reflection and discussion.

When your mission statement declares that you will "do whatever it takes to ensure all students learn at high levels," are your values-guided policies, practices, and behaviors aligned? Are structures and processes in place that would only exist if every person in your organization was deeply committed to your mission? If you are going to publicly declare what you value or what you believe in, work to ensure you are exhibiting behaviors that align!

District leaders, school leaders, and teacher leaders should take note of the clear warning from *Learning by Doing* (DuFour et al., 2024), which says:

> **Nothing will destroy a leader's credibility faster than an unwillingness to address an obvious violation of what the organization contends is vital. Leaders must not remain silent; they must be willing to act when people disregard the purpose and priorities of the organization. (p. 251)**

Therefore, this chapter is meant to ignite your sense of urgency around the need for this ongoing reflection!

## The Impact of Language and Labels

*Words matter.* In a blog post for AllThingsPLC, Jeanne Spiller (2020) states that we have all (educators, parents, students) engaged in the behavior of summing up or labeling students in one word or with phrases that subconsciously can attribute a set of expectations to the label. Some examples of these labels include "limited English proficient" and "SpEd kid." We have heard well-meaning teachers call their students "sweet and lows" and "self-contained kids." While using labels may help us to "explain" low performance or will ensure a student "gets what they need," there are harmful and long-lasting effects of doing so.

As the provision of special education services has evolved and silos between general and special education have been constructed, we have somehow moved away from a core truth: All students are general education students *first*. We have general education students who happen to qualify for services through special education based on an identified disability. When we resort to using labels, they begin to define the student. They reinforce the flawed notion that a diagnosis is who the student is. Unfortunately, what begins to happen is we begin to attribute a set of expectations to the label. "This is a special education student, so I need to alter my expectations and what proficiency should look like for them." Over time, we end up actually adding to learning gaps rather than closing them. Additionally, we are sending messages to our students about whether they can learn.

The lack of high expectations over time begins to impact what advocacy looks and sounds like for students.

## The Role of Advocacy and Productive Struggle

*Merriam-Webster's Dictionary* defines the act or process of *advocating* (Advocate, n.d.) as actively championing or pleading in favor of something or someone. Special educators have historically seen advocating for students with disabilities as one of their most important responsibilities. Most educators tend to embrace their role as advocates. What we need to guard against—and, in many situations, correct for—is allowing the act of "championing or pleading in favor of something or someone" to translate into protecting students from productive struggle (Blackburn, 2018). Our goal must be to ensure accessibility without reducing rigor and champion students' potential without limiting their learning opportunities.

In the not-too-distant past, it was common for special educators to consistently make the case that the students on their caseload "could not possibly" be expected to work on or complete the same activities their peers were asked to complete. They would then spend an inordinate amount of time modifying, modifying, modifying. Instead, we make the case for spending that time proactively designing scaffolds in collaboration with general education peers that will benefit many students, not just students with identified disabilities. We discuss this in further depth in chapter 5 (page 109).

As professionals, it becomes the responsibility of educators to know and recognize the difference between productive and destructive struggle. In *Visible Learning*, John Hattie (2023b) emphasizes that productive struggle promotes growth and resilience by pushing students to engage deeply with challenging but achievable material with appropriate scaffolding. Conversely, destructive struggle leaves students faltering without sufficient support, oftentimes in the dark when it comes to what they are being asked to do. Robert J. Marzano and Debra J. Pickering (2011) also frame productive struggle as an essential part of student learning.

So we would ask this: What does advocacy currently look like for students who receive special education services? Is there consensus on what it should look like among both special and general educators? The collaborative activity (page 59) included at the end of this chapter provides an efficient process for supporting meaningful examination and reflection.

## Summary

When dissecting the concept of aligning beliefs and behaviors, we quickly come to the realization that in order to do so we must be clear as a system regarding what, exactly, we believe in. While most schools and districts have established their purpose through the development of a mission statement and most have identified what they aspire to become through visioning, the critical questions are: Do these foundational elements actively influence and guide day-to-day decisions, policies, and practices? Are they truly living documents that shape the culture and direction of the organization, or do they simply exist as formalities?

Ensuring the ongoing examination of the alignment between beliefs and behaviors can be supported through the ongoing use of the aligned activities at the end of this chapter. We also invite you to use figure 2.3 to engage in a reflective self-assessment of your current reality aligned with this core concept as a way to support the identification of one first action step toward improvement.

| Criteria | 4—Highly Effective | 3—Effective | 2—Developing | 1—Beginning |
| --- | --- | --- | --- | --- |
| Belief in Student Potential | A belief that students can achieve is always shown. | Belief through actions is mostly shown. | Belief and actions are inconsistent. | Belief that all students can achieve is rarely shown. |
| Aligned Practices | Policies and actions fully align with beliefs. | Policies and actions are mostly aligned, with some adjustments made. | Policies and actions have some alignment, but misalignments remain. | Policies and actions have little to no alignment with beliefs. |

| Language and Labels | Labels are not used, and asset-based language is prevalent. High expectations for all are evident. | The use of labels and language has shifted, and high expectations are becoming consistent. | Avoidance of using labels and language that lead to low expectations is inconsistent. | The use of labels and language that lead to low expectations is prevalent. |
|---|---|---|---|---|
| Reflection and Improvement | Reflection, challenging assumptions, and celebrating progress occur regularly. | Reflecting and adjusting, with some celebration of progress, occur sometimes. | Reflection and action taking are inconsistent. Progress is rarely celebrated. | Reflection or taking action seldom happens, and there is no celebration of progress. |

**Figure 2.3:** Reflection rubric for assessing collaborative practices.

*Visit **go.SolutionTree.com/PLCbooks** for a free reproducible version of this figure.*

Through the lens of a school successfully aligning beliefs and behaviors to ensure learning for *all*, use figure 2.4 to reflect on your role, potential challenges, ways to overcome these challenges, and the impact to students both academically and personally.

| Picture a school where . . . | . . . Ongoing examination of espoused beliefs and day-to-day policies, practices, and behaviors ensures alignment and leads to high levels of learning for all |
|---|---|
| Consider your role in making this vision a reality in your context. How would you contribute? | |
| Identify some challenges you may face in achieving this possibility. | |
| Consider ways to overcome these challenges (over, around, and through). | |
| Anticipate the impact on students. How would bringing this possibility to life impact students academically and personally? | |

**Figure 2.4:** Envision What's Possible reflection tool for aligning beliefs and behaviors.

*Visit **go.SolutionTree.com/PLCbooks** for a free reproducible version of this figure.*

Use the following aligned activities included at the end of this chapter to support your work around this chapter's core concept.

- **"Examination of Alignment: Discussion and Planning Tool" (page 55):** Use this reproducible tool as you work to examine the alignment between policies, practices, and day-to-day behaviors and espoused beliefs. Using your mission, vision, and values to guide you, you might use the following format, addressing the questions as listed. We find the process most impactful when evidence of alignment or misalignment is a required part of the analysis and the majority of your conversation is spent on action steps for removing barriers and moving forward.

- **"Beliefs: Mix, Pair, Share" (page 57):** Use this reproducible tool to initiate conversation and reflection about the current reality of beliefs across teams and roles.

- **"Class List Reflection" (page 58):** Use this reproducible tool to examine and begin to deconstruct beliefs and biases about students who are entitled to services.

- **"Collaborative Activity: Defining Advocacy for Students" (page 59):** Use this reproducible tool to get clear on what advocacy accomplishes and should look like in your school.

# Examination of Alignment: Discussion and Planning Tool

**Objective:** Use the grid on this page to review alignment and then answer the alignment examination prompts that follow.

| Aligning Beliefs With Practice  We believe that *all* students can learn at high levels.  We take collective responsibility for the learning of *all* students. | | | | |
|---|---|---|---|---|
| Current policy, procedure, or practice | A = Aligned  M = Misaligned with core beliefs | Evidence or an artifact demonstrating alignment or misalignment | Barriers to moving toward alignment | First next step or first next stop |
| | | | | |
| | | | | |
| | | | | |
| | | | | |
| | | | | |

*All Means All* © 2025 Solution Tree Press • SolutionTree.com
Visit **go.SolutionTree.com/PLCbooks** to download this free reproducible.

**Alignment Examination Prompts**

Collaborate to answer the following alignment examination prompts.

- Does any team or individual in our school intentionally or unintentionally behave in ways that predetermine any student's maximum potential?
- Do any of our practices or processes act as a barrier to any student reaching their maximum potential?
- Do any of our beliefs or practices act as a barrier to students accessing rigor?
- Which policies, procedures, and practices are clearly aligned that we should celebrate?
- Do we have a systematic way to monitor that we are preparing each and every student for success beyond high school?
- What do we do when students are not on track to be successful once they leave us?
- What is the current reality regarding the opportunities to engage in deep professional learning for our adults?
- Have members of our school community had experiences that made them feel as if they were a part of a premier organization?
- When considering whether to allocate precious resources to an initiative or a change, have we asked whether it is something a premier school or district would do?
- Can we provide evidence that we are becoming a top-performing school?
- Do we have tangible evidence that our graduates are benefiting from their experience?
- If we were truly committed to living our values, what would it look like? What would it sound like? What would it feel like?

Examples of policies, processes, and practices to consider include, but are not limited to, the following.

- *Grading and reporting practices*
- *Discipline policies, processes, and practices*
- *Assessment and feedback practices*
- *Practices regarding access to rigor*
- *Examination of teacher expectations*

# Beliefs: Mix, Pair, Share

**Objective:** Assess and monitor current reality regarding beliefs, giving participants the opportunity to hear perspectives from colleagues who serve in various roles.

**Suggested audience:** Full faculty or a team or staff meeting

**Structure:** Stand up, hand up, pair up

**Time:** 10–15 minutes

Introduce and consider the following three high-leverage core beliefs.

1. We believe that all students can learn at high levels.
2. We take collective ownership for the learning of all students in our school.
3. We are committed to doing whatever it takes to ensure high levels of learning for all students.

Use the following steps to conduct the rest of this activity.

1. Participants stand and, with one hand raised, are asked to move around the room until prompted to stop.
2. Prompt participants to stop and high-five someone near them, ensuring it is not someone on their current collaborative team.
3. If participants do not know each other, ask them to introduce themselves and describe their current role in the school or district. If they are familiar with each other, ask them to briefly update their partner on their current role and if they served in other roles in the past.
4. Display and read one core belief, asking each partner to identify the school's current reality on the following Likert scale and what evidence they would use to support the assessment. Provide a timer (three to four minutes).

| 1 | 2 | 3 | 4 | 5 |
|---|---|---|---|---|
| We do not believe this is true at all. | We're not sure we believe this is true. | We believe this is true, but . . . | We believe this is true. | We strongly believe this is true. |

5. Either provide the next prompt, keeping partners together, or ask participants to find a new partner and then provide the next prompt.
6. Continue until partners have discussed each of the prompts you identified.
7. Ask participants to move back to their home tables.
8. Once back at their home tables, ask them to spend three to four minutes discussing anything that they heard from their partners that either surprised them or was an "aha" moment for them.

This activity proves to be powerful, both because it can serve as a way to monitor what the current reality is and because it can help staff members consider the current reality from another staff member's role and perspective.

# Class List Reflection

**Objective:** Examine and reflect on current beliefs regarding every student's ability to learn at high levels.

**Suggested audience:** Full faculty

**Structure:** Partner conversation

**Time:** 10 minutes

Either prior to or immediately following this reflection, facilitate learning around the ladder of inference (Peterson, 2023) to support a deeper level of awareness and understanding. Then, to complete this reflection, follow these steps.

1. Organize participants into pairs.
2. Project the following class list and prompts.
    → A teacher received the class list in the following table the week before school begins.
    → What are some thoughts the teacher may have?
    → What might you have heard from educators who receive this class list?

| Class List | | | | | |
|---|---|---|---|---|---|
| Student | Gender | Supports | Student | Gender | Supports |
| Rashid | B | IEP | Kevin | B | |
| Isabella | G | EL | Luis | B | EL |
| Madeline | G | | Tangenika | G | IEP |
| Louise | G | EL | Patrick | B | |
| Jordan | B | | Dylan | B | IEP |
| Hector | B | IEP and EL | Artem | B | |
| Sally | G | | Jonathan | B | |
| Carina | G | IEP | Josef | B | IEP and EL |
| Amir | B | EL | Cella | G | |
| Kyla | G | EL | Timmy | B | IEP |
| Sam | B | | Elizabeth | G | |
| Students with an individualized education plan (IEP): 7<br>Students who are English learners (ELs): 7 | | | | | |

3. Give pairs three minutes to discuss their reactions.
4. Have each pair connect with one other pair, creating groups of four.
5. Ask new groups to share a summary of each pair's conversation.
6. Ask participants to consider how personal experiences and experiences others share with us may lead to the development of assumptions or generalizations.

Reference

Peterson, R. (2023, November 28). *Understanding the ladder of inference: Navigating cognitive pitfalls*. Accessed at https://gould.usc.edu/news/understanding-the-ladder-of-inference-navigating-cognitive-pitfalls on January 29, 2025.

# Collaborative Activity: Defining Advocacy for Students

**Objective:** Facilitate a group discussion and reflection on the concept of advocacy for students, emphasizing the impact defining it has on student outcomes.

**Time:** 45 minutes

**Materials:**

- *Whiteboard or flip chart*
- *Markers*
- *Sticky notes*
- *Access to research articles on advocacy in education (optional)*

This activity breaks down into the following parts, each with its own set of steps.

### Part 1: Introduction (8 minutes)

Participants get clear on what advocacy is and is not.

1. Begin with a brief overview of advocacy in education. Provide definitions and examples, emphasizing the distinction between advocating for students and enabling them, as discussed in chapter 2 (page 39).
2. Share that the goal of the activity is to collaboratively define what advocacy means within their school and on their teams.

### Part 2: Group Discussion (15 minutes)

Groups facilitate a discussion about advocating for students.

1. Divide participants into small groups (three to five members each or combine two existing collaborative teams).
2. Ask each group to discuss the following questions.
   a. What does advocating for students mean to you?
   b. What actions do you believe are essential to advocate for students, effectively ensuring access to rigor?
   c. How can we ensure our advocacy does not inadvertently lead to rescuing students from struggle?
3. Encourage groups to note key points on sticky notes.

### Part 3: Sharing and Synthesizing (15 minutes)

Groups highlight their thinking and identify themes across groups.

1. After discussions, have each group summarize their conversation to the larger group.
2. As each group speaks, write its key points on the whiteboard or flip chart.
3. Identify common themes and differing perspectives among the groups.

**Part 4: Reflection (7 minutes)**

Provide an opportunity for further learning and reflection.

1. Provide resources that include summaries of best practices in advocacy from research (*The Opportunity Myth* [TNTP, 2018] or Robert J. Marzano's [2017] *The New Art and Science of Teaching*).
2. Ask participants to reflect individually on how a high-leverage definition of advocacy can be integrated into their daily practices.
3. Conclude by having each team identify two or three commitments or actions they plan to take to support this clearer definition of advocacy.

**Part 5: Follow-Up (Optional)**

Participants commit to follow-up discussions.

1. During a meeting sometime in the next four to eight weeks, discuss progress on the group's advocacy commitments and share successes and challenges with each other.

**Key Concepts to Consider**

When conducting this collaborative activity, make sure all participants give consideration to the following key concepts.

- **Advocacy versus rescuing:** Understanding how to provide support without undermining a student's access to rigor and opportunity to develop independence
- **High expectations:** Emphasizing the importance of maintaining rigorous academic expectations while advocating for necessary supports
- **Collaboration:** Building a culture of collaboration where educators have consensus around what advocacy looks like and how they will work together to empower high levels of student learning

We assert that if you move on to the following chapters of this book having minimized the foundational impact of the ongoing reflection on the alignment of beliefs and behaviors, you will be making a mistake your students cannot afford. When educators fail to reflect on their espoused beliefs about high levels of student learning and the corresponding actions taken in the classroom, they risk perpetuating inequities and limiting students' opportunities, not just in school but for a lifetime (DuFour & Eaker, 1998; Hattie, 2012; Schmoker, 2016).

**References**

DuFour, R., & Eaker, R. (1998). *Professional Learning Communities at Work: Best practices for enhancing student achievement*. Solution Tree Press.

Hattie, J. (2012). *Visible learning for teachers: Maximizing impact on learning*. Routledge.

Marzano, R. J. (2017). *The new art and science of teaching*. Solution Tree Press.

Schmoker, M. (2018). *Focus: Elevating the essentials to radically improve student learning* (2nd ed.). ASCD.

# CHAPTER 3

# COLLABORATION BY *ALL* FOR *ALL*

**Envision What's Possible**

| Picture a school where . . . | . . . Collaboration by all for all is observed in every action and is part of the culture |
|---|---|
| At the end of this chapter, you will have the opportunity to further reflect on this vision by considering your role in its achievement, potential challenges along the way, ways to address those challenges, and the positive impact achieving this vision will have on students. ||

There are many different definitions for the word *collaboration*. Consider these examples.

- "The action of working with someone to produce or create something" (*Oxford English Dictionary*; Collaboration, n.d.)
- "To work jointly with others or together especially in an intellectual endeavor" (*Merriam-Webster Dictionary*; Collaborate, n.d.)
- "A deeper level of working together that involves a shared vision, clear objectives, and a mutual understanding of each person's role in achieving those goals" (ThoughtFarmer, n.d.)

The common thread or through line of all these definitions is the act of working together in order to make something happen. When we consider collaboration in a PLC, it becomes clear the "something" we make happen is student learning. *Learning by Doing* defines *collaboration* as "a systematic process in which [people] work together, interdependently, to analyze and impact their professional practice in order to improve individual and collective results" (DuFour et al., 2024, p. 68).

In this chapter's core concept, an observer in a school making the most progress in closing gaps for all learners will see all professionals in the school collaborating around meeting the needs of each and every student. The master schedule identifies time dedicated to collaborative teams. Regardless of the grade level, content area, department, or other structure, these teams include both the general and special educators responsible for student learning.

## The Research on Collaboration

Research related to the power of collaboration expands far beyond that of PLCs. Hattie's (2023b) synthesis of over two thousand meta-analyses related to student achievement defines *collective teacher efficacy* as the collective belief of all adults in a school staff in their ability to positively impact students. His research identifies the effect size of collective teacher efficacy as 1.57 (Visible Learning, 2018). This figure measures the impact on learning versus making no changes to existing practices, with 0.4 indicating one year's worth of expected learning growth for students. The effect size of engaging in collective teacher impact is twice that of giving students feedback (0.72) and almost three times bigger than the effect of classroom management (0.52), which are both effective strategies in their own right (Visible Learning, 2018). These findings show a powerful correlation between collective teacher efficacy—the collective belief that teachers can make a difference—and student achievement, indeed!

While educators working as a group sharing resources has been a long-existing structure, true collaboration by teachers has historically been less frequently observed. Much research affirms the impact of collaboration and having shared norms for that collaboration. In figure 3.1 and figure 3.2, you'll find specific references featured in the fourth edition of *Learning by Doing* (DuFour et al., 2024) relative to collaboration and norms.

| Why Should We Collaborate? |
|---|
| "The single most important factor for successful school restructuring and the first order of business for those interested in increasing the capacity of their schools is building a collaborative internal environment" (Eastwood & Louis, 1992, p. 215). |
| "When groups, rather than individuals, are seen as the main units for implementing curriculum, instruction, and assessment, they facilitate development of shared purpose for student learning and collective responsibility to achieve it" (Newmann & Wehlage, 1995, p. 38). |
| "[High-achieving schools] build a highly collaborative school environment where working together to solve problems and to learn from each other become cultural norms" (WestEd, 2000, p. 12). |
| "The key to ensuring that every child has a quality teacher is finding a way for school systems to organize the work of qualified teachers so they can collaborate with their colleagues in developing strong learning communities that will sustain them as they become more accomplished teachers" (National Commission on Teaching and America's Future, 2003, p. 7). |
| "Collaboration and the ability to engage in collaborative action are becoming increasingly important to the survival of public schools. Indeed, without the ability to collaborate with others, the prospect of truly repositioning schools . . . is not likely" (Schlechty, 2009, p. 237). |
| "It is time to end the practice of solo teaching in isolated classrooms" (Fulton, Yoon, & Lee, 2005, p. 4). |

Teacher collaboration in strong professional learning communities improves the quality and equity of student learning, promotes discussions that are grounded in evidence and analysis rather than opinion, and fosters collective responsibility for student success (McLaughlin & Talbert, 2006).

"Quality teaching is not an individual accomplishment, it is the result of a collaborative culture that empowers teachers to team up to improve student learning beyond what any one of them can achieve alone" (Carroll, 2009, p. 13).

High-performing, high-poverty schools build deep teacher collaboration that focuses on student learning into the culture of the school. Structures and systems are set up to ensure teachers work together rather than in isolation, and "the point of their collaboration is to improve instruction and ensure all students learn" (Chenoweth, 2009, p. 17).

Teachers should be provided with more time for collaboration and embedded professional development during the school day and year. Expanding time for collaboration during the school day "facilitates the development of effective professional learning communities among teachers" (Farbman, Goldberg, & Miller, 2014, p. 25).

"When teachers work together on collaborative teams, they improve their practice in two important ways. First, they sharpen their pedagogy by sharing specific instructional strategies for teaching more effectively. Second, they deepen their content knowledge by identifying the specific standards students must master. In other words, when teachers work together they become better teachers" (Many & Sparks-Many, 2015, p. 83).

"We must stop allowing teachers to work alone, behind closed doors and in isolation in the staffrooms and instead shift to a professional ethic that emphasizes collaboration. We need communities within and across schools that work collaboratively to diagnose what teachers need to do, plan programs and teaching interventions and evaluate the success of the interventions" (Hattie, 2015, p. 23).

*Source: DuFour et al., 2024, p. 87.*
**Figure 3.1:** Why should we collaborate?

---

**Why Should We Create Norms?**

Teams improve their ability to grapple with the critical questions when they clarify the norms that will guide their work. These collective commitments represent the "promises we make to ourselves and others, promises that underpin two critical aspects of teams—commitment and trust" (Katzenbach & Smith, 1993, p. 60).

Explicit team norms help to increase the emotional intelligence of the group by cultivating trust, a sense of group identity, and belief in group efficacy (Druskat & Wolff, 2001).

"When self-management norms are explicit and practiced over time, team effectiveness improves dramatically, as does the experience of team members themselves. Being on the team becomes rewarding in itself—and those positive emotions provide energy and motivation for accomplishing the team's goals" (Goleman, Boyatzis, & McKee, 2004, p. 182).

Norms can help clarify expectations, promote open dialogue, and serve as a powerful tool for holding members accountable (Lencioni, 2005).

Referring back to the norms can help "the members of a group to 're-member,' to once again take out membership in what the group values and stands for; to 'remember,' to bring the group back into one cooperating whole" (Kegan & Lahey, 2001, p. 194).

Inattention to establishing specific team norms is one of the major reasons teams fail (Blanchard, 2007).

After looking at over a hundred teams for more than a year, researchers concluded that understanding and influencing group norms were the keys to improving teams. Researchers noted two norms that all good teams generally shared. First, members spoke in roughly the same proportion. Second, the good teams were skilled at intuiting how others felt based on their tone of voice, expressions, and other nonverbal cues (Duhigg, 2016).

*Source: DuFour et al., 2024, p. 88.*
**Figure 3.2:** Why should we create norms?

The summary of research across contexts leads to a common theory: When teams collaborate, it benefits *all*. In general, "every member of a team has different skills, expertise, and talent. When all the members collaborate together they are able to utilize the experience, knowledge, and skills of everyone involved to achieve the shared goal" (Kissflow, 2025).

## Barriers to Collaboration

If collaboration has been proven to be so valuable, why don't some schools prioritize it? A huge reason for this is a lack of time within the contractual day. In 2018 research findings, only 31 percent of teachers reported that they have sufficient time to collaborate with other teachers (Johnston & Berglund, 2018). This can lead to planning happening in the hallway, in disjointed emails, or not happening in a cohesive way at all. The phenomenon of "Oh, we changed that plan at lunch" happens frequently with the best of intentions, as teachers make the most of the time they have. This can lead to inconsistency in access to standards, invalid assessments, and a sense of frustration for educators. The impact on special educators can be even greater when they are often planning for students at different grade levels in different content areas with different needs. They are often running from room to room, and when plans change, their ability to support learners, to help them access their accommodations to learn, and to provide meaningful instruction decreases dramatically. They have to be reactive instead of proactive, which can lead to frustration, volatility, and a lack of self-efficacy.

Since the publication of *Yes We Can!* (Friziellie et al., 2016), we have seen an increase in teams collaborating. Certainly, the COVID-19 pandemic forced everyone to dig in together to find new ways to do business. Overnight, we were challenged to find ways to plan, teach, assess, and collaborate on virtual platforms, which few educators had used for anything other than joining webinars in the past. Students were learning from home with varying degrees of support or supervision, often with few resources and such weak internet connections that trying to log in to instruction took more time than they actually had interacting with their teachers and classmates. But we did it! We made it happen to keep learning going, collaboration happening, and progress for all continuing to the very best of our abilities.

As a profession, we must celebrate this! However, our work is not yet done. Collaboration by all educators of a content area or course, including special educators and specialists supporting the students and content, occurs far less frequently. We frequently hear that a system might have team structures oriented around grade level, content area or department, job-alike roles, leadership, guiding coalitions, student support, and, yes, even special education. Each of these structures is important for ensuring learning for all students, but too frequently, the teams don't intersect. Student learning takes all of the team structures functioning together to ensure growth at the highest levels possible, with teams operating together as supporting spokes on the same wheel. When, for example, special educators do not have time to collaborate with general educators, we simply cannot guarantee we are meeting student needs. Additionally, general educators do not then have access to the strategies and skills special educators may be able to share to help them meet the needs of students who are not IEP-entitled but who struggle with content. We miss out on shared resources that can make time more efficient and instruction more effective for *all* learners. It also becomes almost impossible for special educators to know how to best support a student in making progress toward grade level when they, as teachers, are not included in planning or conversations targeting the progression of skills, strategies, and measures that lead to grade-level proficiency.

Put simply, collaboration between general and special education teachers is of utmost importance in creating an inclusive and effective learning environment. By working together, educators can share their expertise, resources, and strategies to meet the diverse needs of all students together instead of in isolation (Project IDEA, 2024).

## Conditions for Effective Collaboration

So, if we can identify what presents barriers to collaboration by all for all, what are the conditions in which collaboration is effective for *all*? In our work with schools and districts across the United States, we find the following essential elements are in place and observable in schools where students of all demographics are showing academic growth, and specifically where students with IEPs are closing learning gaps.

- All professionals in the school or system collaborate around meeting the needs of each and every student.
- Collaborative teaming includes general and special educators.
- Collaboration is focused on the four critical questions of a PLC (DuFour et al., 2024).
    a. What knowledge, skills, and dispositions do we expect every student to acquire as a result of this course or grade level?
    b. How will we know when each student has acquired the essential knowledge and skills?
    c. How will we respond when some students do not learn?
    d. How will we extend the learning for students who are already proficient?
- Every effort is made to ensure time for collaboration between general and special educators.
- Special educators are included in strategic preinstruction conversations and data action planning.

- Data discussions include *all* student data.
- When a student with an IEP struggles, all adults supporting the student problem-solve to identify, plan for, and implement a solution.

It's key to note that it is not enough simply to create the time structures and say, "Now, go collaborate!" Groups are often not sure what time is to be used for (such as clarifying learning targets within priority standards, developing formative assessments, identifying scaffolds and supports prior to instruction, or analyzing student assessment data to plan for interventions), what artifacts are expected of the time (such as agendas, unit plans, assessments, intervention plans, or data protocols), and what each person's role is in collaboration (such as facilitator or timekeeper), knowing that all members are expected to share resources and expertise. Without clarity on these things, any teacher is likely to respond by saying, "This is a waste of my time. Can I just have my planning period back?"

It is important that collaboration also involves efforts that serve not only students with disabilities but also their peers without disabilities in the inclusive classroom (Alhossyan, 2023). By clarifying together the benefit that collaboration can have on all educators at the table—general *and* special educators—we can take strides to help each teacher be better at their craft, more ready to support all students, and, hopefully, feel that they thrive in the environment. To do so, clarity on what's expected to happen during the time is key. Highly effective teams focus on the following, all of which are specifically discussed in subsequent chapters with resources to support a team's implementation of the work.

- Clarify and come to consensus on the most essential learning outcomes in a grade level or course.
- Develop common assessments to monitor student progress toward proficiency throughout the unit of instruction.
- Establish common expectations of proficiency.
- Analyze results from formative assessments, including the data of *all* learners.
- Plan for instruction with strategies for higher levels of learning brainstormed together.

## Ways to Strengthen Interdependence

Another challenge teams of any makeup may face is making the personal connections it takes to truly become interdependent. As Dax Grant (2023), the CEO of Global Transform, writes about collaboration and relationships for *Forbes*, "In all scenarios, nurturing key relationships with strategic insight and collaborative strategic understanding remains essential." Simply sharing resources does not require the level of trust that true collaboration demands. Therefore, to truly collaborate as it is defined in this chapter, it's critical to infuse a few key strategies to focus on the human side of team building.

Following are actions we have found in our practice to be critically important to teams truly collaborating. We have also included tools teams can consider to best implement these actions.

- Implement inventories to explore each others' learning preferences, personality styles, and perceived strengths and weaknesses. The Compass Points tool shared later in this section is a great resource for this. You may also consider resources such as Myers-Briggs Type Indicator (www.myersbriggs.org), the Color Code Personality Assessment (www.colorcode.com), the Enneagram (www.enneagraminstitute.com), or a variety of others.

- Utilize a protocol to collaboratively identify what each team member brings to the team, what they need from the team, and how they can contribute to the team's work, given their professional role. We find time and time again that the "Asset Analysis Protocol" (page 74) shared at the end of this chapter works for teams regardless of their size, level, or makeup.

- Establish team norms or operating rules for when the team is meeting and how adults will behave when working together. (Refer to figure 3.2, page 63, for more about team norms.) In addition, the team should proactively determine a way they will positively and gracefully handle a norm breach by any member of the team to ensure commitment to the team norms.

While establishing team norms has been done for a very long time, too often, the process is treated as a "checklist item" where teams comply with the task at the beginning of the school year and then often don't consider the norms again. To make norms more meaningful and living and breathing in teams, we find it helpful to engage in some "heart" work before creating norms. This starts with better understanding each other.

There are many tools available to engage colleagues in discussion about their learning styles, personality, habits, and so on. Earlier in this section, we mentioned the Compass Points preference tool from the Center for Leadership and Educational Equity (CLEE; n.d.). Similar to many other inventories, this exercise uses a set of preferences that relate not to individual but to group behaviors, helping us understand how preferences can impact our group work.

In conducting this activity, participants physically move in one of four directions designated around a room (North, South, East, or West) when prompted by the question, "When you are being your most true and authentic self, which Compass Point reflects your greatest strength?" Each direction is defined as follows (CLEE, n.d.).

- **North (acting):** People who prefer to act, experiment, and generally jump into problem solving, scenarios, and so on

- **East (speculating):** People who prefer to look at the big picture and examine possibilities before they act

- **South (caring):** People who want assurance that the feelings of all participants are factored into decision making and that their voices have been heard before acting
- **West (paying attention to detail):** People who want to know the who, what, when, where, and why before they act

It's important to note that while participants will choose one direction to move in, this does not mean they would never move in a different direction based on circumstances. This exercise is more about determining what a person's dominant direction is.

As participants choose a direction, they form groups based on that choice and discuss a given set of prompts in small conversation clusters, ideally about three to four people within each group. Prompts each group might grapple with might include the following.

- You can count on me to . . .
- Sometimes, it can be hard to work with me because . . .
- For me to trust others when we're working together, I need . . .

These prompts are only suggestions; the facilitator or planning team can certainly revise in any way that may better elicit conversation within the larger group.

When complete, the small groups report back to the whole group. While this strategy can be done in this manner with a large group, it can be just as effective with a small group in a discussion at a table, as well.

After completing a task such as this, participants in a system begin to better understand each other. That, however, does not necessarily create the conditions for effective collaboration. The aforementioned "Asset Analysis Protocol" (page 74) is a tool that can help connect personal attributes and preferences to the context of a team working together. Using this structure, a team can bring to light each other's strengths and then make collective commitments as to how they will work better together. This can lead to far more powerful team norms than those typically seen, simply because they strategically focus on *me* and then shift to the power of *we*. This is especially important as we ask special educators or specialists to join what have typically been collaborative structures made up of general educators, only so that every adult sees the value in each other's work, experience, talents, and perspectives. It is also most powerful when any paraprofessionals supporting learners in the grade level, content area, or team are included in the work. After all, they are often the closest supporters for students and, if included in the general education classroom, can be a resource for *all* learners. Put simply, paraprofessionals are tremendous assets to the collaborative team and add enormous value to collaborative conversations, planning, and problem solving.

It is important to note that while these tools can and (we would argue) should be used any time a new school year or even new semester begins, we encourage systems to also consider using these tools anytime there is a change in team membership—a long-term sub, a new hire, a new paraprofessional—or when a team struggles to get along. These are great structures to use to help build collective efficacy, understanding of each other, and collaboration for the students served.

When considering team structures, we dug into frequently occurring structures in chapter 2 of *Yes We Can!* (Friziellie et al., 2016). We realized, however, that we did not include one key team structure: a collaborative team supporting students who have low-incidence learning challenges. These are teams working with our most complex learners, often students who will need lifelong support to be safe and who may not live independently. To ensure we represent the importance of these teams for the students they serve, we created the conversation guide "Conversations and Activities for Low-Incidence Teams" (page 75). A tool these teams can find extremely beneficial is the Essential Elements within the Dynamic Learning Map (DLM) assessment (Dynamic Learning Maps, n.d.). DLMs are designed to accommodate students with significant cognitive disabilities by tailoring assessments to their abilities and learning needs. They focus on understanding what students know and can do rather than comparing them to grade-level peers. The Essential Elements create learning standards for students at each grade level that align with grade-level standards but at a level of expectation applicable as a starting point for a student with significant complexities in their learning profile.

Additionally, changing structures within a school to find additional time to collaborate may hit roadblocks due to additional time and resources not being readily available. When considering a master schedule change, it is a frequent occurrence that comfort levels may have to shift, and a significant amount of give-and-take is often required. This can lead to a "start at no" mentality for many if the change is too broad in scope to implement without overstressing the system. When considering schedule changes, it may be important to consider the light switch versus dimmer switch analogy. When turning a light switch on or off, the action typically results in an all-or-nothing outcome—the lights are on or off.

Approaching change in this all-or-nothing way can certainly be a fast track to overwhelming the system, moving too fast, getting negative results, and, often, causing frustration for all. However, if we approach changes like shifts in the master schedule, changes in special educator assignments, and adjustments to collaborative team time with the approach of a dimmer switch—a little change at a time—we can be more strategic in the work, reflect on effectiveness, avoid overwhelming educators, implement changes along the way, and ultimately have better outcomes for all involved.

Essential questions to be considered when analyzing the effectiveness of and opportunities for improvement of a master schedule focused on collaboration and high levels of learning for *all* include the following.

- What needs to be in place so we can build the schedule we want and students deserve?
- Does this schedule allow special and general education teachers time to collaborate? If not, how can we get creative to provide that time?
- How do our schedule and class placement practices impact student learning?
- Which students, teachers, or subjects should have priority when developing a master schedule? Should any?
- Are all staff members used in the most effective and efficient way possible?
- Does this schedule allow teaching partners (co-teachers or paraprofessionals) to teach together as much as possible?
- Are all students being served by the most appropriate staff?
- Does this schedule allow for heterogeneously balanced classrooms? Are any classes (content or elective) stacked with students who have academic or behavioral concerns, whether they are special education students or general education?
- Can any changes be made to improve our current schedule?
- Are students currently being pulled from core literacy or mathematics instruction to get supplemental services?

It's key for schools and systems to remember that July isn't the only time to build a schedule. If the dimmer switch metaphor is applied, purposeful midyear changes can certainly be made. For example, the guiding coalition charged with leading the PLC Warren Middle School in Warren, Arkansas, collaboratively made the decision to change the master schedule in October, just a couple of months into the school year. The team did this in order to create flex time where students in need could get access to interventions and to answer the third and fourth critical questions (how to respond when students do or do not learn; DuFour et al., 2024).

Similarly, Lotus Elementary in Spring Grove, Illinois, changed its continuum of services, materials, and model of instruction used for students with IEPs when it was determined their support within the general education classroom was not enough or tailored to student needs so they could close learning gaps. A full grade-level schedule change was implemented midyear! As a result of this more targeted instruction and time, the eight students of focus *all* made more than a year's growth in literacy and mathematics in the eight months of instruction, and three students made two full years of progress in literacy and mathematics within that same eight months.

A tool we have found to be simple but effective in analyzing a master schedule is a SWOT analysis. Originally designed by Robert Franklin Stewart and James E. Lipp

(1962), the SWOT analysis is one of the earliest strategic planning frameworks. It challenges planning participants to consider the *strengths, weaknesses, opportunities*, and *threats* of a potential idea, innovation, or change. When we apply this to master scheduling, whether considering major shifts or minor changes, we can better analyze impact from a place of facts rather than feelings or preferences. A suggested structure for this is as follows.

1. Identify the specific elements of the schedule to investigate. What is the scope of consideration?

2. Identify non-negotiables related to this element. This could include belief statements, data, and facts or any reality factors that may impact the schedule components of focus. The goal is to create a short list of limits or boundaries, not a laundry list of "Yeah, but" statements. If you find that the group identifies a lengthy list, it would be wise to stop, revisit, and collaboratively create a why statement about the reason to examine this schedule element before continuing. Perhaps participants are not yet in agreement on the problem to be solved or why it is important; regardless, this will get in the way of the work if not addressed before beginning the analysis.

3. Consider each element of the SWOT analysis individually first and then discuss as a group. All comments matter, but search for common threads.

4. Based on the findings, create a hypothesis statement that summarizes the consensus of the group related to the identified next step.

You can use the "SWOT Analysis for the Master Schedule" reproducible (page 76) to conduct this exercise. After assembling relevant factors in this analysis, the team can produce a hypothesis statement, such as "We agree that [change, step, innovation] is the logical next step because [rationale]." By establishing this shared commitment, the group can begin to develop the *how* of the change.

To develop the *how*, we encourage you to visit the AllThingsPLC website (https://allthingsplc.info) to explore sample schedules posted by schools who are identified as Model PLCs. You can filter the Model PLC schools database to match your own site demographics and find a school or system that closely matches yours and has shown improvements in data for at least three consecutive years. When you identify a similar school or system, you can access its schedules, resources, and contact information to help inform the decisions you make at your site.

## Summary

Put simply, collaboration between general and special education teachers is key to creating an inclusive and effective learning environment for *all*. It also promotes a school culture focusing on shared responsibility for student success. This, ultimately, is the goal for our students—that they learn and can do more because the educators learn together to know how to do better!

After reading this chapter, please reflect on your context and use the rubric in figure 3.3 to identify your team's strengths and opportunities for improvement.

| Criteria | 4—Highly Effective | 3—Effective | 2—Developing | 1—Beginning |
| --- | --- | --- | --- | --- |
| Collaborative Team Structures | Teams consistently include all educators involved with students. | Teams usually include all relevant educators. | Teams inconsistently include all educators. | Teams show little to no evidence of collaboration among educators. |
| Scheduled Collaboration Time | Regular, dedicated collaboration time is present in the schedule. | Collaboration time is scheduled but is occasionally inconsistent. | Collaboration time is infrequent or inconsistent. | There is no dedicated time for collaboration. |
| Shared Responsibility | All educators share responsibility for problem solving around every student's needs. | Most educators collaborate to solve student issues. | There is some evidence of collaboration, but there are gaps in shared responsibility. | There is little to no shared responsibility for students. |
| Involvement of Special Educators | Special educators are consistently included in planning and data conversations. | Special educators are usually included in planning and discussions. | Special educator involvement in planning and discussions is inconsistent. | Special educators are rarely involved in planning or discussions. |

**Figure 3.3:** Reflection rubric for assessing collaborative practices.

*Visit **go.SolutionTree.com/PLCbooks** for a free reproducible version of this figure.*

Through the lens of a school where educators routinely engage in collaboration by all and for all, use figure 3.4 to reflect on your role, potential challenges, ways to overcome these challenges, and the impact on students both academically and personally.

| Picture a school where . . . | . . . Collaboration by all for all is observed in every action and is part of the culture |
| --- | --- |
| Consider your role in making this vision a reality in your context. How would you contribute? | |
| Identify some challenges you may face in achieving this possibility. | |

**Figure 3.4:** Envision What's Possible reflection tool for aligning beliefs and behaviors.

*Visit **go.SolutionTree.com/PLCbooks** for a free reproducible version of this figure.*

Use the following aligned activities included at the end of this chapter to support your work around this chapter's core concept.

- **"Asset Analysis Protocol" (page 74):** Use this reproducible tool to help connect personal attributes and preferences to the context of a team working together.

- **"Conversations and Activities for Low-Incidence Teams" (page 75):** Use this reproducible tool to explore topics for discussion and outcomes of the work of a team supporting complex-profile learners.

- **"SWOT Analysis for the Master Schedule" (page 76):** Use this reproducible tool to strategically consider any schedule, including a building master schedule, to identify opportunities for improvement.

# Asset Analysis Protocol

Use this reproducible tool to help connect personal attributes and preferences to the context of a team working together.

| Name and Role | | | | | |
|---|---|---|---|---|---|
| **Assets**<br>• What do I bring to the team? (Do this on your own, and then all participants share out.) | | | | | |
| **Roles**<br>• What do I do within the team? (Do this on your own, and then all participants share out.) | | | | | |
| **Commitments**<br>• What do we agree is my purpose on the team?<br>• What do we do together? | | | | | |
| **Behaviors**<br>**(All participants contribute to create one response.)**<br>• How do we all agree to work so everyone contributes as we've agreed? (Include a norms check here! Add new norms or modify existing norms as needed.)<br>• What will we do together? | | | | | |

*All Means All* © 2025 Solution Tree Press • SolutionTree.com
Visit **go.SolutionTree.com/PLCbooks** to download this free reproducible.

# Conversations and Activities for Low-Incidence Teams

| Topics | Potential Conversations and Activities |
| --- | --- |
| Selecting research-based tools and strategies | • What tools or strategies are working?<br>• Should we consider any new tools or strategies?<br>• How do we determine if tools and strategies are working? |
| Determining the scope of curriculum-based instruction | • Review curriculum-based instruction.<br>• Determine locations and purpose.<br>• Scaffold the expectations for each grade level. |
| Creating independence plans for all students | • Determine what each student can do as independently as possible, and create a plan to build on the effort.<br>• Set goals with families and teams on tasks for each student to do yearly as independently as possible.<br>• Train and monitor the paraprofessionals to allow the student to have a productive struggle. |
| Using grade-level priority standards and Essential Elements of Dynamic Learning Map assessments (Dynamic Learning Maps, n.d.) to develop individualized learning plans | • Identify where the student is functioning according to data.<br>• Determine what the team and family believe a student's priorities are.<br>• Create individualized learning progressions for each student.<br>• Monitor student progress regularly, not just for IEP goal updates or annual review. |
| Determining research-based data collection tools | • Look at all data tools for low incidence and determine what makes sense to administer to give valuable data.<br>• Create rubrics aligned to the backward mapping of the learning progressions for the priority standards and Dynamic Learning Map. |

References

Dynamic Learning Maps. (n.d.). *What is a learning map model?* Accessed at https://dynamiclearningmaps.org/model on January 3, 2025.

# SWOT Analysis for the Master Schedule

**Schedule component of focus:**
_____
_____

**Non-negotiable factors:**
_____
_____
_____
_____
_____
_____
_____

| SWOT Analysis ||
|---|---|
| Strengths | Weaknesses |
|  |  |
| Opportunities | Threats |
|  |  |

**Hypothesis Statement**

**Example:** "We agree that [change, step, innovation] is the logical next step because [rationale]."
_____
_____
_____
_____
_____
_____
_____

**All Means All** © 2025 Solution Tree Press • SolutionTree.com
Visit **go.SolutionTree.com/PLCbooks** to download this free reproducible.

# CHAPTER 4

# STANDARDS-FOCUSED PLANNING, INSTRUCTION, ASSESSMENT, AND GRADING FOR *ALL*

| **Envision What's Possible** ||
|---|---|
| **Picture a school where . . .** | **. . . Instruction is standards based, learning progressions guide teaching and learning, and student grading is fair, equitable, and accurate** |
| At the end of this chapter, you will have the opportunity to further reflect on this vision by considering your role in its achievement, potential challenges along the way, ways to address those challenges, and the positive impact achieving this vision will have on students. ||

In *Yes We Can!* (Friziellie et al., 2016) and throughout this book, we emphasize the importance of building a school culture where every educator believes in the potential of each student to reach high levels of achievement. This mindset shift involves moving beyond viewing general and special education as separate entities and instead adopting a unified, collaborative approach to student learning. This mindset is the underlying focus for the collaborative work of general and special educators in establishing a guaranteed and viable curriculum that ensures all students have access to grade-level priority learning standards. When Marzano (2003; Marzano & Hardy, 2023) introduced the concept of a guaranteed and viable curriculum (GVC), he highlighted one of the most effective ways to improve schools. *Guaranteed* means that all students in the same grade, class, or course are taught the same essential content, no matter which teacher they have. If what's being taught varies from classroom to classroom, the curriculum isn't truly guaranteed. *Viable* focuses on the difference between *covering* content and actually *teaching* it. Teachers can race through a lot of material, but that doesn't mean students are learning it. If there's too much content to realistically teach in the time available, then the curriculum isn't viable.

For a curriculum to be both guaranteed and viable, teacher teams need to collaborate and agree on what students should know and be able to do. This shared understanding ensures students get the essential learning they need, regardless of the teacher they have or class they are in.

***Regardless of the teacher they have or class they are in!***

This promise applies to *all* students, including those with disabilities. It is not exclusive to general education; every student deserves this guarantee. The development of priority standards is a critical component of this guarantee and provides the viability to which Marzano refers that allows educators adequate time to teach the priority standards deeply, to intervene and reteach, and then reassess.

Identifying priority standards is particularly beneficial for special educators for several reasons.

- **Focused instruction:** By concentrating on essential learning outcomes, special educators can tailor their teaching strategies to address the most critical skills and knowledge, ensuring students with disabilities receive targeted support that aligns with their IEPs.
- **Efficient resource allocation:** Prioritizing standards allows educators to allocate time and resources more effectively, focusing on areas that will have the greatest impact on student learning and progress.
- **Enhanced collaboration:** A clear set of priority standards facilitates better communication and collaboration between general and special educators, ensuring consistency in instructional goals and methods across different educational settings.
- **Improved assessment and progress monitoring:** With defined priority standards, special educators can develop more precise assessments to monitor student progress, enabling timely interventions and adjustments to instructional approaches.

The identification of priority standards enables special educators to provide more focused, efficient, and collaborative instruction, ultimately enhancing the educational outcomes for students with disabilities. In this chapter, we delve into this process as well as the development of learning progressions, planning and curriculum alignment, assessment, and grading and reporting.

## Making Priority Standards the Focus of Teaching and Learning

In order for the work of identifying priority standards to be effective, these standards must become the cornerstone of daily instruction in every classroom, guiding both teaching and learning daily. Priority standards should receive the majority of instructional time and be the primary focus of assessments, both individual and common. They are central to team discussions and are the basis for interventions when students require additional support to achieve proficiency. By concentrating on priority standards, educators ensure all students meet consistent learning expectations, providing a solid foundation for future academic success.

Moreover, priority standards serve as a guarantee to subsequent grade-level or course teachers regarding what students know and can do. They establish uniform learning goals for all students without modifying expectations, and they play a significant role in communicating learning progress to students and families. By emphasizing priority standards, educators create a cohesive and transparent educational experience, fostering student achievement and facilitating effective communication among all stakeholders.

## The Great Eight

To further communicate the importance of priority standards, we have identified the following Great Eight actions that must be taken to ensure the priority standards are the focus of teaching and learning. The "Great Eight Priority Standard Checklist" reproducible (page 102) provides a means to assess a team's progress with each aspect of the Great Eight.

1. **Priority standards are the focus of teaching and learning every day in every classroom for *all* students:** Priority standards are the primary targets of instruction for *all* students, guiding lesson planning and classroom activities. By centering daily teaching on these standards, educators provide consistent and purposeful learning experiences that align with key educational goals.

2. **Priority standards are what teachers spend the most instructional time on:** General and special educators, working collaboratively, dedicate significant instructional time to priority standards. This collective focus ensures all students receive comprehensive instruction on fundamental concepts, promoting equity and consistency across classrooms.

3. **Priority standards are what teachers assess both individually and commonly:** Priority standards are the basis for both individual and common assessments, though teachers may also assess other standards individually. Teachers design evaluations to measure student understanding and proficiency in these areas, allowing for targeted feedback and instructional adjustments to support student growth.

4. **Priority standards are part of collaborative team discussions at most team meetings:** During team meetings, educators engage in discussions about priority standards to share strategies, analyze student performance

data, and plan interventions. This collaboration fosters a unified approach to addressing student needs and enhancing instructional practices.

5. **Priority standards are the focus of interventions when students need additional support toward proficiency:** When students require additional support, interventions are designed around priority standards. This targeted approach ensures that students receive the necessary assistance to achieve proficiency in critical areas, reinforcing foundational knowledge and skills.

6. **Priority standards are what teachers guarantee the teachers at the next grade level or course that students will know and be able to do:** By emphasizing priority standards, educators ensure students possess the requisite knowledge and skills for success in subsequent grade levels or courses. This continuity supports a seamless transition and ongoing academic achievement.

7. **Priority standards are what we ensure all students learn without modifying expectations:** Priority standards establish consistent learning expectations without modification, ensuring all students are held to the same high standards. Accommodations that level the playing field for some students may be applied, but the learning standard expectation or related tasks are not modified (change the playing field). This approach promotes equity and prepares students for future academic and life challenges.

8. **Priority standards and student proficiency of the essentials are a large part of what teachers use to communicate (report) learning to students and families:** Student proficiency in priority standards is a key component of reporting learning progress to students and families. This transparency fosters a shared understanding of educational objectives and student achievements, strengthening the partnership between educators and families.

These Great Eight actions emphasize the critical role of priority standards in teaching and learning. These standards serve as the central focus of daily instruction, guiding lesson planning, assessments, and interventions to ensure all students achieve proficiency in fundamental concepts. Teachers collaborate to discuss strategies, analyze data, and plan targeted support while maintaining high expectations without modifying standards. Priority standards also drive reporting to students and families, ensuring transparency and shared understanding of learning progress. By dedicating instructional time and resources to these priority standards, educators promote consistency, equity, and long-term student success.

With a clear understanding of the importance of priority standards, the next step is to explore how to identify and develop these standards effectively. Establishing priority standards requires a thoughtful and collaborative process to ensure they align with curricular goals, address essential learning outcomes, and meet the needs of all students.

## Development of Priority Standards

To support the identification of priority standards, we offer a step-by-step process for developing and implementing priority standards. By working together, teacher teams identify the most critical standards, break them down into clear learning targets, and ensure every educator understands and is equipped to teach these priorities effectively. Implementing these strategies helps schools create a more inclusive environment where students are consistently held to high expectations and supported to succeed. Next, we provide a summary of our approach in *Yes We Can!* (Friziellie et al., 2016).

The process begins with the identification of priority standards. We suggest that teams use the "Simple as 1, 2, 3: The Prioritizing Process" (page 103) for determining priority standards. In this process, teams will follow three steps.

1. Individual team members use set criteria to make initial choices about which standards to prioritize.

2. As a team, they discuss their selections and develop an initial list of priority standards.

3. Team members take other sources of information, such as standards from subsequent grade levels and data from accountability assessments, into consideration to guide their final decision about which standards to prioritize.

Once teams complete the prioritizing process and compile their final list of priority standards, it is time to unpack the standards to determine and examine more closely the expectations each learning standard holds about what students need to know and be able to do. Kim Bailey and Chris Jakicic (2023) describe *unpacking* as a strategy that enables collaborative teams "to achieve collective clarity and agreement regarding the overall intent and rigor of the standards and to identify the specific learning targets that lead to their attainment" (p. 51). They further define *learning targets* as the increments of learning—steps of knowledge or concepts and skills—that build on each other and culminate in the attainment of the standard.

Using the protocol in figure 4.1 (page 82), teams follow a seven-step process to unpack their prioritized standards into learning targets: (1) identify the priority standards, (2) identify the verbs (skills) and knowledge (concepts), (3) identify learning targets, (4) determine the level of rigor and examine assessment types, (5) identify key vocabulary, (6) determine a logical learning progression, and (7) determine potential scaffolds and supports. This example shows a fully unpacked mathematics standard. (See page 105 for a blank reproducible version of this figure.)

**Standard:** 6.RP.A.3—Use ratio and rate reasoning to solve real-world and mathematical problems, e.g., by reasoning about tables of equivalent ratios, tape diagrams, double number line diagrams, or equations.

| What Will Students Do (Skills or Verbs) | With What Knowledge or Concept | Level of Thinking or Type of Assessment | Vocabulary | Scaffolds or Supports |
|---|---|---|---|---|
| Use | Ratio and rate reasoning (to solve real-world and mathematical problems) | DOK 2: Multiple choice, constructed response or performance assessment | Ratio<br>Rate | Use vocabulary practice or small-group work.<br><br>Practice mathematical problems with simpler numbers or variables. Once a student demonstrates mastery on these, add problems with more complex numbers or variables.<br><br>Use video clips to demonstrate a process, skill, or concept with student access available for repeated viewings.<br><br>Show and brainstorm the different ways that ratios are written—2 to 5, 2/5, 2:5, 40%, 0.4 are all different ways of describing the same ratio. |
| Solve | Real-world and mathematical problems (using ratio and rate reasoning) | DOK 3: Constructed response or performance task | Solve | Model problem-solving strategies, or practice in small groups.<br><br>Help students visualize the problem, or act out the problem using manipulatives. |
| Reason | About tables of equivalent ratios, tape diagrams, double number line diagrams, or equations | DOK 2: Constructed written response | Equivalent<br>Diagram<br>Reason | Practice reasoning with less complex tables, and so on. |

**Learning Progression:**

- Define and apply the concepts of ratio and rate.
- Understand tables of equivalent ratios, tape diagrams, double number line diagrams, or equations as applied to ratio and rate.
- Understand and apply the concept of reasoning.
- Apply stamina, grit, and perseverance to problem solving.
- Navigate real-world problems, break down the problem into smaller steps, and apply knowledge.

*Source for standard: National Governors Association Center for Best Practices (NGA) & Council of Chief State School Officers (CCSSO), 2010b.*
*Source: Friziellie et al., 2016, p. 58.*

**Figure 4.1:** Example of the unpacking standards process.

# Using Learning Progressions to Plan the Journey to Mastery

In *Yes We Can!* (Friziellie et al., 2016), we communicated the purpose and value of creating learning progressions after completing the initial unpacking steps, as shown in figure 4.1. We expand on that initial thinking here, further showing the value of learning progressions for both general and special educators and how they can be used to check for understanding and develop robust interventions for students as they progress toward mastery of priority standards.

According to W. James Popham (2007), a *learning progression* is a sequence of building blocks or smaller learning targets that lead to mastering a larger curricular aim. By reviewing Depth of Knowledge (DOK; Francis, 2022; Webb, 2025) levels and vocabulary in each learning target, educators can arrange them from simpler to more complex skills, creating a road map for instruction. Additional skills like perseverance and grit may be integrated into the progression, especially when these qualities are essential for tackling complex, real-world problems (Duckworth et al., 2007).

This structured progression supports teachers in planning the journey toward mastery by identifying key stopping points along the way, where students' understanding can be checked and reinforced before moving on to more difficult concepts. This approach ensures students build confidence through early successes with prerequisite concepts, fostering the resilience needed to engage with more challenging material. Although learning progressions can vary among educators, thoughtful planning in this way provides a more beneficial, structured learning path than spontaneous decision making, ultimately enhancing student achievement.

Let's look at some ways the learning progressions support student learning.

## The Power of Learning Progressions for Students Who Struggle

Learning progressions are essential for educators, particularly when working with students who struggle, because they provide a structured pathway that breaks down complex skills and knowledge into manageable, sequential steps. This approach allows teachers to identify where each student is on their learning journey and to tailor instruction in ways that are both accessible and effective. Let's explore further the reasons why learning progressions provide a valuable pathway to the learning of priority standards.

### Clarify Learning Pathways and Set Achievable Goals

Learning progressions outline the specific steps or stages a student needs to master to achieve a particular skill or understanding. For educators, this clarity allows them to establish clear, incremental goals that help students make steady progress. For students who struggle, reaching the larger learning goal may seem overwhelming, but learning progressions break it down into manageable, achievable steps. This scaffolding helps students build confidence as they see themselves progressing, reducing frustration and making learning feel attainable.

### Enable Targeted Instruction and Interventions

Learning progressions provide a road map for pinpointing where each student currently stands and the next steps they need to take. This precision is especially important for struggling students, as it allows teachers to focus on specific skills or concepts that are just within their reach. By targeting instruction to meet students where they are, educators can provide interventions that address immediate needs without overwhelming them. For example, if a student is struggling with reading comprehension, a learning progression can help the teacher focus on foundational skills, like identifying main ideas, before advancing to more complex analysis.

### Facilitate Formative Assessment and Real-Time Feedback

With learning progressions in place, educators can use formative assessments to track students' progress along the pathway. These assessments are aligned with the progression steps, giving teachers specific data on which skills or concepts need more attention. For students who struggle, this real-time feedback allows teachers to make adjustments to their instruction immediately, ensuring students receive timely support. It also helps educators celebrate small victories, since they can track and acknowledge each stage a student masters, encouraging ongoing effort and resilience.

### Provide a Foundation for Differentiation

Learning progressions make it easier for teachers to differentiate instruction by providing multiple entry points for diverse learners. For students who struggle, differentiation often involves addressing gaps in foundational skills. Learning progressions allow educators to identify these gaps and offer personalized activities or resources that target each student's specific needs. Teachers can work with students in different stages of the same progression within one lesson, ensuring everyone is moving forward at a pace that is right for them.

### Promote Student Motivation and Ownership

For students who struggle, learning progressions can transform the learning experience from one of frustration to one of empowerment. When students understand the progression of skills they need to develop, they gain a clearer sense of direction and purpose. Teachers can involve students in tracking their progress along the pathway, helping them take ownership of their learning. By seeing their growth over time, students become more motivated and engaged, building the persistence they need to tackle more challenging material.

### Support Long-Term Skill Development and Mastery

Learning progressions focus on building skills in a logical, cumulative way, which is crucial for struggling learners who may have foundational gaps. By following a progression, teachers ensure students move forward with a strong base of knowledge, reducing the risk of learning gaps that can affect future learning. For example, in mathematics, students need to master addition and subtraction before moving on to multiplication and division. Progressions prevent educators from bypassing these critical steps, ensuring students build a solid understanding over time that will support more complex learning.

### Encourage Reflective Practice for Teachers

Using learning progressions encourages teachers to reflect regularly on their instruction and its effectiveness. When teachers see how students respond to each step of the progression, they gain insights into which instructional strategies work best for different learners. This reflective practice helps teachers refine their approaches and become more adept at anticipating the needs of students who struggle, leading to more impactful and responsive teaching.

## Help With Planning and Curriculum Alignment

Learning progressions provide a framework that aligns curriculum and instruction with specific learning outcomes, making lesson planning more focused and efficient. This alignment is particularly helpful for students who struggle, as it reduces the likelihood of introducing content too quickly or out of sequence. Teachers can plan lessons that build on each other logically, reinforcing foundational skills and preparing students for future concepts in a cohesive, step-by-step manner.

Learning progressions are a powerful tool for educators, especially when teaching students who struggle. By providing a clear, structured pathway for learning, progressions enable teachers to target instruction, differentiate effectively, and support long-term mastery. For students, progressions make learning more manageable and motivating, as they experience success with each step they master. Ultimately, learning progressions help create an educational environment where every student, regardless of their starting point, can experience growth, build confidence, and achieve success.

The chart, featured in figure 4.1 (page 82), details the learning progression for standard 6.RP.A.3 (NGA & CCSSO, 2010b), which focuses on ratio and rate reasoning and serves as a valuable resource for special educators in several key ways.

- **IEP development:** The chart outlines specific learning targets and their progression, enabling special educators to set precise, measurable goals tailored to each student's needs. This alignment ensures IEP objectives are directly connected to grade-level standards, promoting consistency in educational expectations.

- **Targeted instructional planning:** By breaking down complex concepts into manageable steps, the chart assists educators in designing lessons that build on each other. This structured approach allows for the introduction of foundational skills before progressing to more advanced topics, accommodating diverse learning paces.

- **Scaffolding and support strategies:** The detailed progression helps identify potential areas where students may encounter difficulties. Special educators can proactively implement scaffolding techniques—such as visual aids, manipulatives, or step-by-step guides—to support comprehension without diminishing the rigor of the content.

- **Progress monitoring and assessment:** The chart provides clear benchmarks for evaluating student progress. Educators can use these indicators to assess understanding at each stage, facilitating timely interventions and adjustments to instructional strategies as needed.

- **Collaboration with general educators:** Utilizing a common framework fosters effective communication between special and general educators. This shared understanding ensures all students receive cohesive instruction and support, promoting an inclusive learning environment.

The chart serves as a comprehensive guide for special educators, aiding in the development of individualized goals, structured lesson planning, effective scaffolding, ongoing assessment, and collaborative efforts—all aimed at enhancing students' mastery of ratio and rate reasoning.

## How Learning Progressions Connect to Instruction and Assessment

In *Yes We Can!* (Friziellie et al., 2016), we emphasize the importance of incorporating learning progressions into the unpacking process to effectively guide assessment and intervention strategies. Utilizing the learning progression outlined in figure 4.1 (page 82), in this section, we show how educators can systematically approach each step as a formative checkpoint. These checkpoints, assessed through both formal and informal methods, provide valuable evidence of student understanding. When a student encounters difficulties with specific building blocks, these assessments help identify the underlying issues, enabling educators to adjust instruction accordingly to address individual learning needs.

The standard of focus remains 6.RP.A.3, "Use ratio and rate reasoning to solve real-world and mathematical problems, e.g., by reasoning about tables of equivalent ratios, tape diagrams, double number line diagrams, or equations" (NGA & CCSSO, 2010b). Figure 4.2 shows an example of our process for connecting learning progressions to assessment and how it can be used to begin thinking about connecting the steps of the learning progression to assessments and to consider potential scaffolds that might be necessary to ensure students with IEPs can access assessments that measure grade-level standards without lowering the rigor of the assessment. (See page 106 for a blank reproducible version of this figure.) This example depicts the full thinking of a collaborative team as a guide to formative assessment.

*Standards-Focused Planning, Instruction, Assessment, and Grading for* All

| Standard of focus: 6.RP.A.3—Use ratio and rate reasoning to solve real-world and mathematical problems, e.g., by reasoning about tables of equivalent ratios, tape diagrams, double number line diagrams, or equations. | | |
|---|---|---|
| **Learning Progression (Go from least to most complex.)** | **Potential Assessment (Use artificial intelligence to help.)** | **Assessment Scaffolds (Always consider grade-level expectations.)** |
| 1. Define and apply the concepts of ratio and rate. | **Written explanations:** Students write definitions of ratio and rate in their own words.<br><br>**Multiple-choice questions:** Present scenarios where students select the correct definition or identify examples of ratios and rates.<br><br>**Visual representations:** Students create and interpret tape diagrams, double number line diagrams, or tables of equivalent ratios to solve given problems.<br><br>**Graphing activities:** Students plot ratios on a coordinate plane and analyze the relationships, demonstrating their ability to connect ratios with graphical representations. | **Relate to familiar concepts:** Connect ratios and rates to everyday experiences, such as comparing the number of apples to oranges in a basket, to build on existing understanding.<br><br>**Add manipulatives:** Incorporate tools like fraction strips or ratio cubes to provide tangible representations of abstract concepts.<br><br>**Use graphic organizers:** Employ Venn diagrams or T-charts to help students organize and compare information effectively.<br><br>**Provide step-by-step instructions:** Divide complex problems into smaller, manageable steps, guiding students through each phase to build confidence and competence. |
| 2. Understand tables of equivalent ratios, tape diagrams, double number line diagrams, or equations as applied to ratio and rate. | **Problem-solving tasks:** Present real-world scenarios where students must use these representations to find solutions. For example, ask them to determine the best buy between two products by analyzing unit prices using tables of equivalent ratios.<br><br>**Visual representation exercises:** Provide incomplete tape diagrams or double number line diagrams and have students complete them to represent given ratios or rates. This assesses their ability to interpret and construct these visual tools.<br><br>**Equation formulation and solving:** Give students word problems that require setting up and solving equations involving ratios and rates. This evaluates their skill in translating verbal descriptions into mathematical expressions and finding solutions.<br><br>**Matching activities:** Create exercises where students match different representations of the same ratio or rate, such as pairing a table of equivalent ratios with its corresponding tape diagram or equation. | **Activate prior knowledge:** Connect new concepts to students' existing knowledge. For instance, discuss familiar scenarios involving ratios, such as mixing paint colors or cooking recipes, to build a foundation for understanding.<br><br>**Use visual aids and manipulatives:** Incorporate tools like colored counters, fraction strips, or ratio cubes to provide tangible representations of abstract concepts. Visual aids can help students grasp the relationships between quantities.<br><br>**Break down tasks into manageable steps:** Divide complex problems into smaller, sequential steps. Provide clear, step-by-step instructions and guide students through each phase, gradually increasing complexity as their confidence builds.<br><br>**Model problem-solving processes:** Demonstrate solving problems using think-aloud strategies; verbalize your thought process. |

*Source for standard: NGA & CCSSO, 2010b.*
**Figure 4.2:** Example protocol for connecting learning progression to assessment.

*continued →*

| | | | |
|---|---|---|---|
| 3. | Understand and apply the concept of reasoning. | **Problem-solving tasks:** Use real-world scenarios that require the application of ratios and rates. For example, ask them to determine the most cost-effective option between two products by calculating and comparing unit prices.<br><br>**Visual representation exercises:** Provide problems where students must use tape diagrams, double number line diagrams, or tables of equivalent ratios to represent and solve ratio-related questions. This assesses their ability to translate abstract concepts into visual formats.<br><br>**Equation formulation and solving:** Assign tasks that involve writing and solving equations based on ratio and rate problems. For instance, students could set up an equation to find the time required to travel a certain distance at a given speed.<br><br>**Graphing activities:** Have students plot pairs of values from tables of equivalent ratios on a coordinate plane and interpret the resulting graphs to understand proportional relationships. | **Activate prior knowledge:** Begin by connecting new concepts to students' existing knowledge. For instance, discuss familiar scenarios involving ratios, such as mixing paint colors or cooking recipes, to build a foundation for understanding.<br><br>**Use visual aids and manipulatives:** Incorporate tools like colored counters, fraction strips, or ratio cubes to provide tangible representations of abstract concepts. Visual aids can help students grasp the relationships between quantities.<br><br>**Break down tasks into manageable steps:** Divide complex problems into smaller, sequential steps. Provide clear, step-by-step instructions and guide students through each phase, gradually increasing complexity as their confidence builds.<br><br>**Model problem-solving processes:** Demonstrate solving problems using think-aloud strategies, where you verbalize your thought process. This approach helps students understand the reasoning behind each step and encourages them to adopt similar strategies. |
| 4. | Apply stamina, grit, and perseverance to problem solving. | **Extended problem-solving tasks:** Assign complex, multistep problems that require sustained effort over time. Observe how students approach these tasks, noting their persistence in seeking solutions despite difficulties.<br><br>**Process journals:** Encourage students to maintain journals documenting their problem-solving processes, including challenges encountered and strategies employed to overcome them. This reflection provides insight into their perseverance and adaptability.<br><br>**Observation and anecdotal records:** During class activities, observe students' behaviors and attitudes toward challenging tasks. Record instances where they demonstrate resilience, such as persisting after initial failure or seeking alternative solutions.<br><br>**Self-assessment and peer feedback:** Implement self-assessment tools where students evaluate their own perseverance in tasks. Complement this with peer feedback to gain multiple perspectives on their grit and stamina. | **Gradually increase task complexity:** Begin with simpler problems to build confidence, then progressively introduce more challenging tasks. This approach helps students develop resilience incrementally.<br><br>**Deliver explicit instruction on perseverance strategies:** Teach specific techniques for managing frustration and persisting through difficulties, such as breaking problems into smaller steps or employing self-talk to stay motivated.<br><br>**Model processes and think aloud:** Demonstrate problem-solving processes while verbalizing thoughts to showcase how to navigate obstacles and maintain effort. This modeling provides students with concrete examples of perseverance in action.<br><br>**Provide structured reflection opportunities:** Incorporate regular intervals for students to reflect on their problem-solving experiences and discuss challenges faced and strategies used to overcome them. This reflection fosters self-awareness and growth. |

| 5. Navigate real-world problems, break down the problem into smaller steps, and apply knowledge. | **Real-world problem-solving tasks:** Present students with scenarios that require the application of ratio and rate reasoning. For example, ask them to determine the most cost-effective option between two products by calculating and comparing unit prices.<br><br>**Structured problem breakdown:** Provide complex problems and instruct students to outline their approach by breaking the problem into smaller, sequential steps. Assess their ability to identify key components and organize their solution process logically.<br><br>**Application of multiple representations:** Require students to solve problems using various methods, such as tables of equivalent ratios, tape diagrams, double number line diagrams, or equations. This demonstrates their flexibility in applying different strategies to find solutions.<br><br>**Think-aloud protocols:** Have students verbalize their thought process while solving a problem. This allows assessment of their reasoning, decision making, and ability to connect different concepts related to ratios and rates. | **Activate prior knowledge:** Begin by connecting new concepts to students' existing knowledge. For instance, discuss familiar scenarios involving ratios, such as mixing paint colors or cooking recipes, to build a foundation for understanding.<br><br>**Use visual aids and manipulatives:** Incorporate tools like colored counters, fraction strips, or ratio cubes to provide tangible representations of abstract concepts. Visual aids can help students grasp the relationships between quantities.<br><br>**Break down tasks into manageable steps:** Divide complex problems into smaller, sequential steps. Provide clear, step-by-step instructions and guide students through each phase, gradually increasing complexity as their confidence builds.<br><br>**Model problem-solving processes:** Demonstrate solving problems using think-aloud strategies, where you verbalize your thought process. This approach helps students understand the reasoning behind each step and encourages them to adopt similar strategies. |

It is important to reiterate that the purpose of the process and document is to have intentional conversations about the steps of the learning progression and assessment prior to beginning instruction. It is also important to mention that the ideas generated in figure 4.2 (page 87) related to assessment and scaffolds were derived using generative artificial intelligence (AI), specifically ChatGPT (OpenAI, 2024). In a matter of less than two minutes, we were provided with ideas for assessments and scaffolds using the following prompts.

- "In the context of this standard: 6.RP.A.3—'Use ratio and rate reasoning to solve real-world and mathematical problems, e.g., by reasoning about tables of equivalent ratios, tape diagrams, double number line diagrams, or equations' (full standard), how can I assess a student's ability to navigate real-world problems, break down the problem into smaller steps, and apply knowledge (learning target)?"
- "How can I scaffold these assessment ideas without lowering the rigor?"

While the resulting chart may appear to include information that would take a team a large amount of time to generate, the use of generative AI makes the process more efficient. While these outputs must be checked closely and revised as needed, we find that most of the information generated is applicable and useful as a starting point. However, we cannot stress enough that it is vital that teams are discerning and careful to check that the AI platform is providing information that makes sense based on what they were searching for.

## How Learning Progression Assessment Information Can Be Used

Let's walk through how the information gathered and considered by a collaborative team or individual teacher might be used by focusing on the first step in the learning progression in figure 4.2 (page 87). Looking at the first and least complex learning target in the progression, define and apply the concepts of ratio and rate; the assessment ideas to check for understanding are included in the column labeled Potential Assessment. Included in the column are ideas for how to assess this learning target, including the following.

- **Written explanations:** Students write definitions of ratio and rate in their own words.

- **Multiple-choice questions:** Present scenarios where students select the correct definition or identify examples of ratios and rates.

- **Visual representations:** Students create and interpret tape diagrams, double number line diagrams, or tables of equivalent ratios to solve given problems.

- **Graphing activities:** Students plot ratios on a coordinate plane and analyze the relationships, demonstrating their ability to connect ratios with graphical representations.

The collaborative team or individual teacher can decide if they will assess this learning target individually or as a common formative assessment. Since this is the first step in the progression, we generally recommend that this learning target be one that teachers would individually assess during typical classroom assessment versus commonly. For example, to check for whether students can define the concepts of ratio and rate, teachers may have students write definitions as described in figure 4.2 by using whiteboards to check for understanding through observation or by using a checklist.

To check for the ability to apply the concepts of ratio and rate, teachers may ask students to engage in the graphing activity defined in the chart by asking students to plot ratios on a coordinate plane and analyze the relationships as two- or three-question exit slip check-ins. This will provide information to teachers regarding each student's ability to connect ratios with graphical representations. It provides excellent diagnostic information regarding the students who might need additional time and support regarding this learning target.

If you imagine that each step in the progression is a chance to check for understanding, you can see how this intentionality provides valuable information to both general and special educators regarding the specific components of the learning progression with which students may be struggling.

Collaborative teams can decide which steps in the progression they will commonly assess in order to use the collective wisdom of the group to consider responses and to see the overall levels of proficiency for the entire grade level or for all students taking the same course. Generally, we advise that teams choose the components of the learning progression that are most difficult for students to learn and difficult for teachers to teach as the common formative assessment check-in points. We suggest this because the beauty of a common assessment is responding to the data using the collective wisdom of the team. This also drives home the importance of collective responsibility for all students versus just those in a teacher's individual class.

The Assessment Scaffolds column of figure 4.2 asks educators to identify the scaffolds that might be necessary to ensure students with IEPs and others who struggle are able to engage with the rigorous grade-level assessment versus taking an easier, less rigorous assessment. This implies that teachers take the time to carefully review the expectations in the assessment, ensuring the assessment is accurately measuring the priority learning target and standard expectations at the intended level of rigor. For example, if measuring the application of rates and ratios, multiple-choice questions that ask students to define rates and ratios would not match the rigor of *application* but would match the rigor of *define*.

With that said, scaffolds, like the one identified in the first row of figure 4.2 in the column Assessment Scaffolds, give educators the direction to relate the concepts of rates and ratios to familiar concepts and connect ratios and rates to everyday experiences, such as comparing the number of apples to oranges in a basket, to build on existing understanding. This could be extremely helpful for a student who is struggling to make sense of these concepts.

Figure 4.2 continues with each of the learning targets in the learning progression from least to most complex with potential assessments and assessment scaffold ideas. We suggest that this process of connecting each step in the progression to potential assessments and scaffolds will be beneficial in keeping expectations high versus giving students who struggle something easier or less complex.

By systematically identifying and creating learning progressions based on priority standards, educators can provide focused, coherent instruction that meets the diverse needs of all students, including those with special needs. This collaborative approach fosters a shared understanding of learning expectations and promotes consistency across classrooms. While maintaining grade-level expectations is essential, the challenges in grading students with IEPs reflect the need for continued conversations and thoughtful solutions. In the next section, we will explore specific processes and strategies designed to help educators assign fair and meaningful grades to students with disabilities in both standards-based and traditional grading contexts.

# Grading and Reporting Student Learning for Students With IEPs

As more students with disabilities are included in general education classrooms, grading practices have become more complex. General education teachers often handle report card grades, while special education teachers monitor progress toward IEP goals. For example, an eighth-grade student may not meet grade-level standards due to significant disabilities but has made progress on IEP goals. Failing this student seems unfair, given their effort and growth, but passing them without meeting grade-level standards raises questions about fairness and accuracy. This complexity prompts an essential question: *Do we grade a student with an IEP based on their proficiency related to grade-level expectations, or do we grade them based on proficiency in below-grade-level work?*

For example, if a fifth-grade student with a mild to moderate disability demonstrates proficiency on a below-grade-level task (such as a third-grade task), should they receive a proficient score? The answer is *no*; the student's grade should reflect their proficiency based on fifth-grade standards. This approach aligns with our belief that all students, including those with disabilities, are general education students first and deserve clear, accurate assessments of their progress toward grade-level standards.

## The Principle That Students With IEPs Are General Education Students First

Given that a foundational belief in inclusive education is that *students with IEPs are general education students first*, this means the general education classroom is their primary learning environment, where they benefit academically, socially, and emotionally from learning alongside their peers. IDEA (2004) supports this principle, affirming students' right to be educated in the least restrictive environment to the greatest extent possible.

By treating students with IEPs as general education students first, educators are encouraged to create inclusive instructional practices that make the curriculum accessible to all. This approach affirms students' belonging in the general education setting, emphasizes high expectations, and promotes academic rigor with individualized support. General education teachers are essential members of the IEP team, collaborating with special educators to implement accommodations that support student success.

## The Importance of Grade-Level Alignment for Students With Disabilities

Grading students with mild to moderate disabilities in alignment with grade-level expectations promotes equity, access, and meaningful learning outcomes, including the following.

- **Equity and high expectations:** Aligning grading with grade-level standards reinforces that all students can achieve high standards with the right support.

Consistent expectations affirm that students with disabilities are entitled to rigorous education, helping counter any potential biases or low expectations.

- **Inclusive and accessible curriculum:** Holding students to grade-level standards requires educators to make the curriculum accessible through supports, accommodations, and modifications. This approach, aligned with Universal Design for Learning (UDL; CAST, 2024), allows students to engage with the same material as their peers, enhancing their sense of belonging.
- **Preparation for future academic and career goals:** Grade-level alignment helps students develop skills for future educational and career opportunities. By learning in a rigorous, inclusive environment, students with disabilities build competencies essential for postsecondary education or employment.
- **Clear communication of progress and needs:** Grading aligned with grade-level standards provides consistency in measuring a student's progress in relation to peers, which is essential for setting IEP goals and monitoring growth toward grade-level skills.
- **Self-advocacy and confidence:** When students meet grade-level standards, it boosts their self-confidence and promotes a growth mindset. They learn that effort, persistence, and the right supports enable them to succeed, building resilience for future challenges.
- **Legal and policy compliance:** IDEA (2004) and Section 504 (Rehabilitation Act, 1973) require that students with disabilities access the general education curriculum. Aligning grading practices to grade-level standards upholds these policies, ensuring students receive instruction based on age-appropriate standards, along with the supports they need.

## The Challenge of Grading Students With IEPs in a General Education Context

Aligning grading practices with grade-level expectations for students with IEPs requires a thoughtful approach that balances equity with inclusivity. Here are some core considerations.

- **Grading for equity and inclusivity:** Grades should reflect a student's progress toward grade-level standards with any necessary accommodations rather than lowering rigor or using different grading criteria. This approach maintains grading integrity, ensuring grades accurately represent a student's achievements in the general education curriculum.
- **Consistent expectations with supportive differentiation:** Emphasizing general education first underscores that students with IEPs deserve the

same high expectations as their peers, along with supports like specially designed instruction (SDI) and accommodations to reach these standards. Grading should measure progress toward grade-level goals, acknowledging accommodations that make the curriculum accessible.

- **Clear communication of progress:** Grades, paired with IEP progress reports, should give families a comprehensive view of a student's academic performance and growth toward individualized goals. Accurate grading enables teachers and families to understand the student's current progress and what supports are needed, fostering a bridge between general education standards and individualized instruction.

- **Strength-based grading and feedback:** Emphasizing strengths in grading and feedback shifts focus from limitations to progress. Grading should highlight a student's successes within the general education curriculum, along with specific feedback on growth areas. This approach reinforces students' sense of belonging and fosters self-efficacy within the general education setting.

## Concerns About Grading and Self-Esteem

Concerns often arise that grading students with IEPs at grade-level standards may lead to discouragement or affect their self-esteem. Educators may feel pressured to inflate grades, worrying that low grades could harm students' motivation. However, while well meaning, inflating grades can ultimately undermine the accuracy of feedback, leading to a mismatch between report card grades and standardized assessment results.

In fact, as both school and district administrators, we have often been asked by parents of students with disabilities why their child has consistently received As or marks indicating proficiency but then scores below the 20th percentile on norm-referenced assessments, such as a state end-of-year assessment. Accurate grading provides clear, honest feedback that benefits students' long-term learning and self-efficacy. It reinforces that setbacks are a natural part of growth, helping students build resilience, skills, and confidence grounded in realistic expectations.

Inclusive grading practices are essential for fostering equitable learning environments that support all students, including those with IEPs. Educators can adopt several strategies to provide fair and meaningful grades for students with IEPs while addressing their individual needs. We have included the following seven strategies that provide a structured approach. Each strategy includes a rubric that provides a framework for implementation. Each criterion includes clear indicators for performance levels, from emerging to advanced, providing a road map for educators to implement and refine inclusive grading practices. Using these rubrics, schools can create a culture of fairness, accuracy, and collaboration that benefits all learners.

1. **Use standards-based grading to clarify expectations (figure 4.3):**
   - *Align grades with priority standards*—Identify and prioritize priority standards to ensure grading reflects progress toward critical grade-level skills. For students with IEPs, focus grading on these standards, separating IEP goal progress from core academic standards.
   - *Assess skill mastery*—Rather than relying on traditional letter grades, use proficiency scales (for example, "emerging," "approaching," "proficient") to show a student's current mastery level. This approach is especially useful for communicating specific growth areas without artificially inflating or lowering scores.

| Criteria | 4—Highly Effective | 3—Effective | 2—Developing | 1—Beginning |
| --- | --- | --- | --- | --- |
| Identification of Priority Standards | Standards are prioritized, consistently aligned, and communicated to stakeholders. | There is clear identification and prioritization of grade-level priority standards. | Some priority standards are identified, but they are not consistently aligned with grading. | Standards are unclear or misaligned with grade-level priorities. |
| Focus on IEP Goals | There is clear distinction between IEP goals and grade-level skill; these are communicated effectively. | IEP progress and core standard mastery are assessed and reported separately. | There is limited separation of IEP goals from core standards; some clarity is provided. | IEP goal progress is mixed with academic grades, creating confusion. |

**Figure 4.3:** Rubric for using standards-based grading to clarify expectations.

*Visit **go.SolutionTree.com/PLCbooks** for a free reproducible version of this figure.*

2. **Provide differentiated assessments with the same standards (figure 4.4, page 96):**
   - *Modify the approach, not the standard*—Create assessments that allow students to demonstrate understanding of grade-level standards but with accommodations, such as extended time, scaffolding, or modified response formats. This allows students to engage with grade-level content in a way that suits their unique needs.
   - *Use formative assessments for feedback and growth*—Formative assessments give students ongoing feedback, guiding learning and showing progress over time. This approach emphasizes growth and effort, allowing educators to highlight student strengths and identify areas for improvement.

| Criteria | 4—Highly Effective | 3—Effective | 2—Developing | 1—Beginning |
| --- | --- | --- | --- | --- |
| Proficiency Scales | Proficiency scales are fully embedded, emphasizing growth and mastery of standards. | Proficiency scales (such as emerging, approaching, and proficient) clearly reflect mastery. | There is some use of proficiency scales but with limited connection to standards. | Traditional letter grades are used without clarity on skill mastery. |
| Differentiation of Assessments | Assessments are tailored with appropriate accommodations and consistent scaffolding. | Accommodations modify the approach but not the standard, ensuring grade-level alignment. | Some accommodations are provided, but they don't consistently align with the standard. | Assessments are modified in ways that alter the grade-level standard. |

**Figure 4.4:** Rubric for providing differentiated assessments with the same standards.

*Visit **go.SolutionTree.com/PLCbooks** for a free reproducible version of this figure.*

3. **Collaborate on IEP-driven accommodations and modifications (figure 4.5):**

    - *Embed accommodations in general education settings*—Work closely with special education staff to understand and consistently implement each student's accommodations. For example, if a student requires visual aids or a quiet environment, these should be incorporated in general education settings and assessments to accurately reflect their capabilities.

    - *Provide specially designed instruction as part of the general curriculum*—Use SDI to support learning within grade-level standards. For instance, if a student struggles with reading comprehension, provide targeted SDI that reinforces skills needed for grade-level texts. Document these supports so families understand how accommodations and SDI contribute to their child's grade.

| Criteria | 4—Highly Effective | 3—Effective | 2—Developing | 1—Beginning |
| --- | --- | --- | --- | --- |
| Implementation of Accommodations | Accommodations are seamlessly implemented, reflecting full collaboration across staff. | Accommodations are consistently embedded in general education assessments and settings. | Some accommodations are embedded, but they are not fully integrated into general education settings. | Accommodations are inconsistently implemented or poorly understood. |
| Targeted SDI Within the Curriculum | SDI is fully integrated and well documented, enhancing access to grade-level content. | Targeted SDI supports mastery of grade-level standards; documentation is clear. | Limited SDI is provided; it is not clearly aligned with grade-level standards. | SDI is separate from the general curriculum and standards. |

**Figure 4.5:** Rubric for collaborating on IEP-driven accommodations and modifications.

*Visit **go.SolutionTree.com/PLCbooks** for a free reproducible version of this figure.*

4. **Separate academic achievement from effort and behavior (figure 4.6):**

    - *Grade academic skills independently*—Avoid factoring in effort, participation, or behavior in academic grades for students with IEPs. This separation ensures grades reflect true academic proficiency, allowing students and families to understand academic growth specifically.

    - *Offer feedback on effort and growth separately*—While effort is important, communicate it in a way that doesn't inflate or detract from academic performance. Use narrative feedback or separate grading categories for effort and participation, helping students see the connection between effort and progress without conflating it with academic achievement.

| Criteria | 4—Highly Effective | 3—Effective | 2—Developing | 1—Beginning |
| --- | --- | --- | --- | --- |
| Grading Academic Skills Independently | Clear and consistent distinction ensures accurate reporting of academic proficiency. | Academic grades reflect only skill mastery and are separate from effort, participation, and behavior. | There is limited separation of academic grades and effort, participation, and behavior. | Effort, participation, or behavior factor into academic grades. |
| Feedback on Effort and Growth | Feedback clearly highlights effort, growth, and progress, inspiring student ownership. | Effort and growth are communicated separately through narrative or feedback. | Limited feedback is provided on effort or growth. | Feedback on effort is unclear or conflated with academic grades. |

**Figure 4.6:** Rubric for separating academic achievement from effort and behavior.

*Visit **go.SolutionTree.com/PLCbooks** for a free reproducible version of this figure.*

5. **Engage in transparent, two-way communication with families (figure 4.7, page 98):**

    - *Explain grading criteria and standards*—Proactively communicate how grading reflects progress toward grade-level expectations and the role of accommodations in making learning accessible. For instance, share that while the student may use supports, their grade still reflects grade-level standards.

    - *Share IEP progress alongside report card grades*—Update families on both IEP goal progress and grade-level academic performance. This dual reporting clarifies areas of strength and growth, providing a comprehensive view of their child's development and helping families set realistic expectations.

| Criteria | 4—Highly Effective | 3—Effective | 2—Developing | 1—Beginning |
|---|---|---|---|---|
| Clarity of Grading Criteria | Families fully understand grading practices, standards alignment, and all provided supports. | Grading practices reflect clear progress toward standards, and accommodations are explained. | Grading criteria are shared with families, but they lack clarity or detail on accommodations. | Grading criteria and accommodations are not communicated to families. |
| Dual Reporting of IEP Goals and Academic Progress | Dual reporting of IEP progress and academic performance is detailed, comprehensive, and supports family collaboration. | IEP progress and academic performance are reported alongside each other. | There are limited updates on IEP goals; reporting lacks detail or clarity. | There is no distinction between IEP goal progress and core academic grades. |

**Figure 4.7:** Rubric for engaging in transparent, two-way communication with families.

Visit **go.SolutionTree.com/PLCbooks** *for a free reproducible version of this figure.*

6. **Use descriptive, constructive feedback to support growth (figure 4.8):**

   - *Highlight progress and next steps*—Descriptive feedback helps students understand their strengths and how they can improve, which is particularly valuable for students with IEPs. Instead of focusing solely on correct answers, guide students by offering next steps they can take toward proficiency.

   - *Encourage reflection and self-assessment*—Engage students in reflecting on their work and setting personal goals. Self-assessment builds ownership over learning and can boost motivation, helping students with IEPs recognize their achievements and areas for growth.

| Criteria | 4—Highly Effective | 3—Effective | 2—Developing | 1—Beginning |
|---|---|---|---|---|
| Quality of Feedback | Feedback is constructive, specific, and drives continuous student reflection and growth. | Feedback is descriptive, highlighting strengths and actionable next steps. | Feedback highlights mistakes, but it offers limited guidance for improvement. | Feedback is vague or focuses solely on correct and incorrect answers. |
| Student Reflection and Ownership | Students consistently reflect, self-assess, and set personal learning goals. | Students are guided in reflection and goal setting to build ownership. | There are limited opportunities for students to reflect on learning or set goals. | Students are not engaged in reflection or goal setting. |

**Figure 4.8:** Rubric for using descriptive, constructive feedback to support growth.

Visit **go.SolutionTree.com/PLCbooks** *for a free reproducible version of this figure.*

7. **Build an inclusive grading culture through team collaboration (figure 4.9):**

    - *Collaborate regularly with special education staff*—Meet with special education teachers to align grading practices and expectations for students with IEPs. Discuss how IEP goals can support general education curricula and grading, and ensure consistency in implementing supports across classrooms.

    - *Provide professional development on inclusive grading*—As grading practices evolve, offer training to help all staff understand and implement inclusive, standards-aligned grading for students with IEPs. Professional development can focus on strategies like standards-based grading, UDL, and data-informed instruction.

| Criteria | 4—Highly Effective | 3—Effective | 2—Developing | 1—Beginning |
| --- | --- | --- | --- | --- |
| Collaboration With Special Education Staff | Collaboration is embedded in school culture, ensuring seamless student support across staff. | Regular collaboration between general and special education staff ensures aligned expectations and consistent support. | Some collaboration occurs between general and special education staff, but alignment on supports is inconsistent. | Minimal collaboration occurs between general and special education staff. |
| Professional Development | Ongoing training empowers staff to consistently apply inclusive, standards-aligned grading. | Professional development supports an understanding of standards-based grading, Universal Design for Learning, and inclusive practices. | Limited professional development exists, but it lacks a clear focus on grading practices. | Staff lack training on inclusive grading or supports for students with IEPs. |

**Figure 4.9:** Rubric for building an inclusive grading culture through team collaboration.

*Visit **go.SolutionTree.com/PLCbooks** for a free reproducible version of this figure.*

Through these steps, educators can create grading practices that are both equitable and inclusive, providing students with IEPs and their families with meaningful, accurate feedback on academic progress and growth.

## Summary

This chapter clarifies the importance of building a unified school culture that supports all students, including those with disabilities, through collaborative work between general and special education teachers focused on a guaranteed and viable curriculum that includes the development of priority standards, learning progressions, and grading practices that are equitable and inclusive.

A guaranteed and viable curriculum ensures all students learn the same essential content and there is adequate time for deep learning and interventions. Priority standards serve as the cornerstone of instruction, interventions, and assessments. Identifying priority standards allows educators to focus on essential learning outcomes, allocate resources efficiently, and collaborate effectively. Learning progressions break down standards into smaller steps, allowing targeted instruction, formative assessments, and support for struggling students on the pathway to mastery of priority standards. Learning progressions help clarify goals, guide instruction, and monitor growth. The development of priority standards and learning progressions plays a significant role in providing clarity for grading practices by offering a structured and transparent approach to assessing student learning for all students. Seven strategies were shared for providing clear, honest feedback regarding academic progress for students with disabilities. To assess your progress toward these outcomes, use the full set of rubrics in the Concerns About Grading and Self-Esteem section (page 94).

Through the lens of a school where educators routinely use a standards-focused approach to planning, instruction, assessment, and grading, use figure 4.10 to reflect on your role, potential challenges, ways to overcome these challenges, and the impact on students both academically and personally.

| Picture a school where . . . | . . . Instruction is standards based, learning progressions guide teaching and learning, and student grading is fair, equitable, and accurate |
|---|---|
| Consider your role in making this vision a reality in your context. How would you contribute? | |
| Identify some challenges you may face in achieving this possibility. | |
| Consider ways to overcome these challenges (over, around, and through). | |

| Anticipate the impact on students. How would bringing this possibility to life impact students academically and personally? | |

**Figure 4.10:** Envision What's Possible reflection tool for standards-focused planning, instruction, assessment, and grading.

*Visit **go.SolutionTree.com/PLCbooks** for a free reproducible version of this figure.*

Use the following aligned activities included at the end of this chapter to support your work around this chapter's core concept.

- **"Great Eight Priority Standard Checklist" (page 102):** Use this reproducible tool to assess a team's progress with each aspect of the Great Eight.

- **"Simple as 1, 2, 3: The Prioritizing Process" (page 103):** Use this reproducible tool to support your work when determining priority standards.

- **"Unpacking Document" (page 105):** Use this reproducible tool to give teams a structure for each step of the unpacking process.

- **"Protocol for Connecting the Learning Progression to Assessment" (page 106):** Use this reproducible tool to ensure each step in the learning progression has a clear and appropriate assessment aligned with it and includes scaffolds to ensure all students can access the assessments, regardless of their starting point. By using this tool, teachers can create a structured approach to assessing students' progress in mastering complex skills while also considering the supports students might need at different stages.

# Great Eight Priority Standard Checklist

| Action | Summary | Current Status |
|---|---|---|
| 1. Priority standards are the focus of teaching and learning every day in every classroom for *all* students. | Priority standards are the primary targets of instruction for all students, guiding lesson planning and classroom activities. By centering daily teaching on these standards, educators provide consistent and purposeful learning experiences that align with key educational goals. | ☐ We got this!<br>☐ We are getting there.<br>☐ We need to take action. |
| 2. Priority standards are what teachers spend the most instructional time on. | General and special educators, working collaboratively, dedicate significant instructional time to priority standards. This collective focus ensures all students receive comprehensive instruction on fundamental concepts, promoting equity and consistency across classrooms. | ☐ We got this!<br>☐ We are getting there.<br>☐ We need to take action. |
| 3. Priority standards are what teachers assess both individually and commonly. | Priority standards are the basis for both individual and common assessments, though teachers may also assess other standards individually. Teachers design evaluations to measure student understanding and proficiency in these areas, allowing for targeted feedback and instructional adjustments to support student growth. | ☐ We got this!<br>☐ We are getting there.<br>☐ We need to take action. |
| 4. Priority standards are part of collaborative team discussions at most team meetings. | During team meetings, educators engage in discussions about priority standards to share strategies, analyze student performance data, and plan interventions. This collaboration fosters a unified approach to addressing student needs and enhancing instructional practices. | ☐ We got this!<br>☐ We are getting there.<br>☐ We need to take action. |
| 5. Priority standards are the focus of interventions when students need additional support toward proficiency. | When students require additional support, interventions are designed around priority standards. This targeted approach ensures students receive the necessary assistance to achieve proficiency in critical areas, reinforcing foundational knowledge and skills. | ☐ We got this!<br>☐ We are getting there.<br>☐ We need to take action. |
| 6. Priority standards are what teachers guarantee the teachers at the next grade level or course that students will know and be able to do. | By emphasizing priority standards, educators ensure students possess the requisite knowledge and skills for success in subsequent grade levels or courses. This continuity supports a seamless transition and ongoing academic achievement. | ☐ We got this!<br>☐ We are getting there.<br>☐ We need to take action. |
| 7. Priority standards are what we ensure all students learn without modifying expectations. | Priority standards establish consistent learning expectations without modification, ensuring all students are held to the same high standards. Accommodations that level the playing field for some students may be applied, but the learning standard expectations or related tasks are not modified (change the playing field). This approach promotes equity and prepares students for future academic and life challenges. | ☐ We got this!<br>☐ We are getting there.<br>☐ We need to take action. |
| 8. Priority standards and student proficiency of the essentials are a large part of what teachers use to communicate (report) learning to students and families. | Student proficiency in priority standards is a key component of reporting learning progress to students and families. This transparency fosters a shared understanding of educational objectives and student achievements, strengthening the partnership between educators and families. | ☐ We got this!<br>☐ We are getting there.<br>☐ We need to take action. |

# Simple as 1, 2, 3: The Prioritizing Process

The Simple as 1, 2, 3 process provides teams with a step-by-step plan for developing priority standards.

To prioritize step 1, individuals make initial choices based on criteria. Each team member makes an initial assessment of what standards should be prioritized by studying the three criteria Douglas B. Reeves (2002) outlines: (1) endurance, (2) leverage, and (3) readiness for the next level of learning.

**The standard must meet one of these criteria:**

1. **Endurance** means that the standard reflects learning that will be important now and for a long time to come. For example, in mathematics, a deep understanding of place value is important for students over their entire lifetime. It isn't something that they will need to know only for a grade level or for a summative assessment.

2. **Leverage** refers to learning that has cross-curricular implications; something that is taught in one subject but used in another subject. For example, we teach students about unit rate in mathematics but use that concept to solve problems in physical science classes.

3. **Readiness for the next level of learning** identifies prerequisite skills. For example, students are taught letter and sound recognition in early literacy, which is an important skill when learning to read. Students who don't learn letter and sound recognition have a difficult time with future reading skills. (as cited in Bailey, Jakicic, & Spiller, 2014, p. 49)

After analyzing and discussing these three criteria, each team member reviews the full list of unit standards created in action step 1 and is given no more than ten minutes to make her or his initial individual choices regarding what standards should be prioritized. The team member will be applying professional knowledge and judgment to mark or highlight the standards she or he believes meet one or more of the criteria. It is important that this silent time to think is provided to foster individual accountability and avoid groupthink. Special educators should be full participants in this process if they teach the content and should approach this process with typical grade-level expectations in mind. While they will naturally consider their students' current gaps, the process of determining priority should not be based on individual student considerations. Priority should be based on high expectations for all grade-level students.

Prioritizing step 2 means developing an initial list of priority standards. Teams come to initial conclusions regarding the priority standards list. Teachers share their individual choices using a round-robin structure. One person begins by identifying a standard he or she chose as priority, giving an explanation for his or her choice. Explanations should include how the person's choice reflects the three criteria of endurance, leverage, and readiness for the next level of learning. What teams do not want to hear is, "I chose this standard because it is something we already do, and it will be easy for students to learn." As each team member shares, others reveal if they also marked that standard and give their explanation and thinking. It is unlikely that there will be full agreement on a particular standard, but if there is, celebrate! If not, the discussion that ensues is often very robust and enlightening. Teachers discover understandings and misunderstandings about the standards that they may not have thought about before. In order for this conversation to be productive and include all voices, determine ahead of time how the team will handle a lack of consensus. The team may decide to develop or use a previously developed list of behavioral norms to guide these professional debates. This process continues until all team members are satisfied with their initial list of priority standards.

Prioritizing step 3 entails reviewing other sources of information to make final decisions. In this step, team members gather information that will be helpful in making a final decision regarding what students need to know and be able to do. A review of the previous and subsequent grade-level, subject-area, and course standards is critical in determining appropriate vertical alignment. For instance, in reviewing the subsequent grade-level standards for mathematics, the team may find that demonstrating a strong understanding of the division of fractions will be necessary for students to be able to master the next learning level. If the team members prioritized division of fractions, they have taken a positive step toward aligning standards vertically. If not, the team will need to consider whether to add the standard to its prioritized list. Whenever possible, consider sharing your initial set of priority standards with the grade levels or courses prior to and after your grade level or course (for example, third grade shares with second grade and fourth grade) to properly ensure strong vertical alignment. Teams can facilitate this process by sharing the list of priority standards electronically and asking the team members to provide feedback, or by having at least one team member from each grade level or course come together to discuss the vertical progression. If the entire school or district is participating in this process, the vertical alignment component becomes its own step, and teams analyze full priority lists from grade to grade. When engaging in smaller-scale work, this is not always feasible.

Team members will also want to pay attention to information they have from accountability assessments, such as state end-of-year tests. This information may include test blueprints, released assessment items and practice tests, or other documents indicating the amount of emphasis placed on certain standards for state assessment purposes. Team members may decide to add other documents to consider, depending on which documents guide teaching and learning in their setting.

References

Bailey, K., Jakicic, C., & Spiller, J. (2014). *Collaborating for success with the Common Core: A toolkit for Professional Learning Communities at Work.* Solution Tree Press.

Reeves, D. B. (2002). *The leader's guide to standards: A blueprint for educational equity and excellence.* Jossey-Bass.

# Unpacking Document

This reproducible gives teams a structure for each step of the unpacking process. We have found that most teams recreate this document electronically, making it easier for them to access the information after the process is complete.

| Standard: | | | | |
|---|---|---|---|---|
| What Will Students Do (Skills or Verbs) | With What Knowledge or Concept | Level of Thinking or Type of Assessment | Vocabulary | Scaffolds or Supports |
| | | | | |
| | | | | |
| | | | | |
| Learning Progression: | | | | |

*Source: Friziellie, H., Schmidt, J. A., & Spiller, J. (2016). Yes we can! General and special educators collaborating in a professional learning community. Solution Tree Press.*

# Protocol for Connecting the Learning Progression to Assessment

Use this protocol to align the steps of a learning progression with potential assessments and assessment scaffolds. The Learning Progression column captures the sequence of skills or knowledge from least to most complex. It represents the developmental stages students go through as they master a concept or skill. The Potential Assessment column identifies possible assessments for each step in the learning progression. We suggest using generative artificial intelligence to design, evaluate, or analyze these assessments. For example, tools like Gemini and ChatGPT can help generate formative assessment questions, analyze student responses, or provide adaptive assessments. The Assessment Scaffolds column emphasizes scaffolding strategies for assessments, ensuring they are appropriate for the grade-level expectations and support students who may need additional help. Scaffolds might include visual aids, sentence starters, guided practice, or differentiated questions.

| Standard of focus: | | |
| --- | --- | --- |
| **Learning Progression** (Go from least to most complex.) | **Potential Assessment** (Use artificial intelligence to help.) | **Assessment Scaffolds** (Always consider grade-level expectations.) |
| | | |
| | | |

page 1 of 2

**All Means All** © 2025 Solution Tree Press • SolutionTree.com
Visit **go.SolutionTree.com/PLCbooks** to download this free reproducible.

page 2 of 2

**All Means All** © 2025 Solution Tree Press • SolutionTree.com
Visit **go.SolutionTree.com/PLCbooks** to download this free reproducible.

# CHAPTER 5
# TAILORING INSTRUCTION

**Envision What's Possible**

| Picture a school where... | ...Initial grade-level or course instruction is intentionally and proactively planned to meet the needs of the variety of learners in a classroom |
|---|---|
| At the end of this chapter, you will have the opportunity to further reflect on this vision by considering your role in its achievement, potential challenges along the way, ways to address those challenges, and the positive impact achieving this vision will have on students. ||

When designing initial grade-level instruction to keep expectations high for all students and provide scaffolds for support, questions about *how* always arise like clockwork. "How do I teach a student at grade level when they're not yet reading at that level?" "How do I help students tackle rigorous standards when basic skills aren't solid?" "How can students learn grade-level mathematics if foundational mathematics skills aren't secure?"

These are just a few of the questions we regularly encounter, and often, the answer from many well-intended educators has been to match instruction more closely with students' current abilities, even if that means lowering expectations.

Every day, teachers work hard to meet students' diverse needs. They wrestle with how to support students who are behind, balancing the desire to maintain high expectations with the need to avoid overwhelming them. Many worry that struggle could become destructive rather than constructive. We believe, however, that struggle is essential to learning.

This notion is supported by Norman Doidge's (2007) work focused on neuroplasticity. This work demonstrates that the brain adapts and grows when faced with challenges. Struggle activates neural processes that form, strengthen, and reorganize connections. For students who are behind, this means that effort and persistence are not just about catching up—they are opportunities for their brains to develop in meaningful ways. His research reveals that error signals in the brain during struggle are essential for learning. These signals prompt the brain to seek solutions, refine strategies, and consolidate learning. When teachers allow students to grapple with complex tasks, they are giving their brains the chance to build resilience and deepen understanding.

A core tenet of Doidge's (2007) work is that neuroplasticity applies to all individuals, regardless of ability or starting point. This means that even students who are far behind can make significant progress when their brains are engaged through meaningful struggle. Teachers who embrace this understanding can shift from seeing struggle as a potential harm to recognizing it as an essential component of learning.

With careful planning, strategic scaffolding, and a range of supports, the struggle becomes productive rather than discouraging (Blackburn, 2018). Unfortunately, this tension—between protecting students from frustration and challenging them to grow— too often leads to lower expectations, creating barriers to grade-level learning. By lowering the bar, we risk widening learning gaps and denying students access to rigorous, grade-level content.

We first discussed this idea of productive struggle in chapter 5 of *Yes We Can!* (Friziellie et al., 2016), and we emphasize it here once again: Maintaining high expectations, thoughtfully scaffolding learning, and enabling students to face challenges head-on foster resilience and growth, keeping rigorous learning within reach for all students. This is discussed further when we describe the STAGES process on page 113.

It is difficult for teachers to watch students struggle, just like it is difficult for parents to watch their children struggle, but we must always remember that struggle can be a good thing. Confirming Doidge's (2007) assertions, Dylan Wiliam (2018), in his book *Embedded Formative Assessment*, emphasizes that students must engage in tasks that push their cognitive boundaries to develop a deeper understanding and resilience. This perspective underscores the necessity of incorporating productive struggle into educational practices to enhance student learning. We must provide experiences for students that offer just the right amount of struggle so that they make progress.

When we, as educators, continue to rescue students who struggle, we are in danger of creating learned helplessness. Learned helplessness is a psychological phenomenon where individuals come to believe they have little or no control over the outcomes of their actions, often as a result of repeated experiences of failure or perceived lack of influence. This mindset leads them to stop trying to change or improve their circumstances, even when opportunities for success are available. *Learned helplessness* is defined as a conditioned response to circumstances that appear out of one's locus of control (Gordon & Gordon, 2006). Students who have developed this condition have learned to attribute their failures to internal factors that can affect academic achievement. Although students with disabilities are more susceptible to this condition, Robert Gordon and Myrna Gordon (2006) explain that learned helplessness is not a learning problem and can be remedied with the appropriate amount of support. Furthermore, this condition is more likely to be amplified in a school setting because of the probability of being exposed to failure, success, and criticism (Walling & Martinek, 1995).

In an educational context, and specifically for students with disabilities, learned helplessness can develop when these students encounter challenges without the support or success needed to overcome them. Over time, they may feel that no amount of effort will lead to success, leading to disengagement, avoidance of challenges, and decreased motivation to learn. They may stop participating in class, avoid difficult tasks, or express negative self-beliefs like "I'm just not smart enough" or "I'll never get this." This cycle can perpetuate poor performance and a lack of confidence, as they see each new challenge as evidence of their inability.

On the other hand, too much support can compound this problem. When well-meaning teachers and support staff provide too much assistance, students might become overreliant on teachers, support staff, or peers for help, believing they cannot succeed independently. This dependence can perpetuate the belief that they are incapable of completing tasks on their own. By stepping in too quickly, teachers or support staff may unintentionally communicate to the student that they are not capable of managing on their own. This can erode students' self-confidence and discourage them from attempting tasks independently, as they assume failure is inevitable. Examples of this in the classroom might include the following.

- A student struggles with a mathematics problem, and the teacher, support staff, or peer quickly provides the answer. The student learns that they don't need to think critically or attempt the problem because the answer will always be provided.

- A student is assigned the task of writing a paragraph, and the teacher or support staff fills in all the missing words or phrases for them. The student never practices organizing their own thoughts or learning how to use tools like graphic organizers to support their writing.

Breaking the cycle of learned helplessness involves providing students with experiences of success and gradually building their confidence. Teachers can counter learned helplessness by setting achievable goals, offering constructive feedback, and fostering a growth mindset, which emphasizes that abilities can develop with effort and practice. By teaching students resilience and encouraging them to view setbacks as part of the learning process, educators can help them regain a sense of agency and motivation, allowing them to engage in learning with a renewed belief in their ability to succeed.

Because they care about the social and emotional well-being of their students, teachers do not want students to be frustrated or angry, so they sometimes swoop in and rescue them.

We often hear, "It's too hard for these babies; we can't expect them to do this on their own. We need to help and make it doable." Unfortunately, this can backfire and actually cause the student more frustration when the student is working at home or any time the teacher or support staff are unavailable. These strategies aim to support students through the discomfort of learning without allowing that discomfort to become counterproductive. By fostering an environment that ensures productive struggle, educators can help students thrive in school and beyond. One of the key ways to ensure this happens is to keep expectations high by focusing on rigorous grade-level expectations. The rest of the chapter offers guidance on how to plan initial instruction that considers individual student needs and ensures productive struggle.

## Rigorous Grade-Level Expectations

In addition to the ideas focused on productive struggle and learned helplessness in the preceding sections, we believe effective instructional planning can help avoid destructive struggle and promote productive struggle. We offer the STAGES planning process later in the chapter to address this (page 113). Keep in mind that, as stated in chapter 4 (page 77), the planning process begins with clarity around the priority standards and careful development of learning progressions. Clarity about the priority standards and learning progressions will help educators think through instruction, determining what each student may need to be successful.

Learning progressions will help educators consider a plan for how and when they will intervene with students who still need some support while at the same time working to develop students' learning so they have the grit and stamina to persevere through challenging tasks. If we want our students to be prepared for college and careers, we should foster independence as much as we foster academic content. This is part of rigorous teaching and learning. Robyn R. Jackson, coauthor of the book *How to Support Struggling Students* (Jackson & Lambert, 2010) and author of the handbook *How to Motivate Reluctant Learners* (Jackson, 2011), points out: "Rigor requires rigor—if we want to develop rigorous learning and thinking for our kids, than [sic] we have to be more rigorous in our teaching" (as cited in Allen, 2012). To help foster independence, it is vital to allow students to struggle, but educators must discern between productive and destructive struggle and intervene appropriately.

To be clear, we believe educators genuinely want to maintain high expectations for all students. When they occasionally lower these expectations, it's often out of love and care, hoping to foster a learning environment where students feel comfortable, successful, and accomplished. However, true learning often thrives when it pushes us out of our comfort zones, challenging us just enough to grow, which is how questions are valid and deeply understood.

So, how do we design rigorous, grade-level learning experiences that keep expectations high for *all* students, address individual needs, and build independence, gradually shifting responsibility from teacher to student? We believe that the key lies in thoughtful initial instructional planning at Tier 1 (grade- and course-level learning). We were purposeful in beginning with excellent Tier 1 instruction because it really is the key to success and improved outcomes for all students. Excellent Tier 1 instruction improves outcomes for all students.

Page 18 of *Improving Special Education* (Costello & Crowell, 2023) presents research that underscores a critical insight: When the overall quality of education improves, it benefits all students, including those with IEPs. This finding supports the importance of strengthening Tier 1 instruction to ensure it is both robust and inclusive. Enhancements in teaching quality, resources, and instructional strategies within general education settings contribute to better outcomes for all learners. The research highlights the interconnectedness of student performance, reinforcing the idea that efforts to elevate the educational experience for general education students can also lead to meaningful gains for students receiving special education services.

General and special educators share responsibility for ensuring rigorous, high-quality instruction for all students. Recognizing that most students who struggle, including those with special needs, spend the majority of their day in general education classrooms, core instruction must address the needs of the majority. This highlights the critical power of collaboration between general and special educators. Both general and special educators work together to ensure the learning of all students in the classroom, combining their expertise to deliver inclusive and differentiated instruction. Together, they focus on ensuring equitable access to the curriculum and fostering opportunities for meaningful engagement and success for all students.

By embracing this shared responsibility, they ensure every student—regardless of ability—thrives in a supportive, inclusive learning environment. We addressed this relationship further in chapter 3 (page 61). In the next section, we share an instructional planning process that general and special educators can work through together in order to ensure instruction is thoughtful, rigorous, engaging, and meets the needs of all students in the classroom.

## The STAGES Planning Process

We firmly believe that the key to high-quality instruction is a thoughtful, intentional, and focused planning process that collaborative teams engage in well before instruction begins. Ideally, the collaborative team would consist of all educators who are responsible for ensuring students master grade-level material. This includes general educators, special educators, English learner specialists, instructional coaches, and possibly others. You might be thinking, "How will we find the time to plan together?" Or, "Since we have to follow the plans identified in the purchased curricular resource, the planning is already done for us."

To address the first question, we acknowledge that finding time is not always easy to do, but there is nothing more critical than collaborative, thoughtful planning between general and special educators (others, too) for creating inclusive and effective learning environments. The collective wisdom that both general and special educators bring to the planning process is critical when working to address the diverse needs of all students, particularly those with disabilities.

We suggest the following ways to find time.

1. Designate during the school day team and (or) individual planning time for joint planning sessions.

2. Accommodate varying schedules by using collaboration platforms like Google Workspace or Microsoft Teams to share documents, plan lessons, and communicate asynchronously.

3. Arrange for substitute teachers or support staff to cover classes, freeing educators for collaborative planning.

4. Merge staff meetings with planning sessions to maximize time efficiency.

5. Dedicate portions of existing meetings specifically to collaborative instructional planning.

6. Allocate portions of in-service or professional development days specifically for collaborative planning.

7. Allow teachers to observe each other's classes, followed by joint planning sessions to discuss observations and strategies.

To address the second statement ("The planning is already done for us"), we argue that curricular resources provide a valuable place to start when planning, but teachers, who are actually doing the work every day in classrooms, know more specifically what students in their classrooms need. While the curricular resource typically provides detailed planning, collaborative teams must consider the needs of students and align instruction with priority standards. We are discouraged when we see collaborative teams divide the lessons of a curricular resource among the members of the team to develop lessons and then share with each other, sometimes with no time for discussion and collaborative planning.

The STAGES planning process we provide here is intended to be used as a guide for collaborative teams as they navigate instructional planning with or without a curricular resource. It should be used to consider a plan for each lesson. We believe that once teams begin to use the STAGES planning process, they may begin to see gaps in many lessons, including those provided by the curricular resource. While we call it a process and include a planning template (page 140), the intention is that teams begin by following the process, but eventually, after using it over time, the elements included in the process should become a natural part of collaborative instructional planning, therefore taking less planning time.

The STAGES planning process is adapted from the standards-based education planning process originally developed by Paula Rutherford (2008) and shared in her book *Instruction for All Students*. The process includes the elements of instruction we believe must be present to ensure lessons are crafted with high expectations in mind, incorporating the principles of UDL (CAST, 2024) and the gradual release of responsibility (GRR; Fisher & Frey, 2021). It's essential to remember that all plans are made in pencil, ready to adjust as new data and observations emerge. If we are truly focused on learning, not just teaching, we'll let assessment data and real-time student responses guide our instructional path.

We incorporate UDL because the premise of UDL is that initial instruction is centered on designing instruction that addresses the broad range of needs and learning styles of all students from the outset. Rather than only tailoring lessons for specific students later, UDL proactively incorporates diverse methods and materials into instruction to ensure every learner can access, engage with, and express their understanding of the content. At its core, UDL focuses on three key areas.

1. Multiple means of representation (how information is presented)
2. Various means of engagement (how students connect with the material)
3. Multiple means of action and expression (how they demonstrate their knowledge)

By embedding these options into the initial lesson design, UDL makes learning accessible to students with varied needs—such as those with different learning abilities, language backgrounds, or attention spans—and supports the growth of each student by meeting them where they are while still holding high expectations.

In addition, we include the four elements of GRR using the model proposed by Douglas Fisher and Nancy Frey (2021). This framework for scaffolding instruction gradually shifts responsibility for learning from the teacher to the student. It provides a structured way to guide students toward independence, helping them develop the skills and confidence to apply what they've learned on their own.

Now, let's look at how both UDL and GRR are reflected in the STAGES process using the "STAGES Lesson Planning Template" (page 140). Each letter in STAGES represents a step in the instructional planning process.

## Step 1: Standards Identification

Pinpoint and understand the priority learning standards that are included in the lesson. If the team has engaged in the unpacking of a standard in the past, use the unpacking time to review the learning targets embedded into each standard. If the team has not unpacked a standard in the past, identify what students must know and do for the standards embedded in the lesson. Also, if a team has developed learning progressions, the team should review the learning progression for each of the standards in the lesson during this stage of the process.

## Step 2: Thinking Through Assessment

Review unit assessments to understand the end in mind. What will students have to know and be able to do on the common formative assessments during the unit of instruction and the end-of-unit assessment? Teams should also consider how they will check for understanding during the lesson.

Reviewing common formative and end-of-unit assessments before instruction begins is crucial, particularly for students in special education, for several reasons, such as the following.

- **Alignment with learning objectives:** Pre-unit assessment review ensures instructional plans are directly aligned with the desired learning outcomes, providing a clear road map for both teachers and students.

- **Identification of necessary accommodations:** By examining assessments in advance, educators can identify and implement appropriate accommodations or modifications, ensuring students with disabilities can demonstrate their knowledge effectively.

- **Differentiated instructional planning:** Understanding assessment expectations allows teachers to design differentiated instruction that meets the diverse needs of all students, promoting equitable access to the curriculum.

- **Consistency across educational settings:** Collaborative review fosters consistency in instructional approaches and assessment criteria, which is particularly beneficial for students who may transition between different educational environments.

- **Enhanced data-driven decision making:** Early familiarity with assessment tools enables educators to collect and analyze data more effectively, informing instructional adjustments and targeted interventions throughout the learning process.

- **Multiple means of action and expression:** This element of UDL is here, as it addresses the how of learning, focusing on the various ways students can demonstrate their knowledge and skills. This offers the opportunity for the collaborative team to consider other ways for students to demonstrate understanding. This is addressed further in step 5 (page 118).

## Step 3: Activity Design

It is only after we have a clear articulation of learning standards and assessment expectations that we can move into instructional design and develop a meaningful learning experience that engages students. It is here that we start to examine how the learning experiences will be structured. How will the material be presented? How will students make sense of and practice learning? How will we design instruction for those who already possess extraordinary background experience and knowledge? How will we design instruction for those with gaps in experience and background knowledge? As we gather formative assessment data along the way, how will we incorporate opportunities to address what the data tell us about our students' learning to date?

We can use the elements of GRR and UDL to develop robust instructional activities.

## Step 4: Gradual Release of Responsibility

Use gradual release of responsibility to guide students from dependence to independence. The GRR model is typically divided into four key phases (Fisher & Frey, 2021).

1. **Focused instruction (I do):** In this phase, the teacher takes on most of the responsibility by explicitly modeling and explaining a skill or concept. The teacher demonstrates the thought processes, strategies, and procedures needed to understand or complete a task, making the learning target clear. This phase ensures students understand what is expected and have a strong foundation before they begin working independently.

2. **Guided instruction (We do):** Here, the teacher begins to involve students more directly, often through questioning, prompting, and leading discussions. The teacher provides support and scaffolding as students practice new skills or concepts with guidance. This phase encourages students to think critically while receiving feedback and corrections, which helps deepen their understanding.

3. **Collaborative learning (You do it together):** At this stage, students work together in pairs or small groups to practice and apply what they've learned. Collaboration allows them to share ideas, problem-solve collectively, and deepen their understanding of the material through interaction with peers. This phase fosters confidence as students gain experience applying skills in a social context.

4. **Independent practice (You do it alone):** Finally, students practice and apply the skill or concept independently. This phase reinforces learning as students demonstrate their ability to perform the task or understand the idea independently. It serves as a measure of student mastery, indicating they can apply their knowledge without assistance.

The GRR model supports a gradual shift from teacher-led instruction to student autonomy, ensuring students have the tools and confidence they need to succeed independently. This approach is practical across various subjects and helps build self-efficacy, accountability, and critical-thinking skills in students.

## Step 5: Elements of Universal Design for Learning

Integrate Universal Design for Learning principles to make learning accessible for all. UDL is a research-based framework that guides the design of inclusive learning environments to accommodate the diverse needs of all learners. Rooted in neuroscience and supported by educational research, UDL emphasizes proactive planning to ensure curriculum, materials, and instructional methods are accessible and effective for students with varying abilities, preferences, and cultural backgrounds (CAST, 2024). The framework is built on three primary principles: (1) multiple means of engagement to stimulate motivation and interest, (2) multiple means of representation to present information in diverse ways, and (3) multiple means of action and expression to provide varied options for demonstrating learning (Meyer, Rose, & Gordon, 2014). By incorporating these principles, educators can minimize barriers to learning and foster environments where every student has equitable opportunities to succeed.

The UDL process encourages educators to anticipate learner variability and integrate flexibility into their teaching practices. This involves using technology, differentiated strategies, and universally accessible materials to support all students, including those with disabilities or unique learning needs (Hall, Meyer, & Rose, 2012). For example, providing digital texts with adjustable font sizes, embedding multimedia resources, or offering both verbal and written instructions can make learning more inclusive and effective. UDL aligns closely with the principles of equity and inclusivity in education, fostering a culture where learners are empowered to achieve their potential through purposeful design and intentional instruction (CAST, 2024). Ultimately, the UDL framework not only benefits students with diverse needs but also enhances the overall learning experience for all students by promoting flexibility, creativity, and innovation in teaching. Following this, we define each element of UDL further.

- **Multiple means of representation** refers to offering diverse ways of presenting information to accommodate the varied ways learners perceive and comprehend content. This approach acknowledges that students have different sensory abilities, cultural backgrounds, and learning preferences and aims to make learning accessible to all. Multiple means of representation can be incorporated into planning by using videos, podcasts, and interactive simulations to present information in engaging ways; employing supports like charts, graphs, and mind maps to visually organize and represent data; providing translations or definitions for learners with diverse linguistic backgrounds; and utilizing screen readers, closed captioning, or Braille materials to support learners with disabilities.

- **Multiple means of engagement** focuses on the why of learning, emphasizing the importance of motivating students and sustaining their interest. This principle recognizes that learners have varied preferences and needs when it comes to engagement. To address this, collaborative teams can allow students to select from various project formats, such as essays, presentations, or creative works, to demonstrate their understanding and provide a range of topics or themes for assignments, enabling students to explore areas that interest them and offer different methods for completing tasks, such as individual work, group projects, or digital platforms, catering to diverse learning preferences. In addition, teams can incorporate examples and case studies that reflect students' backgrounds and experiences and design assignments that require teamwork, promoting peer interaction and collective problem solving.

- **Multiple means of action and expression** addresses the how of learning, focusing on the various ways students can demonstrate their knowledge and skills. Recognizing that learners differ in how they express themselves, this principle encourages educators to allow students to showcase their understanding through essays, presentations, videos, or artistic creations; incorporate tools like speech-to-text software or alternative keyboards to support diverse expression methods; supply templates, checklists, or exemplars to guide students in organizing and expressing their ideas effectively; and promote self-assessment and reflection to help students evaluate their learning processes and outcomes. We include this element of UDL in the assessment portion of the STAGES planning process, as it is considered during the assessment review and design.

## Step 6: Struggle

Ensure productive struggle and avoid destructive struggle. Identifying whether a student is engaging in a productive struggle or slipping into a destructive struggle is the crucial first step in providing adequate support. Table 5.1 (page 120) introduces five key indicators of productive struggle and illustrates how each can shift into destructive struggle, as well as what actions to take when it does. We explore each of these indicators in the sections that follow.

**Table 5.1:** Productive and Destructive Struggle Characteristics and Taking Action

| Productive Struggle | Destructive Struggle | Taking Action When Destructive |
|---|---|---|
| Persistence in problem solving | Stubbornness without progress | • Offer timely support.<br>• Model flexible problem-solving strategies.<br>• Encourage goal setting. |
| Active engagement | Passivity or avoidance | • Provide timely encouragement.<br>• Break down the task into manageable parts.<br>• Offer alternative strategies to reignite the student's engagement. |
| Strategic effort | Reliance on ineffective or random approaches | • Help students develop a reflective mindset.<br>• Guide students to pause and evaluate their approaches.<br>• Encourage them to consider why a strategy isn't working and consider alternatives.<br>• Monitor and adjust the level of difficulty. |
| Risk taking and resilience | Reluctance to take risks and fear of mistakes | • Create a supportive environment where mistakes are normalized as part of learning.<br>• Encourage a growth mindset.<br>• Celebrate efforts rather than just outcomes.<br>• Provide constructive feedback.<br>• Model resilience. |
| Positive attitude toward challenge | Negative, defeatist attitude | • Reinforce the idea that learning takes effort and that progress often comes through overcoming difficulties.<br>• Reframe challenges as beneficial rather than threatening.<br>• Provide encouragement.<br>• Highlight past successes. |

*Persistence in Problem Solving Versus Stubbornness Without Progress*
Persistence in problem solving is a critical component of productive struggle, as it reflects a student's ability to tackle challenging tasks with resilience. Productive persistence involves viewing difficulties as part of learning rather than obstacles to avoid. Students engaged in productive struggle adapt their strategies, maintain focus, and regulate their emotions, allowing them to stay motivated despite setbacks. They use goal-oriented thinking to remind themselves of their purpose and apply self-reflection to assess what's working, making them more effective problem solvers over time.

On the other hand, destructive struggle occurs when students' persistence turns into rigidity, resulting in a lack of progress and heightened frustration. Students in destructive struggle may repeatedly use the same ineffective methods without adjusting their approach, leading to feelings of being stuck. This "blind struggle" can cause mental exhaustion, a buildup of negative emotions, and a sense of defeat, causing students to disengage or give up on tasks. Without the necessary support to adapt their approach, they struggle in a way that is unproductive, reinforcing negative beliefs about their abilities.

Teachers can help students foster productive persistence by offering timely support, modeling flexible problem-solving strategies, and encouraging goal setting. Recognizing early signs of frustration allows teachers to provide guidance or hints that keep students moving forward without taking over the problem-solving process. Celebrating small successes also reinforces students' efforts, helping them build confidence and see the value of persistence. These strategies not only promote resilience but also create an environment where students feel empowered to approach challenges with a positive, growth-oriented mindset.

### Active Engagement Versus Passivity or Avoidance

In productive struggle, active engagement is central to meaningful learning. When students engage productively, they are fully immersed in the task at hand, mentally exploring various strategies and actively questioning their approaches. They often experiment with different methods to find solutions, and this hands-on exploration allows them to deepen their understanding and build confidence. Productive engagement like this reflects a growth mindset (Dweck, 2016), as students see challenges as opportunities to learn and develop new skills.

Conversely, destructive struggle arises when students lose this active engagement and shift toward passive or avoidant behaviors. Instead of tackling challenges head-on, they may daydream, disengage, or simply go through the motions without any real investment in the task. These students often avoid the problem, lacking the mental engagement necessary for genuine problem solving. This disengagement might stem from feelings of frustration, self-doubt, or a belief that they cannot succeed, causing them to view the challenge as an insurmountable obstacle rather than a learning opportunity.

Teachers who aim to support productive struggle must recognize the signs of both active engagement and disengagement. Educators can intervene when they notice signs of destructive struggle by providing timely encouragement, breaking down the task into manageable parts, or offering alternative strategies to reignite the student's engagement. This support helps students shift from avoidance to active participation, allowing them to view challenges more positively and continue building problem-solving skills. Ultimately, fostering active engagement in productive struggle helps students develop resilience, creativity, and a sense of accomplishment.

### Strategic Effort Versus Reliance on Ineffective or Random Approaches

Students demonstrate strategic effort by experimenting with various approaches and thoughtfully adapting their strategies. They assess their progress as they go, analyzing what works and making adjustments based on their observations. This flexibility reflects a willingness to shift methods when necessary, a key trait of effective problem solvers. By being open to new paths, these students build resilience and learn that multiple routes can lead to a solution, reinforcing a growth-oriented mindset.

In contrast, destructive struggle often lacks this strategic effort. Students caught in destructive struggle may resort to random or ineffective methods without clear direction. They tend to use a trial-and-error approach, repeatedly attempting the same incorrect tactics without analyzing or learning from their mistakes. This repetitive cycle can result from frustration or confusion, where students feel stuck but lack the support or skills needed to change course. If they ignore feedback or refuse to adjust their approach, they often spiral further into disengagement.

Supporting students in shifting from destructive to strategic efforts involves helping them develop reflective mindsets. Educators can guide students to pause and evaluate their approaches, encouraging them to consider why a strategy isn't working and explore alternatives. Providing structured feedback and modeling adaptive thinking can help students move beyond aimless trial-and-error to more purposeful problem solving. With these supports, students gain the skills to analyze their efforts thoughtfully, fostering greater independence and effectiveness in tackling challenges.

### Risk Taking and Resilience Versus Reluctance to Take Risks and Fear of Mistakes

Productive struggle encourages students to take risks and embrace mistakes as part of the learning process. In this mindset, students understand that errors are valuable opportunities for growth, leading them to experiment with new approaches without fear of failure. This risk taking is paired with resilience; students in productive struggle view setbacks as temporary, allowing them to bounce back, learn from their experiences, and refine their methods. Their ability to recover from mistakes and try again builds confidence and a deeper understanding of the task at hand.

On the other hand, destructive struggle is often marked by a fear of failure that prevents students from engaging fully. Reluctant to take risks, these students may hold back, avoiding strategies that might lead to mistakes. When they do encounter errors, they tend to internalize them as personal failures, feeling discouraged and questioning their abilities. This low resilience can trap students in a cycle of self-doubt, making it harder for them to persist through challenges and diminishing their willingness to learn from mistakes.

To foster risk taking and resilience, educators can create a supportive environment where mistakes are normalized as part of learning. Encouraging a growth mindset and celebrating efforts rather than just outcomes can help students see value in their attempts, regardless of immediate success. By providing constructive feedback and modeling resilience, teachers can guide students toward viewing setbacks as stepping stones rather than barriers, reinforcing their confidence to take risks and persevere through challenges.

*Positive Attitude Toward Challenge Versus Negative, Defeatist Attitude*
A positive attitude toward challenge is a hallmark of productive struggle, where students maintain a growth-oriented mindset that fuels their motivation. These students understand that hard work and persistence are essential components of improvement, so they approach challenges with confidence and a willingness to persevere. Rather than viewing difficulty as an obstacle, they see it as an opportunity to learn and grow, which helps them tackle tasks with energy and resilience. This mindset allows them to stay focused on their goals and remain open to feedback, enhancing their overall learning experience.

Alternatively, destructive struggle often stems from a fixed, defeatist mindset that sees challenges as threats to self-worth rather than as opportunities. Students in destructive struggle are more likely to express self-doubt, frustration, and negative beliefs about their abilities with statements like "I can't do this" or "I'll never be good at this." This negative self-talk can sap motivation, causing students to give up easily or avoid tasks that seem too difficult. Their belief that ability is fixed rather than developed through effort makes it hard for them to see value in working through challenges, creating a cycle of disengagement and discouragement.

To help students shift from a defeatist to a growth-oriented mindset, educators can reinforce the idea that learning takes effort and that progress often comes through overcoming difficulties. By normalizing the struggles inherent in learning and celebrating effort, teachers can help students reframe challenges as beneficial rather than threatening. Providing encouragement and highlighting past successes can also build students' confidence, gradually transforming their approach to challenges from one of reluctance to one of eager engagement and resilience.

STAGES implies a well-thought-out progression through the instructional process, helping students succeed at each of the "stages" of their learning journey. We encourage teams to start slowly by embedding one or two of the instructional components of the process at a time. For example, a team may choose to embed GRR into their lesson planning first and then add UDL later. We also encourage teams to engage in at least some elements of the process to plan all of the lessons in a full unit of instruction. This should allow them the opportunity to become familiar enough with the embedded elements so they can naturally consider them in their planning without having to follow the process precisely. We have included elementary, middle, and high school examples in the sections that follow.

## Elementary STAGES Example

The lesson plan titled "Exploring Rhyming Words With *The Cat in the Hat*," created using the STAGES planning process and depicted in figure 5.1 (page 124), is designed to help students recognize, produce, and understand rhyming words through engaging and interactive activities. (See page 140 for a blank reproducible version of this figure.)

| Lesson Name | Exploring Rhyming Words With *The Cat in the Hat* |
|---|---|

**Standards Identification**

*What should students know and be able to do?*

| List standards and learning progression, if applicable. | Know | Do |
|---|---|---|
| **Standard:** Recognize and produce rhyming words.<br><br>**Learning Progression:**<br><br>• Listen to rhyming stories, songs, and poems to build familiarity with rhyming sounds.<br>• Identify pairs of words that rhyme from a given list or set of pictures.<br>• Identify rhyming words within spoken sentences or familiar rhymes.<br>• Generate a rhyming word when given a prompt word.<br>• Create pairs of rhyming words in both spoken and simple written form. | Understand that rhyming words have the same ending sounds. | Identify and produce pairs of rhyming words. |

**Thinking Through Assessment**

*How will we know when students are successful? How will the students know? (UDL: Consider multiple means of action and expression.)*

- Observe student participation during discussions and activities. Use a checklist.
- Monitor responses during guided practice with rhyming word pairs. Use a checklist.
- Students complete a worksheet where they match pictures of rhyming words.
- Students create their own rhyming word pairs through drawing or writing.

**Activity Design**

**Gradual Release of Responsibility**

*What learning experiences will facilitate student success? (GRR in any order)*

| I Do It | We Do It | You Do It Together | You Do It Alone |
|---|---|---|---|
| • Introduce the concept of rhyming words, using examples from the book *The Cat in the Hat* by Dr. Seuss.<br><br>• Read selected passages aloud, emphasizing rhyming word pairs.<br><br>• Explain that rhyming words have the same ending sounds. | • Engage the class in identifying rhyming words from the story.<br><br>• Create a list of rhyming word pairs on the board, discussing the common ending sounds.<br><br>• Provide a category, like animals, then give a nonsense word, like *log* for *dog*, in a sentence. For example, "I walked my log this morning before work." Students correct the rhyming word. | • In small groups, students use picture cards to match pairs of rhyming words.<br><br>• Encourage discussion about why the words rhyme and any patterns they notice. | • Individually, students complete a worksheet where they draw lines connecting pictures of rhyming words.<br><br>• Students create their own illustrations of rhyming word pairs and share them with the class or a small group. |

**Elements of Universal Design for Learning (UDL)**

**Multiple Means of Representation:** How will I give learners various ways of acquiring knowledge and skills?

- Use visual aids, like picture cards and illustrations from the book, to illustrate rhyming words.
- Provide audio recordings of rhyming songs or poems for auditory learners.

| |
|---|
| **Multiple Means of Engagement:** How will I incorporate students' interests, encourage their efforts, and promote self-regulation? <br> • Incorporate hands-on activities with manipulatives to maintain student interest. <br> • Relate rhyming words to familiar songs or nursery rhymes to make the concept relatable. |
| **Struggle** <br> *How do we ensure productive struggle rather than destructive struggle?* |
| **Do less closed questioning and include more open-ended questions to extend student thinking.** |
| To encourage critical thinking, ask questions like, "What are words that rhyme with *cat*?" |
| **Implement think-aloud modeling.** |
| Demonstrate the thought process of identifying rhyming words by verbalizing each step. |
| **Break down tasks using scaffolding and then gradually remove the scaffolding.** |
| Begin with simple, familiar words and gradually introduce more complex rhyming pairs as students build confidence. |
| **Teach and encourage self-questioning techniques.** |
| Teach students to ask themselves, "Do these words sound the same at the end?" |
| **Limit immediate help and encourage perseverance.** |
| Provide positive reinforcement and remind students that recognizing rhymes takes practice. |
| **Reframe mistakes as learning opportunities.** |
| Discuss incorrect rhyming pairs as learning opportunities, analyzing why certain words do not rhyme. |

**Figure 5.1:** Example of using the STAGES process at the elementary level.

Using Dr. Seuss's classic book as a foundation, the lesson progresses through a GRR model. It begins with the teacher introducing the concept of rhymes and modeling examples from the story, followed by class collaboration to identify and discuss rhyming word pairs. Students then work in small groups using picture cards to match rhyming words, ultimately completing individual tasks, such as drawing or writing their own rhyming word pairs. Assessment methods include observation, checklists, and creative student outputs. The lesson integrates UDL by incorporating visual aids, auditory materials, and hands-on activities to engage all learners. This type of intentional planning is particularly valuable for general and special educators because it provides a structured yet flexible framework that addresses diverse learning needs. By embedding scaffolding, differentiated tasks, and multimodal instruction, educators can ensure all students, including those with learning differences, can access and succeed in the lesson. The emphasis on collaboration, open-ended questioning, and reframing mistakes as opportunities also fosters an inclusive learning environment, allowing both general and special educators to work together effectively to support all students' language development.

## Middle School STAGES Example

The middle school example featured in this section employs the STAGES framework to design a lesson focused on exploring ratios and proportional relationships. The Standards Identification section outlines key learning targets, such as understanding the concept of ratios, using ratio language, and solving real-world ratio problems. A comprehensive learning progression is included, starting with identifying situations where quantities can be compared and culminating in interpreting the results of ratio problems in context. Specific examples include writing ratios in various forms (such as 3:2 or 3 to 2) and translating real-world scenarios, like adjusting recipes or scaling maps, into ratio notation.

The Thinking Through Assessment section ensures both teachers and students can evaluate progress. Strategies include observing participation in discussions, using checklists during group work, and assessing responses to quick-write prompts about real-life applications of ratios. Tools such as worksheets, student-created word problems, and interactive simulations (for example, virtual cooking activities) are incorporated to assess understanding.

The Activity Design follows the GRR model, beginning with teacher-led demonstrations (such as introducing ratios using visuals of fruit comparisons), progressing to collaborative problem solving (like adjusting recipe proportions as a group), and ending with independent practice, such as creating and solving personalized word problems. Additionally, the Elements of Universal Design for Learning (UDL) section enriches the lesson with options for representation, like visuals, video tutorials, and manipulatives as well as varied means of engagement, such as using sports statistics or video games to make ratio examples relatable and motivating.

The chart, shown in figure 5.2, also emphasizes productive struggle and scaffolding, with open-ended questioning, think-aloud modeling for complex problems, and gradually reduced scaffolding. It promotes perseverance and reframes mistakes as learning opportunities, ensuring students develop both their conceptual understanding and problem-solving resilience.

| Lesson Name | Exploring Ratios and Proportional Relationships | | |
|---|---|---|---|
| **Standards Identification** *What should students know and be able to do?* | | | |
| **List standards and learning progression, if applicable.** | **Know** | **Do** | |
| **Standard:** Understand the concept of a ratio and use ratio language to describe a ratio relationship between two quantities.<br><br>**Learning Progression:**<br><br>• Identify situations where two quantities can be compared.<br>• Understand that a ratio shows a relationship between two amounts.<br>• Write ratios in various formats (such as 3 to 2, 3:2, 3/2).<br>• Translate real-world scenarios into ratio notation.<br>• Interpret ratios to explain relationships (such as, "For every 3 pencils, there are 2 erasers"). | Understand that a ratio is a relationship between two quantities and can be expressed in different forms (such as 3:2 and 3 to 2). | Use ratio language to describe relationships between quantities in real-world contexts (such as, "There are 3 apples for every 2 oranges"). | |

| | | |
|---|---|---|
| • Describe ratios in words, emphasizing their meaning in context.<br>• Compare two or more ratios to determine which represents a greater or lesser relationship.<br>• Use equivalent ratios to scale quantities up or down.<br>• Use ratio reasoning to solve real-world problems (such as adjusting a recipe or scaling a map).<br>• Interpret the results of a ratio problem in context. | | Identify and write ratios from diagrams, word problems, and real-life scenarios. |

**Thinking Through Assessment**

*How will we know when students are successful? How will the students know? (UDL: Consider multiple means of action and expression.)*

- Observe participation during discussion and guided practice.
- Use a checklist to monitor understanding during group work.
- Check responses to quick-write prompts on how ratios apply to their daily lives.
- Students complete a worksheet to solve real-world ratio and proportion problems.
- Assess student-created word problems involving ratios and their solutions.

**Multiple Means of Action and Expression:**

- **Choice boards:** Provide a menu of problems, allowing students to choose how they demonstrate their understanding (such as writing, building, or presenting).
- **Simulations:** Use interactive simulations, like virtual cooking, to adjust recipes based on ratios.
- **Student choices:** Allow students to choose how they express ratios (such as writing, speaking, or using visuals).

**Activity Design**

**Gradual Release of Responsibility**

*What learning experiences will facilitate student success? (GRR in any order)*

| I Do It | We Do It | You Do It Together | You Do It Alone |
|---|---|---|---|
| • Introduce the concept of ratios with visuals (such as comparing oranges to apples in a fruit basket).<br>• Model how to write a ratio and solve a simple proportion. Demonstrate how to interpret ratios in graphs and tables. | • Collaboratively solve problems using everyday scenarios (such as recipe adjustments or comparing prices).<br>• Discuss the strategies and patterns observed in solving proportions. | • In small groups, students work on a set of problems requiring them to identify proportional relationships from tables, graphs, and equations.<br>• Groups present one problem and their solution to the class or another small group, explaining their reasoning. | • Students independently complete a worksheet involving proportional relationships in various formats.<br>• Students create and solve their own word problems involving ratios. |

**Elements of Universal Design for Learning (UDL)**

**Multiple Means of Representation:** How will I give learners various ways of acquiring knowledge and skills?

- Use visuals, graphs, and manipulatives (for example, fraction tiles or ratio cubes).
- Provide video tutorials for additional explanations.

**Multiple Means of Engagement:** How will I incorporate students' interests, encourage their efforts, and promote self-regulation?

- Incorporate topics of interest, such as sports statistics or video game character strengths, for ratio examples.
- Offer competitive and cooperative problem-solving games to boost engagement.

**Figure 5.2:** Example of using the STAGES process at the middle school level.

*continued →*

| |
|---|
| **Struggle** <br> *How do we ensure productive struggle rather than destructive struggle?* |
| **Do less closed questioning and include more open-ended questions to extend student thinking.** |
| Use open-ended questions, such as, "How can we determine if these two quantities are proportional?" |
| **Implement think-aloud modeling.** |
| Model think-alouds for solving complex ratios step by step. |
| **Break down tasks using scaffolding and then gradually remove the scaffolding.** |
| Gradually reduce scaffolding by first solving simpler problems, then moving to more complex scenarios. |
| **Teach and encourage self-questioning techniques.** |
| Encourage self-questioning: "Does my solution make sense in the context?" |
| **Limit immediate help and encourage perseverance.** |
| Provide positive reinforcement for perseverance. |
| **Reframe mistakes as learning opportunities.** |
| Analyze incorrect solutions as learning opportunities. |

## High School STAGES Example

This section's high school example using the STAGES framework provides a lesson on the causes of the American Revolution, emphasizing each of the elements of the STAGES framework. It includes a standards-based design, scaffolded learning, and UDL principles. It also outlines a clear learning progression that begins with understanding basic definitions of economic, political, and social factors and progresses toward deeper skills, such as analyzing sources, formulating inquiry questions, and constructing nuanced arguments. The lesson is structured around priority standards, such as identifying and analyzing key causes of the American Revolution, and incorporates varied assessment strategies, including discussions, essays, and quizzes, to gauge student understanding. By integrating multiple means of representation, the plan ensures students can access the material in diverse ways, such as through videos, interactive maps, and primary source excerpts.

Additionally, the chart, as shown in figure 5.3, emphasizes active student engagement and gradual skill-building using GRR. The I Do It stage involves teacher-led activities, such as mini-lectures and source analysis demonstrations, while the We Do It stage transitions to collaborative discussions and group categorization of causes. Students move to the You Do It Together stage, working in groups to analyze sources and present findings before advancing to independent work, such as writing essays that synthesize their learning. Activities like role-playing historical figures, creating interactive timelines, and analyzing political cartoons foster engagement and critical thinking. The framework also highlights strategies to balance productive struggle, encouraging perseverance and reframing mistakes as learning opportunities while scaffolding tasks to build confidence and autonomy. This multifaceted approach ensures all students can develop a deep understanding of the complex causes of the American Revolution.

| Lesson Name | Understanding the Causes of the American Revolution | | |
|---|---|---|---|
| **Standards Identification** ||||
| *What should students know and be able to do?* ||||
| **List standards and learning progression, if applicable.** | | **Know** | **Do** |
| **Standard:** Identify key concepts and ideas that shape inquiry about historical events (such as, "What were the economic, political, and social causes of the American Revolution?"). **Learning Progression:**<br>• Understand the basic definitions of economic, political, and social factors.<br>• Learn to categorize causes.<br>• Identify and describe key events using teacher-provided examples.<br>• Begin to use primary and secondary sources to gather basic evidence.<br>• Practice grouping causes into economic, political, and social categories.<br>• Explore the role of historical context in understanding these causes.<br>• Evaluate primary and secondary sources for reliability and bias.<br>• Develop and answer inquiry questions (such as, "How did taxation policies unify the colonies?").<br>• Begin constructing arguments supported by multiple sources.<br>• Understand how economic, political, and social factors interact to create systemic change.<br>• Analyze how individual and collective actions shaped historical outcomes.<br>• Evaluate the legacy and interpretation of causes over time.<br>• Formulate complex, open-ended inquiry questions that guide deeper research (such as, "What does the American Revolution reveal about the relationship between political power and economic control?").<br>• Compare and contrast multiple interpretations of historical events.<br>• Use evidence to construct nuanced arguments acknowledging counterclaims. | | Identify key economic, political, and social causes of the American Revolution. | Analyze primary and secondary sources to evaluate the significance of events leading to the American Revolution. |
| **Thinking Through Assessment** ||||
| *How will we know when students are successful? How will the students know? (UDL: Consider multiple means of action and expression.)* ||||
| • Monitor student participation in discussions and group activities.<br>• Use exit tickets with open-ended questions demanding analysis of the causes discussed.<br>• Students complete a short essay analyzing a specific event's role in leading to the revolution.<br>• Issue a quiz with source-based questions to evaluate comprehension of economic, political, and social causes. ||||

**Figure 5.3:** Example of using the STAGES process at the high school level.

*continued →*

**Multiple Means of Action and Expression:**
- **Interactive timelines:** Students create physical or digital timelines of key events leading to the revolution. Use tools like Padlet, Google Slides, or physical posters.
- **Gallery walks:** Students display their analysis of primary sources (such as political cartoons or acts like the Stamp Act) and participate in a class gallery walk to discuss their findings.
- **Interactive maps:** Use interactive maps to track the geographical impact of laws and events (such as the Proclamation Line of 1763 and tea imports).

## Activity Design

### Gradual Release of Responsibility

*What learning experiences will facilitate student success? (GRR in any order)*

| I Do It | We Do It | You Do It Together | You Do It Alone |
|---|---|---|---|
| • Provide a mini-lecture using visuals (such as timelines and maps) to outline major causes of the American Revolution.<br>• Model source analysis by examining an excerpt from the Stamp Act and identifying its significance. | • Facilitate a class discussion on the Boston Tea Party using guided questions to evaluate its impact.<br>• In pairs, students categorize provided events as economic, political, or social causes and share their reasoning. | • In small groups, students analyze different primary sources (such as political cartoons and letters) and present findings on how they reflect revolutionary causes. | • Students write an essay responding to the question, "What was the most significant cause of the American Revolution, and why?" |

## Elements of Universal Design for Learning (UDL)

**Multiple Means of Representation:** How will I give learners various ways of acquiring knowledge and skills?

- Use a combination of videos, interactive timelines, and printed primary source excerpts to present the material.
- Provide definitions for complex terms and offer translated materials for English learners.

**Multiple Means of Engagement:** How will I incorporate students' interests, encourage their efforts, and promote self-regulation?

- Use a role-playing activity where students take on personas of historical figures to debate causes.
- Incorporate a gamified quiz platform for students to review key events and causes.

## Struggle

*How do we ensure productive struggle rather than destructive struggle?*

**Do less closed questioning and include more open-ended questions to extend student thinking.**

Example: "Why do you think 'no taxation without representation' became such a rallying cry for the colonists?"

**Implement think-aloud modeling.**

Demonstrate analyzing a political cartoon, verbalizing thought processes and interpretations.

**Break down tasks using scaffolding and then gradually remove the scaffolding.**

Provide sentence starters and graphic organizers for categorizing causes.

**Teach and encourage self-questioning techniques.**

Encourage students to ask, "How does this event reflect broader revolutionary tensions?"

**Limit immediate help and encourage perseverance.**

Share stories of historical figures who persevered through challenges, tying it to the lesson's theme (such as colonial resilience against British policies).

**Reframe mistakes as learning opportunities.**

Celebrate effort and progress over correctness. Encourage students to view incorrect answers as steps in learning (such as, "This is a great start. Let's explore why _____ doesn't quite fit").

## Tailoring the STAGES Process With Scaffolding Supports During or After Instruction

In addition to intentional planning, before instruction begins, there will be times when we must consider how to support students who struggle during and after instruction. We must also bridge between specialized instruction and scaffolding. The bridge between specialized instruction in special education and scaffolding lies in their shared goal of supporting student learning by addressing individual needs while progressively fostering independence. Specialized instruction, often delivered through a student's IEP, is tailored to the specific learning needs, strengths, and goals of students with disabilities. It typically includes explicit teaching methods, targeted strategies like phonics-based reading interventions, social skills training, behavior management techniques, and accommodations such as extended time or modified content. This instruction is designed to help students access and progress in the general education curriculum by addressing their unique challenges. Scaffolding strategies refer to temporary instructional supports provided to students as they learn new concepts or skills. These supports are gradually removed as students become more proficient and independent. Scaffolding may involve breaking tasks into manageable steps; providing visual aids, sentence starters, or graphic organizers; and using prompts, modeling, or guided practice.

While both specialized instruction and the use of scaffolding strategies are geared toward student access to grade-level content, the focus for each can be slightly different. For example, specialized instruction might focus on developing prerequisite skills (such as decoding for reading comprehension), while scaffolding ensures students can engage with grade-level material despite gaps in foundational knowledge, bridging the gap between intervention and general curriculum.

To define this further, let's consider how this might play out in schools through the lens of a reading comprehension example.

- **Specialized instruction:** A student with a reading comprehension disability receives explicit instruction in identifying main ideas and using graphic organizers.
- **Scaffolding:** In the general education classroom, the teacher provides the student with a partially completed graphic organizer and sentence starters while reading a complex text, gradually reducing these supports as the student demonstrates proficiency.

By combining the structured, intentional strategies of specialized instruction with the adaptive, real-time nature of scaffolding, educators create a seamless continuum of support that fosters both immediate success and long-term growth for students with disabilities.

The rest of this section focuses on typical instructional challenges for students with disabilities and all students in general in both literacy and mathematics. We have included research-based strategies to consider regarding each of the challenges. The charts that follow include common challenges in literacy for elementary, divided by grades K–2 and 3–5, and then secondary grades 6–12. For mathematics, we have included elementary (K–5) and secondary (6–12) charts. You can access live links for all URLs in these charts online (visit **go.SolutionTree.com/PLCbooks**).

## Elementary Grades (K–2) Common Challenges, Strategies, and Resources

To support students in kindergarten through grade 2 in overcoming common literacy challenges, educators can implement the research-based strategies in figure 5.4. Implementing these strategies can effectively support young learners in developing essential literacy skills, laying a solid foundation for their future academic success.

| Challenge | Strategies | Resources |
|---|---|---|
| Phonemic Awareness | **Sound-manipulation activities:** Engage students in exercises that involve adding, deleting, or substituting sounds in words to enhance their ability to recognize and manipulate individual phonemes.<br><br>**Rhyming games:** Incorporate activities that focus on identifying and generating rhyming words to strengthen phonemic awareness. | **University of Florida Literacy Institute:** https://ufli.education.ufl.edu/resources/teaching-resources/instructional-activities/phonemic-awareness |
| Phonics | **Explicit phonics instruction:** Systematically teach letter-sound relationships, progressing from simple to more complex patterns.<br><br>**Decodable texts:** Use reading materials that align with the phonics skills being taught, allowing students to apply their knowledge in context. | **What Works Clearinghouse:** https://ies.ed.gov/ncee/wwc/Document/265 |
| Vocabulary Development | **Interactive read-alouds:** Read books aloud and discuss new words, encouraging students to use them in sentences to build vocabulary.<br><br>**Word walls:** Create a visual display of high-frequency and thematic words in the classroom to reinforce vocabulary learning. | **Texas Center for Learning Disabilities:** https://texasldcenter.org/teachers-corner/five-research-based-ways-to-teach-vocabulary |
| Reading Fluency | **Repeated reading:** Have students read the exact text multiple times to improve speed, accuracy, and expression.<br><br>**Choral reading:** Practice reading aloud together as a group to build confidence and fluency. | **National Center on Improving Literacy:** www.improvingliteracy.org/post/how-to-build-fluency-with-text-in-your-classroom |
| Reading Comprehension | **Graphic organizers:** Use tools like story maps and Venn diagrams to help students organize and understand information from texts.<br><br>**Questioning strategies:** Teach students to ask and answer questions about the text to deepen comprehension. | **What Works Clearinghouse:** https://ies.ed.gov/ncee/wwc/PracticeGuide/14 |

| Writing Skills | **Guided writing practice:** Provide structured opportunities for students to write sentences and short paragraphs, offering feedback to improve their skills.<br><br>**Spelling instruction:** Teach spelling patterns and rules explicitly, and encourage practice through writing activities. | **Tech and Learning:** www.techlearning.com /news/new-research-16 -writing-interventions-that -work |
|---|---|---|

**Figure 5.4:** Research-based strategies for overcoming common literacy challenges in grades K–2.

## Elementary Grades (3–5) Common Challenges, Strategies, and Resources

To support students in grades 3 through 5 in overcoming common literacy challenges, educators can implement the research-based strategies featured in figure 5.5.

| Challenge | Strategies | Resources |
|---|---|---|
| Reading Comprehension | **Explicit strategy instruction:** To enhance understanding, teach students specific comprehension strategies, such as summarizing, questioning, and predicting.<br><br>**Graphic organizers:** Utilize tools like story maps and Venn diagrams to help students organize information and identify main ideas. | **Reading Rockets:** www.readingrockets.org /topics/comprehension /articles/seven-strategies -teach-students-text -comprehension |
| Vocabulary Development | **Contextual analysis:** Encourage students to use context clues to infer the meanings of unfamiliar words during reading.<br><br>**Word learning strategies:** Teach methods such as analyzing word parts (prefixes, suffixes) and using dictionaries to build vocabulary. | **Edutopia:** www.edutopia.org/article /4-ways-to-teach -vocabulary-and-reading -comprehension |
| Critical Thinking | **Questioning techniques:** Encourage students to ask and answer higher-order questions that require analysis, synthesis, and evaluation of texts.<br><br>**Comparative analysis activities:** Design tasks that involve comparing and contrasting themes, characters, or events across different texts to deepen understanding. | **Walden University:** www.waldenu.edu/online -bachelors-programs/bs -in-elementary-education /resource/seven-ways-to -teach-critical-thinking-in -elementary-education |
| Fluency | **Repeated reading:** Have students read passages multiple times to improve speed, accuracy, and expression.<br><br>**Choral reading:** Engage students in group reading activities to build confidence and fluency. | **National Center on Improving Literacy:** https://wifacets.org/wp -content/uploads/2025 /02/4-Steps-to-Building -Fluency-with-Text.pdf |
| Writing Skills | **Process writing approach:** Guide students through the stages of writing—prewriting, drafting, revising, editing, and publishing—to develop organized and coherent texts.<br><br>**Grammar instruction:** Provide explicit teaching of grammar rules and sentence structures, integrating practice into writing activities. | **Tech and Learning:** www.techlearning.com /news/new-research-16 -writing-interventions-that -work |

**Figure 5.5:** Research-based strategies for overcoming common literacy challenges in grades 3–5.

## Middle School and High School Common Challenges, Strategies, and Resources

To address the literacy challenges commonly faced by middle and high school students, educators can implement the research-based strategies shown in figure 5.6.

| Challenge | Strategies | Resources |
|---|---|---|
| Reading Comprehension | **Explicit strategy instruction:** To enhance understanding, teach students specific comprehension strategies, such as summarizing, questioning, and predicting.<br><br>**Graphic organizers:** Utilize tools like story maps and Venn diagrams to help students organize information and identify main ideas. | **AdLit:** www.adlit.org/topics/comprehension/teach-seven-strategies-highly-effective-readers<br><br>**Lexia:** www.lexialearning.com/blog/top-5-intervention-strategies-for-reading-comprehension |
| Vocabulary Development | **Contextual analysis:** Encourage students to use context clues to infer the meanings of unfamiliar words during reading.<br><br>**Word learning strategies:** Teach methods such as analyzing word parts (prefixes, suffixes) and using dictionaries to build vocabulary. | **Edutopia:** www.edutopia.org/article/4-ways-to-teach-vocabulary-and-reading-comprehension |
| Critical Thinking | **Questioning techniques:** Encourage students to ask and answer higher-order questions that require analysis, synthesis, and evaluation of texts.<br><br>**Comparative analysis activities:** Design tasks that involve comparing and contrasting themes, characters, or events across different texts to deepen understanding. | **American Institute for Learning and Human Development:** www.institute4learning.com/2017/02/07/6-metacognitive-strategies-for-middle-and-high-school-classrooms |
| Fluency | **Repeated reading:** Have students read passages multiple times to improve speed, accuracy, and expression.<br><br>**Choral reading:** Engage students in group reading activities to build confidence and fluency. | **Great! Schools.org:** www.greatschools.org/gk/articles/improving-older-kids-reading-speed-and-comprehension |
| Writing Skills | **Process writing approach:** Guide students through the stages of writing—prewriting, drafting, revising, editing, and publishing—to develop organized and coherent texts.<br><br>**Grammar instruction:** Provide explicit teaching of grammar rules and sentence structures, integrating practice into writing activities. | **Keys to Literacy:** https://keystoliteracy.com/blog/teaching-secondary-students-to-write-effectively |

**Figure 5.6:** Research-based strategies for overcoming common literacy challenges in middle and high school.

## Elementary Mathematics (K–5) Common Challenges, Strategies, and Resources

To support students in kindergarten through grade 5 in overcoming common mathematics challenges, educators can implement the research-based strategies in figure 5.7.

| Challenge | Strategies | Resources |
|---|---|---|
| Number Sense and Counting | **Visual representations:** Incorporate tools like number lines, counters, and visual aids to help students understand numerical relationships and counting sequences.<br><br>**Number talks:** Facilitate discussions in which students explain their thought processes for solving numerical problems, enhancing their conceptual understanding. | **What Works Clearinghouse:** https://ies.ed.gov/ncee/wwc/Docs/PracticeGuide/WWC2021006-Math-PG.pdf |
| Basic Operations | **Explicit and systematic instruction:** Provide clear, step-by-step teaching of addition and subtraction using consistent language and procedures.<br><br>**Word problem practice:** Introduce word problems that require addition and subtraction to help students apply operations in real-world contexts. | **Education Northwest:** https://educationnorthwest.org/resources/mathematics-interventions-what-strategies-work-struggling-students |
| Place Value | **Base-ten blocks:** Employ manipulatives to represent ones, tens, and hundreds, aiding in the visualization of place value concepts.<br><br>**Decomposition and composition:** Guide students in breaking down numbers into tens and ones and combining them, reinforcing place value understanding. | **National Center on Intensive Intervention:** https://intensiveintervention.org/resource/place-value-concepts-instructional-videos |
| Word Problems | **Problem-solving strategies:** Instruct students on identifying essential information, choosing appropriate operations, and devising solution plans for word problems.<br><br>**Visual representations:** Encourage drawing pictures or diagrams to represent the problem scenario, which will facilitate comprehension and solution planning. | **National Center on Intensive Intervention:** https://intensiveintervention.org/resource/mathematics-word-problem-solving-late-elementary-and-middle-school-evidence-based |
| Mathematical Language | **Explicit vocabulary instruction:** Directly teach mathematical terms and symbols, using consistent definitions and examples to build students' mathematical language proficiency.<br><br>**Mathematical discussions:** Promote classroom conversations where students use and apply mathematical vocabulary in context. | **Council for Learning Disabilities:** www.council-for-learning-disabilities.org/wp-content/uploads/2014/12/Math_Disabilities_Support.pdf |
| Measurement and Data | **Hands-on measurement activities:** Provide opportunities for students to measure objects using standard units, fostering practical understanding.<br><br>**Data collection and interpretation:** Engage students in gathering data and creating simple graphs and then guide them in interpreting the information presented. | **What Works Clearinghouse:** https://ies.ed.gov/ncee/wwc/Docs/PracticeGuide/WWC2021006-Math-PG.pdf |
| Geometry | **Shape exploration:** Allow students to handle and examine various geometric shapes, discussing their properties and differences.<br><br>**Use of geometric vocabulary:** Integrate terms like *sides*, *vertices*, and *angles* in discussions to familiarize students with geometric language. | **What Works Clearinghouse:** https://ies.ed.gov/ncee/wwc/Docs/PracticeGuide/WWC2021006-Math-PG.pdf |

**Figure 5.7:** Research-based strategies for overcoming common mathematics challenges in grades K–5.

## Secondary Mathematics (Grades 6–12) Common Challenges, Strategies, and Resources

To address the mathematical challenges commonly faced by middle and high school students, educators can implement the research-based strategies shown in figure 5.8.

| Challenge | Strategies | Resources |
|---|---|---|
| Algebraic Concepts | **Use of solved problems:** Incorporate solved problems into instruction to help students analyze algebraic reasoning and strategies. Discussing these problems enables students to understand various solution methods and common errors.<br><br>**Algebraic structure:** Encourage students to recognize and utilize the structure of algebraic expressions and equations. This approach helps simplify complex problems and helps students understand underlying patterns. | **What Works Clearinghouse:** https://ies.ed.gov/ncee/wwc/Docs/practiceguide/wwc_algebra_040715.pdf |
| Visual Representation and Concrete Models | **Structured sentence frames or mathematics talk prompts:** Use sentence starters to help students explain their logic and build confidence with mathematics vocabulary. | **What Works Clearinghouse:** https://ies.ed.gov/ncee/wwc/Docs/practiceguide/wwc_algebra_040715.pdf |
| Geometry and Spatial Reasoning | **Hands-on activities:** Engage students in activities that involve constructing and manipulating geometric shapes to enhance spatial visualization skills.<br><br>**Multiple representations:** Present geometric concepts through various representations, such as diagrams, physical models, and real-life applications, to deepen understanding. | **Teaching in the Fast Lane:** https://teachinginthefastlane.com/2015/02/seven-super-strategies-for-geometry.html<br><br>**Math Giraffe:** www.mathgiraffe.com/blog/teaching-geometry-for-deeper-understanding-using-the-5-van-hiele-levels |
| Functions and Graphs | **Graphical analysis:** Teach students to interpret and analyze different types of graphs by exploring their features, such as intercepts, slopes, and asymptotes.<br><br>**Function notation practice:** Provide exercises that involve evaluating and manipulating functions using proper notation to build familiarity and confidence. | **Achieve the Core:** https://tools.achievethecore.org/coherence-map/HS/F |
| Word Problems and Mathematical Modeling | **Structured problem solving:** Guide students through a step-by-step approach to solving word problems, including identifying relevant information, selecting appropriate operations, and interpreting results.<br><br>**Real-world applications:** Incorporate problems that relate to real-life scenarios to make mathematical modeling more engaging and meaningful. | **What Works Clearinghouse:** https://ies.ed.gov/ncee/wwc/Docs/practiceguide/wwc_algebra_040715.pdf |
| Advanced Arithmetic and Number Theory | **Conceptual understanding:** To enhance problem-solving abilities, focus on building a deep understanding of number properties and operations rather than rote memorization.<br><br>**Interactive tools:** Utilize digital platforms and manipulatives to explore number theory concepts dynamically. | **PBS LearningMedia:** https://wisconsin.pbslearningmedia.org/subjects/mathematics/high-school-number--quantity/complex-numbers |

| Probability and Statistics | **Data analysis projects:** Engage students in collecting, analyzing, and interpreting data sets to apply statistical concepts practically.<br><br>**Probability simulations:** Use simulations and experiments to demonstrate probability principles and reinforce theoretical understanding. | **National Council of Teachers of Mathematics:** https://illuminations.nctm.org/Search.aspx?view=search&type=ls&st=d&gr=6-8_9-12 |
|---|---|---|
| Mathematical Reasoning and Proof | **Logical reasoning exercises:** Incorporate activities that require constructing and evaluating logical arguments to strengthen reasoning skills.<br><br>**Proof writing practice:** Provide opportunities for students to write and critique mathematical proofs, starting with simple statements and progressing to more complex ones. | **What Works Clearinghouse:** https://ies.ed.gov/ncee/wwc/Docs/practiceguide/wwc_algebra_040715.pdf |

**Figure 5.8:** Research-based strategies for overcoming common mathematics challenges in grades 6–12.

# Summary

By combining scaffolding, targeted interventions, intentional proactive planning, and a supportive classroom environment, educators can give struggling students the tools they need to access and succeed with challenging material, building confidence and competence along the way.

Educators can evaluate their progress in designing instruction that prioritizes tailored support without compromising high expectations by using the rubric in figure 5.9. The rubric reflects the integration of several educational frameworks that emphasize equity, access, and high expectations for all learners. The principles of UDL (CAST, 2024)

| Criteria | 4—Highly Effective | 3—Effective | 2—Developing | 1—Beginning |
|---|---|---|---|---|
| High Expectations for All | Instruction consistently challenges all students to meet grade-level standards. | Most instruction is designed to meet grade-level standards for all. | Some students receive challenging instruction, but not consistently. | Few students are challenged to meet grade-level standards. |
| Access to Grade-Level Materials | All students, including those with IEPs, use grade-level texts and materials. | Most students with IEPs use grade-level texts and materials. | There is inconsistent use of grade-level texts and materials for IEP students. | IEP students rarely use grade-level texts or materials. |
| Support for Productive Struggle | Students receive support when they struggle but are not rescued from difficult tasks. | Students who struggle are supported but are occasionally rescued from struggle. | Students who struggle receive some support, but this support often leads to rescuing students. | Students are regularly rescued from difficult tasks. |

**Figure 5.9:** Reflection rubric for tailoring instruction.

*continued →*

| Proactive Instructional Planning | Instruction is tailored to meet individual needs while maintaining high expectations. | Instruction is often tailored to individual needs, with high expectations. | Tailoring of instruction is inconsistent, and expectations vary. | Instruction is rarely tailored and displays lowered expectations. |

*Visit **go.SolutionTree.com/PLCbooks** for a free reproducible version of this figure.*

are evident in its focus on providing access to grade-level materials for all students, including those with IEPs, and ensuring instruction is proactively tailored to meet diverse needs. For instance, an educator might use the rubric to evaluate their curriculum and identify areas where grade-level materials need to be made more accessible, such as incorporating text-to-speech tools or scaffolds for comprehension. The emphasis on maintaining high expectations for all learners aligns with UDL's commitment to designing learning environments that remove barriers while promoting rigorous standards. Additionally, the rubric reflects PLC principles by encouraging educators to collaborate in evaluating their practices, such as using common assessments to measure how effectively students are being challenged and supported across classrooms. The rubric also incorporates key elements of special education inclusion frameworks, such as IDEA (2004) and the principle of the least restrictive environment (LRE). For example, a special education teacher might use the rubric to guide their collaboration with general educators, ensuring students with disabilities are not only included in grade-level instruction but also supported in a way that promotes independence and productive struggle. Frameworks from resources like Charlotte Danielson (2013) emphasize proactive instructional planning, which the rubric helps bring to life by prompting teachers to anticipate student needs and design differentiated strategies accordingly. For example, during a planning session, teachers could use the rubric to reflect on their use of scaffolding strategies—such as providing graphic organizers or modeling problem-solving processes—to ensure struggling learners are supported without being rescued. By providing a structured approach to assessing and refining instructional practices, the rubric serves as a valuable tool for educators committed to creating equitable, inclusive, and high-impact learning environments.

Through the lens of a school where educators routinely tailor instruction, use figure 5.10 to reflect on your role, potential challenges, ways to overcome these challenges, and the impact on students both academically and personally.

| Picture a school where . . . | . . . Initial grade-level or course instruction is intentionally and proactively planned to meet the needs of the variety of learners in a classroom |
|---|---|
| Consider your role in making this vision a reality in your context. How would you contribute? | |
| Identify some challenges you may face in achieving this possibility. | |
| Consider ways to overcome these challenges (over, around, and through). | |
| Anticipate the impact on students. How would bringing this possibility to life impact students academically and personally? | |

**Figure 5.10:** Envision What's Possible reflection tool for tailoring instruction.

*Visit **go.SolutionTree.com/PLCbooks** for a free reproducible version of this figure.*

Use the following aligned activities included at the end of this chapter to support your work around this chapter's core concept.

- **"STAGES Lesson Planning Template" (page 140):** Use this template as a structured framework designed to guide educators in planning and delivering effective and inclusive lessons. Together, the STAGES components create a comprehensive road map for instructional design that ensures alignment with learning goals, thoughtful assessment strategies, engaging activities, and accessibility for diverse learners.

# STAGES Lesson Planning Template

| Lesson Name: | | | |
|---|---|---|---|
| **Standards Identification** <br> *What should students know and be able to do?* | | | |
| List standards and learning progression, if applicable. | | Know | Do |
| Standard: <br><br><br><br> Learning Progression: <br> • <br> • <br> • <br> • <br> • <br> • <br> • <br> • <br> • | | | |
| **Thinking Through Assessment** <br> *How will we know when students are successful? How will the students know? (UDL: Consider multiple means of action and expression.)* | | | |
| • <br> • <br> • <br> • | | | |
| Multiple Means of Action and Expression: <br> • <br> • <br> • <br> • <br> • | | | |
| **Activity Design** <br> **Gradual Release of Responsibility** <br> *What learning experiences will facilitate student success? (GRR in any order)* | | | |
| I Do It | We Do It | You Do It Together | You Do It Alone |
| • <br> • <br> • | • <br> • <br> • | • <br> • <br> • | • <br> • <br> • |

page 1 of 2

| Elements of Universal Design for Learning (UDL) |
|---|
| **Multiple Means of Representation:** How will I give learners various ways of acquiring the knowledge and skills? |
|  |
| **Multiple Means of Engagement:** How will I incorporate students' interests, encourage their efforts, and promote self-regulation? |
|  |

| Struggle |
|---|
| *How do we ensure productive struggle rather than destructive struggle?* |
| Do less closed questioning and include more open-ended questions to extend student thinking. |
|  |
| Implement think-aloud modeling. |
|  |
| Break down tasks using scaffolding and then gradually remove the scaffolding. |
|  |
| Teach and encourage self-questioning techniques. |
|  |
| Limit immediate help and encourage perseverance. |
|  |
| Reframe mistakes as learning opportunities. |
|  |

# CHAPTER 6

# RESPONDING WHEN STUDENTS HAVEN'T YET LEARNED

| **Envision What's Possible** | |
|---|---|
| **Picture a school where . . .** | **. . . All students, regardless of eligibility, have access to a timely, strategic, and robust system of interventions** |
| At the end of this chapter, you will have the opportunity to further reflect on this vision by considering your role in its achievement, potential challenges along the way, ways to address those challenges, and the positive impact achieving this vision will have on students. | |

Response to intervention (RTI), which is embedded within the reauthorization of IDEA (2004), aims to provide a framework that helps schools identify and support students with learning and behavioral needs early on, before they fall too far behind. Noting a lack of focus on early intervention instead of relying on a "what to fail" model (which points to the traditional discrepancy model as a way to qualify students as having a specific learning disability), the recommendations contained in the President's Commission on Excellence in Special Education (2002) report laid the groundwork for RTI to help address overidentification for and heavy reliance on special education despite a lack of consistent data indicating effectiveness. The fact that it was attached to the reauthorization of IDEA (2004) led to the misperception that RTI is a special education requirement. For some time, the interpretation of its implications appeared on the agenda at special education and school psychologist conferences. It took some time for schools and districts to come to the understanding that RTI was not a special education or a general education "thing." It was a systemwide process meant to support all learners as they need more time and support.

In 2004, schools who had begun their PLC journey began to understand that RTI, when specifically addressed in a systematic way, supported answering critical questions three and four (how to respond if students do not or do learn; DuFour et al., 2024). It was not a bureaucratic distraction; it was a framework for early intervention and prevention. This foundation established, it's important to note that this book generally, and this chapter specifically, is not meant to be a how-to book on RTI. Exceptional resources exist that serve as a comprehensive guide to designing and implementing RTI in a PLC. If answering critical questions three and four is where your school is on its PLC journey, we strongly recommend the following resources.

- ***Taking Action: A Handbook for RTI at Work, Second Edition* (Mattos et al., 2025):** This handbook provides a comprehensive guide to implementing RTI within the PLC at Work framework, detailing core concepts for educators.
- ***The Big Book of Tools for RTI at Work* (Ferriter, Mattos, & Meyer, 2025):** Coauthored by William M. Ferriter, Mike Mattos, and Rob J. Meyer, this publication provides educators with targeted, ready-to-use tools for achieving a multitiered system of supports (MTSS).
- ***It's About Time: Planning Interventions and Extensions in Secondary School* (Mattos & Buffum, 2015):** This book provides strategies for secondary schools to design effective intervention and extension schedules, ensuring timely support for students.
- ***It's About Time: Planning Interventions and Extensions in Elementary School* (Buffum & Mattos, 2015):** Also edited by Austin Buffum and Mike Mattos, this companion volume focuses on elementary education, offering practical examples and tools for implementing interventions and extensions.
- ***RTI at Work Plan Book* (Buffum & Mattos, 2020):** This is a practical plan book with weekly planning pages and tools to guide teachers and teams in implementing RTI within a PLC.
- ***Behavior Solutions: Teaching Academic and Social Skills Through RTI at Work* (Hannigan, Hannigan, Mattos, & Buffum, 2021):** This book delves into the strategic actions educators can take to reduce behavioral issues and boost students' social-emotional learning to improve metacognition and meet their psychological needs through the integrated processes of PLC at Work and RTI at Work.

In this chapter, we focus on the components of an intervention system that are critical to continually examine in order to ensure that your students entitled to special education services are being supported in a way that is equitable, strategic, and focused. It delves into some of the intricacies of RTI and MTSS, emphasizing Tier 1 instruction as the foundation for addressing diverse student needs while minimizing overidentification. By exploring best practices, common mistakes, and strategies for overcoming systemic challenges, it highlights the critical role of collaboration among educators, clear processes, and data-driven decision making. The ultimate goal is to create a robust framework that not only prevents students from unnecessarily entering special education but also ensures those already eligible receive appropriate, high-quality support to thrive academically and personally.

## The Importance of Tier 1

*Taking Action* illustrates RTI at Work through the inverted pyramid illustrated in figure 6.1.

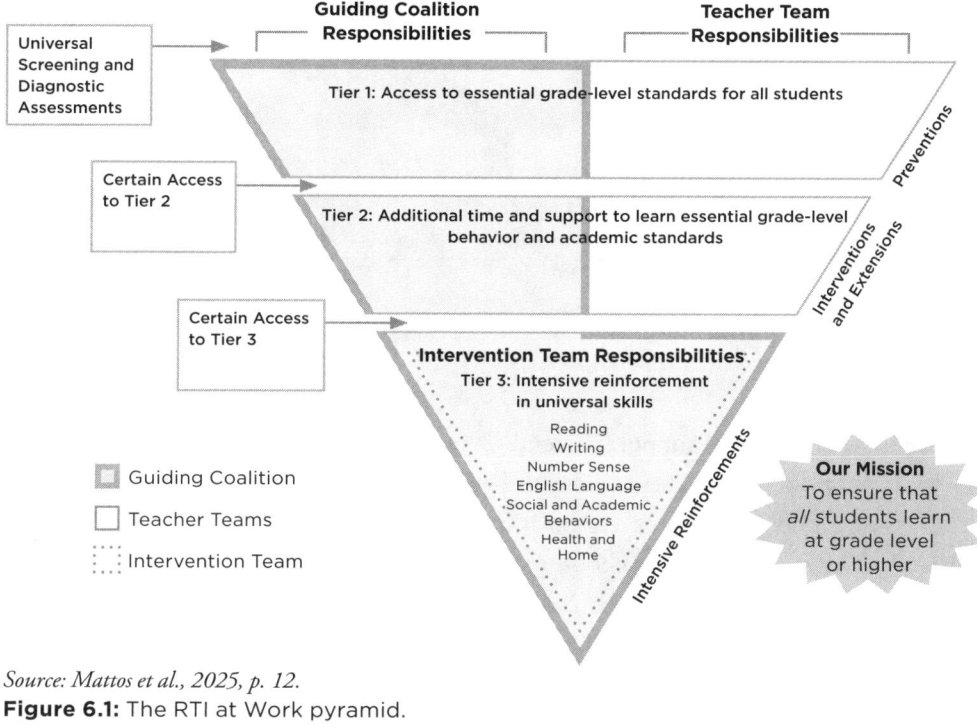

Source: Mattos et al., 2025, p. 12.
**Figure 6.1:** The RTI at Work pyramid.

The top of the pyramid of interventions (Tier 1) intentionally inverts the foundation on which a pyramid is typically built. For RTI to be effective, it requires that all students receive high-quality, research-based Tier 1 instruction in the general education classroom. Teachers use proven strategies to engage and teach all students effectively, aiming to minimize the need for additional interventions while offering universal screening and diagnostic assessments to determine which students *also* need access to a higher tier of intervention.

Any focus on Tier 2 and Tier 3 cannot divert time and attention away from working to develop a robust cycle of instruction that includes high-leverage Tier 1 instruction and intervention. Figure 6.2 (page 146) illustrates the need for *at least one* team-developed common formative assessment embedded in each unit, resulting in a timely data review

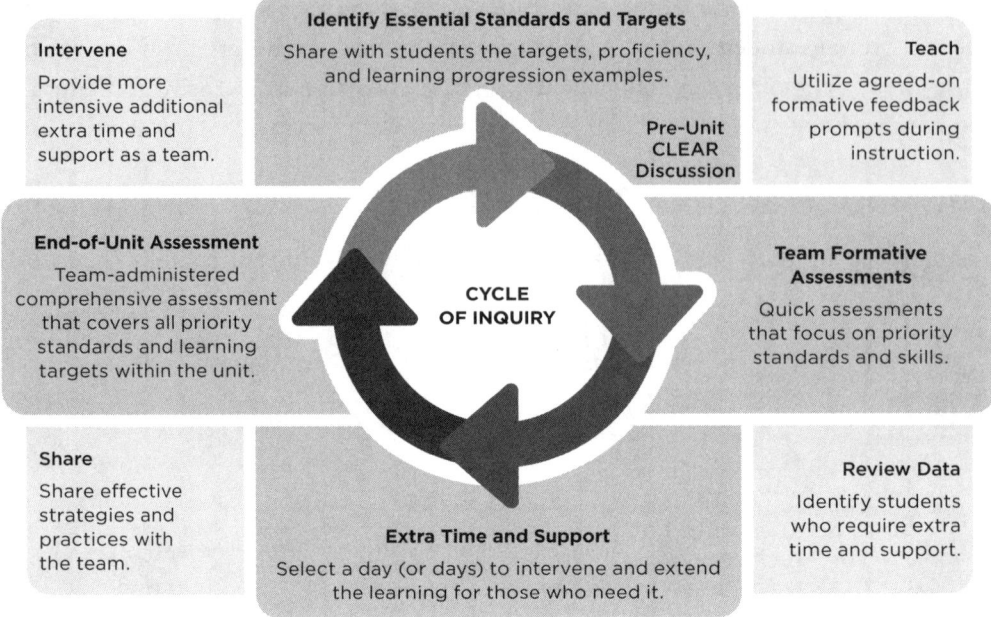

Source: Adapted from Sonju, Powers, & Miller, 2023.
**Figure 6.2:** Unit cycles of instruction.

and provision of time and support driven by that data. This is the purest illustration of Tier 1 intervention. In fact, the *only* way to significantly lower the percentage of students needing Tier 2 and Tier 3 intervention is by working toward meeting the needs of all students in Tier 1. By doing so, schools reduce the percentage of students needing more time and intensity over time. Tiers 2 and 3 intervention must not be a Band-Aid for ineffective Tier 1 instruction.

When teams and schools spend the vast majority of their time, energy, and resources on developing and implementing complex systems of Tier 2 and Tier 3 intervention, it is most often at the expense of Tier 1, and the likelihood is low of achieving the desired outcome of a declining need for Tier 2 and Tier 3.

When students who are eligible for special education services are placed in a special education setting for core instruction in literacy or mathematics, the result is that, often, they actually get *less*! The amount of time they are assigned to that special education setting for literacy or mathematics is most often equal to one class period. During the same fifty minutes (for example) that students in a general education classroom are receiving subject-specific core instruction, special education teachers are typically trying to (1) teach to content standards and (2) work to address underlying skill deficits as identified in the student's IEP. The result, again, is *less* core instruction and *less* access to essential learning.

Given this reality, it is essential that when at the IEP table and considering the least restrictive environment, the team always *start* with the general education setting. Access to the general education classroom should always be the *first* consideration and eliminated only when the team determines that a student's specific identified needs cannot be met within that setting. In this way, all students are considered general education students first, even if they happen to qualify for additional special education services. Put another way, special education is not a place but a service. When a student's needs call for a more restrictive setting, schools must allocate time for general and special educators to collaborate. This collaboration should enable the special education teacher to gain a thorough understanding of the Priority standards taught in the general education setting.

## The Role of Tier 2 and Tier 3

The first essential regarding access to Tier 2 and Tier 3 intervention for students who qualify for special education services is to understand that it is an *and*, not an *or*. Access to *all* tiers for *all* is the key. Students who are eligible for special education services must also have access to tiered intervention. We recognize that some students need everything. At times, teams must prioritize what students have access to and when. When faced with this challenge, the team should first consider the highest leverage skills and concepts first.

What are the skills and concepts that, if mastered, would be life-changing for the student academically, personally, socially, or emotionally? For example, for a special education–eligible student at the elementary level who has significant deficits in decoding and phonemic awareness, receiving the service minutes as stipulated in the IEP is a legal mandate. But the team must also maximize the use of tiered intervention time while not missing core instruction, and the Tier 1 intervention that happens following the administration of a common formative assessment is essential to that learning. We have supported teams who have done the following in this situation.

- Prioritize literacy and mathematics core instruction while tapping into science and social studies time for additional work on decoding and phonemic awareness, realizing that the student must close these gaps in order to be successful in literacy moving forward. The team used science and social studies texts to work on reading skills, an elementary version of double-dosing core content.

- Take a forty-minute daily intervention block and use it as two twenty-minute blocks in order to provide a more differentiated approach to intervention. The team worked to clearly identify which blocks of time throughout the week could be used to provide necessary support.

- Push an adult into specials or electives in order to provide literacy support through elective content, continuing to focus on the prioritized skill deficit area.
- Use the "more isn't always better" approach. For a student with extensive needs, having multiple adults address the same reading deficits separately doesn't guarantee improvement. Instead, a strategic and consistent approach is likely more effective. Limiting the number of adults involved reduces inconsistencies, and if multiple adults are needed, their support must be carefully coordinated to ensure consistent vocabulary and strategies. Any approach should adapt based on data, with progress monitoring shared among all team members to ensure alignment. If not carefully focused, you may be just throwing everything against a wall, hoping something will stick. It rarely does. Less can, at times, be more.

Figure 6.3 summarizes how assessment, instruction, and monitoring fit together as students progress through the tiers.

| Step 1 | Step 2 | Step 3 | Step 4 |
| --- | --- | --- | --- |
| All Students, All Grade Levels<br><br>Universal Screening Fall-Winter-Spring<br><br>Data Result in Identification of Need for Tiered Intervention | Additional Diagnostic Assessment | Instruction | Results Monitoring |
| Tier 1: Core Instruction and Prevention | None | Core instruction | Formative, common formative, and summative classroom assessments; yearly assessments |
| Tier 2: Supplemental Instruction | None | Small group | Two to four times per month |
| Tier 3: Intensive Reinforcements | Individual diagnostic | Individual or very small group with the same identified need | One to two times per week |

**Figure 6.3:** How assessment, instruction, and monitoring fit together.

## Clear Processes and Criteria

Designing and implementing clear processes and procedures for a school's system of interventions are essential for ensuring *all* students receive timely, equitable, and effective support. When schools have a well-structured intervention system, it helps streamline identification, monitoring, and support for students who may be struggling, *especially* those at risk of a special education referral due to academic or behavioral challenges. Defining and consistently applying clear processes simultaneously, with entry and exit criteria, streamline identification and support while helping to ensure fairness. A consistent approach also helps to address the issue of disproportionality, as described in chapter 1 (page 9).

Some of the key components of a clear process include the following.

- **Screening and assessment:** Screening tools and assessment data are essential for identifying students who need more time and support and the specific areas in which they need them. The National Center on Response to Intervention (2010) and the National Center on Intensive Intervention (2013) offer guidelines on these foundational practices, emphasizing their importance in identifying students needing support and tracking their progress.

- **Clear criteria for decision making:** Establishing entry and exit criteria and decision rules for when to move students to higher levels of support or to less time and support is essential. This helps avoid overreliance on subjective judgment and ensures what was supposed to be an intervention does not turn into a remediation or placement. The power of the intervention pyramid lies in its fluidity.

Research widely supports that using multiple data points to determine whether students qualify for Tier 2 and Tier 3 interventions is a best practice (Fuchs & Fuchs, 2006; National Center on Intensive Intervention, 2013; National Center on Response to Intervention, 2010; Shinn & Walker, 2010). This could include universal screening data, classroom observations and performance on classroom assessments, summative assessments, yearly accountability assessments, norm-referenced assessment data (such as the NWEA Measures of Academic Progress [MAP]), and criterion-referenced assessment data (such as the State of Texas Assessments of Academic Readiness [STAAR]).

Once tiered interventions are engaged, data to support decisions regarding movement among the tiers could include classroom formative assessments, common formative assessments, and progress-monitoring data. Figure 6.4 is an example of what a criteria grid for fourth grade might look like.

| Grade and Tier | MAP | Accountability Assessment | R-CBM | | | MAZE | | | QRI (Administered only if needed) |
|---|---|---|---|---|---|---|---|---|---|
| Grade 4, Tier 2 | 11th to 25th percentile | Below 750 | Fall 68 to 104 | Winter 87 to 119 | Spring 103 to 135 | Fall 8 to 12 | Winter 13 to 18 | Spring 13 to 18 | "Frustrational" at fourth-grade level |
| Grade 4, Tier 3 | 1st to 10th percentile | Below 750 | Fall 67 or below | Winter 86 or below | Spring 102 or below | Fall 7 or less | Winter 12 or less | Spring 12 or less | "Frustrational" at fourth-grade level |

**Figure 6.4:** Example criteria matrix.

Once decision-making criteria are clearly established, schools and teams should memorialize them in a way that is easily accessible and understandable to all stakeholders, including staff, students, and parents.

In order to examine a school's level of clarity around the intervention process, we recommend creating a one-page description for dissemination (see the suggested activities in the Summary section on page 155). If the task of doing so proves difficult, it will certainly support the school's identification of next steps in their journey.

Once clear criteria have been applied and students begin receiving additional time and support, clear and consistent processes for monitoring the effectiveness of intervention strategies and documenting and updating the intervention plan are essential.

## Progress Monitoring

Regular, data-driven progress monitoring enables educators to evaluate the effectiveness of interventions and adjust as needed. This is especially important in tracking how students respond to interventions, helping avoid unnecessary referrals to special education. It can also lead to the closing of gaps and the dismissal from special education services. It is important to note that when students are receiving both special education services and intervention support, data should not be analyzed and considered in isolation. The data a special educator collects as they monitor progress toward goals, along with the data collected during interventions, must be examined as a whole picture. Decisions should not be made in isolation but collaboratively, creating a whole and accurate picture of a student, their needs, and their successes.

Best practice indicates that students receiving Tier 2 intervention should be progress-monitored every two to four weeks, and those students receiving Tier 3 intervention should be progress-monitored every week (Mattos et al., 2025; National Center on Response to Intervention, 2010). The student's team, including general education, special education, and those providing intervention, should consider the data and any adjustments based on that data at least every six to eight weeks for an individual student.

## Process Monitoring and Record Keeping

A clear and consistent method for documenting the intervention process, student data, and the decisions made is essential for both accountability and for communication. While progress monitoring and the examination of the trendline are the bedrock of process monitoring, other data should be collected and examined. A team that has the responsibility for monitoring a school's system of intervention must be identified, and that team must evaluate its effectiveness on an ongoing basis to ensure decisions are data driven. Figure 6.5 is the agenda of one such team that meets once per quarter.

| Meeting Type | Goal | Duration and Frequency | Participants | Agenda Items |
|---|---|---|---|---|
| School-Based Intervention System Data Review | Evaluate the effectiveness of schoolwide intervention practices. | Once per quarter (every nine weeks) for two hours | • Principal<br>• Assistant principal<br>• School psychologist<br>• All team leaders (ensure special education representation)<br>• Representative from the language support team | • Examine the percentage of students adequately served by core instruction.<br>• Examine equity of core instruction (across demographics, grades, and classrooms).<br>• Examine student body growth and movement among tiers.<br>• Evaluate the quality of intervention delivery.<br>• Plan for improvement. |

**Figure 6.5:** Example meeting agenda.

Note that this team monitors the movement of students on the tiers to ensure fluidity and effectiveness. Team members also monitor access to and success in core instruction by demographics, including students who are learning another language and students who qualify for special education services. When they note trends or data that indicate the need for improvement, they move on to the last agenda item: the development of a plan to improve.

Last, it is essential that such a team note the successes and celebrations in the data and that they publicly share these celebrations with the entire staff. This should include celebrations big and small, such as the following examples.

- Eight second-grade students exited Tier 2 intervention and returned to solely Tier 1 support.
- Ten seventh-grade students met the criteria to move up the inverted pyramid from Tier 3 to Tier 2.
- Only five eighth-grade students entered Tier 2 intervention after the midyear universal screener.

Table 6.1 (page 152) offers a final summary of the components of each intervention tier.

## Common RTI Mistakes

Despite the best intentions to support students, many schools and districts are struggling to implement effective MTSS and RTI models. Issues such as inconsistent implementation, a lack of focus on Tier 1 instruction and intervention, insufficient data collection, and a lack of collaboration between general and special education teams have hindered the effectiveness of these interventions and have led to ongoing high percentages of students needing Tier 2 and Tier 3 intervention on an ongoing basis.

**Table 6.1:** Summary of Intervention Tiers

| Tier 1 | Tier 2 | Tier 3 |
|---|---|---|
| Guaranteed and viable curriculum | Universal screening | Universal screening |
| Formative assessment driving Tier 1 instruction and intervention | Progress monitoring | Additional diagnostic assessment to ensure a match to a discreet skill deficit |
| Closely tied to priority standards and targets being taught | Clear criteria for entry and exit | More frequent progress monitoring |
| Robust cycle of instruction | Problem-solving process | Problem-solving process |
|  | Systematic | Systematic |

Henry Ford is often credited with the statement that "The only real mistake is the one from which we learn nothing" (as cited in Andersen, 2013). In our practice, we've discovered that examining missteps has provided some of the most important lessons in improving systems of intervention. In this section, we explore some of the common mistakes we see educators across the United States make regarding systems of intervention, particularly those that apply directly to students receiving special education services. By examining these missteps, we aim to identify key areas for improvement to help schools refine their systems and shift the weight of the pyramid up to Tier 1 (refer to figure 6.1, page 145). The missteps described in the following sections are in addition to the critical mistake that happens when students receiving special education services are pulled during core instruction in order to receive services as stipulated in their IEP. While we do not intend to delve into each mistake as outlined in the activity included at the end of the chapter (see "Common RTI Mistakes," page 159), we chose to highlight a few here that are particularly relevant when considering RTI and MTSS systems through the lens of students who are or may become eligible for special education services.

### RTI Is Viewed as a Hoop to Jump Through to Get Students Into Special Education

When RTI was included in the reauthorization of IDEA (2004), and for several years thereafter, many assumed it to be a special education piece of legislation. One reason for that was because it was embedded in the 2004 reauthorization of IDEA. However, RTI was specifically intended to address general education by strengthening classroom instruction and providing *proactive* systematic intervention for all students in order to *limit the number* of students needing to be evaluated for special education eligibility, thus avoiding overidentification.

The President's Commission on Excellence in Special Education (2002) makes it clear that special education has become a life sentence rather than a gateway to specialized instruction that leads to students no longer requiring intervention or special education services. RTI is meant to provide a tiered approach to addressing gaps identified so there is something available between what individual teachers do in their classroom and special education for students who struggle. There is no evidence to suggest that students becoming eligible for special education services is a "magic" solution—quite the opposite.

## RTI Schedules or Structures Result in Students Who Need the Most Getting *Less*

When students qualify for more time and support but that additional support is being provided at the same time that *new instruction* is being provided in the general education classroom, we compound the problem. When a school has intervention time built into the school day, but students who need Tier 3 support receive that support while others are receiving critical Tier 1 or Tier 2 intervention, we compound the problem. When legally required services, as indicated in an IEP, are provided while other students receive critical intervention across all three tiers, we compound the problem. In any of these scenarios, the students who need the most get less.

We recognize that we all support students who need *everything*. This requires that we come to consensus on how to prioritize for these students. Considerations should include which skills, if mastered, would be the most impactful for future learning and the most life-changing for the student. Start there and prioritize your time, focusing on the highest leverage skills and concepts.

## RTI Does Not Provide Clear Collaborative Structures, Careful Coordination, or Ongoing Communication Protocols Essential for Effective Intervention

A lack of careful coordination inevitably leads to multiple adults providing various interventions using inconsistent vocabulary and practice. Less is more when interventions are carefully, diagnostically, and strategically coordinated. When digging into individual intervention plans for students during a leadership meeting, a middle school principal shared concerns regarding the lack of progress being made by a seventh-grade student receiving Tier 3 intervention. The plan involved the student receiving intervention during four different identified time slots each day, yet progress monitoring indicated there was no improvement. The fact of the matter was that four different adults were working with the student on reading comprehension, but they were each using different strategies—and, at times, different vocabulary—without any knowledge of what the other was doing. In essence, they were throwing everything up against the wall and hoping that something would stick!

A high level of collective ownership is required in order for a system of interventions to be highly effective. If key personnel (individual teachers, teacher teams, special education teachers, instructional coaches, interventionists, counselors, administrators, and so on) are unable to articulate the desired outcome for the student, the specific steps of the intervention plan, the responsibilities of all those who provide support, how progress will be monitored, and the standard the student must achieve to no longer require intervention support will all be ineffective. More is not always better, but coordinated strategies are!

## RTI Focuses on Symptoms Rather Than Causes and Lacks the Consideration of Gathering Additional Diagnostic Information

When educators assign students to an intervention because they are failing English, they are responding to a symptom. Without greater clarity regarding what is causing the failure, they will be unable to intervene effectively.

When students receive Tier 1 intervention, it should be directly aligned to a target they are struggling to demonstrate proficiency in within a unit of instruction. Data should drive exactly what intervention is being provided for students who qualify for Tier 2. When students are considered for movement from Tier 2 to Tier 3 because the data indicate they need more time and support with universal skills, there is a lack of consistency regarding the collection of additional diagnostic information to ensure the intervention provided matches the discrete skill deficit. Using the same strategy or program for every student struggling in reading comprehension, for example, will not meet the individual needs of each student.

RTI allows schools to administer diagnostic assessments to identify students' academic or behavioral needs without requiring parental consent. These assessments should be part of routine instructional practices intended to inform general education interventions and progress monitoring. Under the Family Educational Rights and Privacy Act (FERPA; 1974) and IDEA (2004), parental consent is typically not required for interventions and assessments that are universally applied or are not used to determine special education eligibility. However, if the diagnostic assessment results suggest that the student may need special education services, or if the school wants to conduct a formal evaluation to determine eligibility under IDEA (2004), then parental consent *is* required.

## RTI Assigns the Least-Skilled Adults to Work With the Students Who Need Expert Teaching the Most

In many schools, interventions for students who struggle are provided by well-intentioned people who lack pedagogical skill and content expertise to address students' learning difficulties. While this mistake often presents one of the greatest challenges for schools, volunteers, paraprofessionals, and even some certified staff members lack an in-depth knowledge of the progression of skills a particular subject area requires.

When a lack of time and human resources requires that interventions be supported by professionals who do not possess the deep knowledge needed in any given academic area, they must be *directed and supervised* by someone who is. This means the highly qualified professional should design what the intervention will look like and supervise the administration of it. When determining who will work with each group when providing team-driven intervention, teams should use their formative data to support those decisions.

### RTI Lacks Flexibility and Fluidity

Hattie (2023b) notes that one of the most powerful things about RTI as it is intended to work is that educators are flexible and fluid in their approach. In other words, we continually monitor whether what we are doing with a student is working. If it is, we keep doing it. If it is not, we stop, reevaluate, and do something different. This also reinforces the importance of not being married to one program or strategy for every student who struggles in a similar area. Students all learn in different ways, and RTI requires that we be responsive to each student's unique needs.

A lack of flexibility and fluidity when it comes to how intervention time in the school day is used may also result in the inability to provide timely intervention. For example, if a team has forty minutes of intervention time each day built into the schedule, and they have committed to a fixed schedule regarding the use of that time (Mondays and Wednesdays are for literacy, Tuesdays and Thursdays are for mathematics, and so on), they are not able to respond to the immediate needs driven by where the team is in its instructional cycle. High-functioning teams flex how intervention time will be spent based on their instructional cycle and when they will have updated data to act on.

## Summary

After reading this chapter, please reflect on your context and use the rubric in figure 6.6 (page 156) to identify your team's strengths and opportunities for improvement. We invite you to engage in a reflective self-assessment of your current reality aligned to this core concept as a way to support the identification of one first action step toward improvement.

Through the lens of a school where *all* students, regardless of eligibility, have access to a timely, strategic, and robust system of intervention, use figure 6.7 (page 156) to reflect on your role, potential challenges, ways to overcome these challenges, and the impact on students both academically and personally.

| Criteria | 4—Highly Effective | 3—Effective | 2—Developing | 1—Beginning |
|---|---|---|---|---|
| Access to Support | All students have access to all levels of support, regardless of eligibility. | Most students have access to appropriate levels of support. | Student access to support is inconsistent or unclear. | Few students access the necessary levels of support. |
| Effective Tier 1 Instruction | Tier 1 instruction is consistently strong, providing all students with access to grade-level content. | Tier 1 instruction is generally effective, but some students need more support. | Tier 1 instruction shows gaps in effectiveness. | Tier 1 instruction is ineffective for many students. |
| Clear Tier 2 and Tier 3 Processes | Processes for accessing and exiting Tier 2 and Tier 3 support are clear and consistently applied. | Tier 2 and Tier 3 processes are mostly clear, but they are not consistently followed. | Tier 2 and Tier 3 processes lack clarity or consistency. | There are little to no clear processes for Tier 2 and Tier 3 support. |
| Least Restrictive Environment (LRE) | Continuum of services ensures students receive IEP support in the LRE, with regular reviews. | LRE is generally prioritized, with services regularly reviewed. | LRE is considered, but services are not regularly reviewed. | LRE is not prioritized or reviewed consistently. |

**Figure 6.6:** Reflection rubric for responding when students don't learn.

*Visit **go.SolutionTree.com/PLCbooks** for a free reproducible version of this figure.*

| Picture a school where . . . | . . . All students, regardless of eligibility, have access to a timely, strategic, and robust system of interventions |
|---|---|
| Consider your role in making this vision a reality in your context. How would you contribute? | |
| Identify some challenges you may face in achieving this possibility. | |
| Consider ways to overcome these challenges (over, around, and through). | |

| Anticipate the impact on students. How would bringing this possibility to life impact students academically and personally? | |

**Figure 6.7:** Envision What's Possible reflection tool for responding when students haven't yet learned.

*Visit **go.SolutionTree.com/PLCbooks** for a free reproducible version of this figure.*

Use the following aligned activities included at the end of this chapter to consider your system of interventions through the lens of your students, who oftentimes need them the most.

- **"Collaborative Activity: Analyzing Common RTI Mistakes" (page 158):** Use this reproducible tool to self-assess your current celebrations and areas of vulnerability.

- **"Common RTI Mistakes" (page 159):** Use this reproducible, with its expanded list of RTI mistakes, to support your use of the "Collaborative Activity: Analyzing Common RTI Mistakes" reproducible.

- **"Collaborative Activity: Design a One-Page RTI Process Guide or Flowchart" (page 163):** Use this reproducible tool to illustrate that your system of interventions is systemic and identify where you need further clarity.

# Collaborative Activity: Analyzing Common RTI Mistakes

**Objective:** Educators will collaborate to reflect on frequent RTI implementation mistakes and develop next steps for improving RTI practices at their school.

**Time:** 50 minutes

**Materials:**

- *Printed or digital copies of the "Common RTI Mistakes" reproducible (see page 159)*
- *Sticky notes or virtual collaboration tools (like Google Jamboard or Padlet)*
- *Chart paper or whiteboard space for group sharing*

Use the following steps to complete this activity.

1. **Read and reflect (5 minutes):** Individually, each participant reviews the "Common RTI Mistakes" list and identifies one or two mistakes that resonate for them, either because they believe the mistakes are local areas for improvement or celebration!

2. **Form small groups of three to five members each to discuss (15 minutes):**
   - → Which mistakes resonate most with their current reality
   - → Which are areas of celebration given their current reality
   - → Examples of the mistakes they've seen or experienced
   - → How these mistakes may impact students and overall RTI effectiveness

3. **Identify next steps (15 minutes):** As a group, select one common RTI mistake to address. Use the "What is your current reality regarding this potential mistake?" column in the "Common RTI Mistakes" reproducible as a starting point. Brainstorm and write down one or two actionable steps each team member can implement or advocate for to help prevent or correct the chosen mistake.

4. **Share out and commit to action (10 minutes):** Each group presents its chosen mistake and their proposed next steps. Individuals then write down a personal commitment on how they will apply this reflection in their RTI practice, creating accountability.

5. **Debrief (5 minutes):** Reflect as a full group on what team members learned and discuss any common patterns or challenges identified. Encourage open dialogue on needed resources or support for future RTI improvement efforts.

# Common RTI Mistakes

Use this reproducible, with its expanded list of RTI mistakes, to support your use of the "Collaborative Activity: Analyzing Common RTI Mistakes" reproducible (page 158).

| RTI Mistake | Description | What is your current reality regarding this potential mistake? What is the first next step? |
|---|---|---|
| RTI is viewed as a checklist to complete or a program to be purchased to comply with regulations rather than an ongoing process to improve student learning. | If educators believe that RTI simply requires completing steps on a checklist, purchasing a new program, or assigning students who struggle to a computer-based program of learning in order to meet the stipulations of regulations, the schools will fail to develop effective systems of intervention.<br><br>As Austin Buffum, Mike Mattos, and Chris Weber (2012) write, "If there is one thing that traditional special education has taught us, it is that staying compliant does not necessarily lead to improved student learning; in fact, the opposite is more often the case" (p. 5). | |
| RTI is viewed as a hoop to jump through to get students into special education. | RTI was specifically intended to address general education by strengthening classroom instruction and providing proactive systematic intervention for all students in order to limit the number of students needing to be evaluated for special education eligibility, thus avoiding overidentification.<br><br>The President's Commission on Excellence in Special Education (2002) makes it clear that special education has become a life sentence rather than a gateway to specialized instruction that leads to students no longer requiring intervention or special education services. RTI is meant to provide proactive early intervention. | |

| | | |
|---|---|---|
| RTI schedules or structures result in students who need the most getting less. | When students qualify for more time and support, but that additional support is being provided at the same time that new instruction is being provided in the general education classroom, we compound the problem. When a school has intervention time built into the school day, but students who need Tier 3 support receive that support while others are receiving critical Tier 1 or Tier 2 intervention, we compound the problem. When legally required services, as indicated in an IEP, are provided while other students receive critical intervention across all three tiers, we compound the problem. In any of these scenarios, the students who need the most get less. | |
| RTI lacks a systematic approach. | When something is systematic, it is organized and intentional and has a comprehensive effect on a system. This requires that all stakeholders be aware of and able to articulate the details of the plan to those it impacts. In schools, this means teachers, students, and parents should have clarity around identification criteria, how interventions will be delivered and by whom, how progress will be monitored, and criteria for exiting. | |
| RTI does not provide clear collaborative structures, careful coordination, or ongoing communication protocols essential for effective intervention. | A high level of collective ownership is required in order for a system of interventions to be highly effective. If key personnel (individual teachers, teacher teams, special education teachers, instructional coaches, interventionists, counselors, administrators, and so on) are unable to articulate the desired outcome for the student, the specific steps of the intervention plan, the responsibilities of all those who provide support, how progress will be monitored, and the standard the student must achieve to no longer require intervention support will all be ineffective.<br><br>A lack of careful coordination will lead to multiple adults providing various interventions using inconsistent vocabulary and practice. Less is more when carefully, diagnostically, and strategically coordinated. | |

| | | |
|---|---|---|
| RTI energy and efforts are focused on Tier 2 and Tier 3 interventions. | When teams and schools spend the vast majority of their time, energy, and resources on developing and implementing complex systems of Tier 2 and Tier 3 intervention, it is most often at the expense of Tier 1 instruction and prevention.<br><br>The focus on Tier 2 and Tier 3 cannot divert time and attention away from working to develop a robust cycle of instruction that includes high-leverage Tier 1 instruction and prevention. In fact, the only way to significantly lower the percentage of students needing Tier 2 and Tier 3 intervention is by working toward meeting the needs of all students in Tier 1. | |
| RTI focuses on symptoms rather than causes and lacks the consideration of gathering additional diagnostic information. | When educators assign students to an intervention because they are failing English, they are responding to a symptom. Without greater clarity regarding what is causing the failure, they will be unable to intervene effectively.<br><br>When students receive Tier 1 instruction, it should be directly aligned to a target in which they are struggling to demonstrate proficiency within a unit of instruction. Data should drive exactly what intervention is being provided for students who qualify for Tier 2. When students are considered for movement from Tier 2 to Tier 3 because the data indicate they need more time and support with universal skills, there is a lack of consistency regarding the collection of additional diagnostic information to ensure the intervention provided matches the discrete skill deficit. Using the same strategy or program for every student struggling in reading comprehension, for example, will not meet the individual needs of each student. | |
| RTI assigns the least-skilled adults to work with the students who need expert teaching the most. | In many schools, interventions for students who struggle are provided by well-intentioned people who lack pedagogical skill and content expertise to address students' learning difficulties. This mistake often presents one of the greatest challenges for schools because volunteers, paraprofessionals, and even some certified staff members lack an in-depth knowledge of the progression of skills a particular subject area requires. | |

| | | |
|---|---|---|
| RTI lacks flexibility and fluidity. | John Hattie (2023) notes that one of the most powerful things about RTI as it is intended to work is that educators are flexible and fluid in their approach. In other words, we continually monitor whether what we are doing with a student is working. If it is, we keep doing it. If it is not, we stop, reevaluate, and do something different. This also reinforces the importance of not being married to one program or strategy for every student who struggles in a similar area. Students all learn in different ways, and RTI requires that we be responsive to each student's unique needs. | |
| RTI lacks clear entry and exit criteria supported by ongoing progress monitoring. | RTI is meant to be fluid and flexible and driven by data. All involved should be clear on why a student qualifies and, specifically, for what. The plan should include when and how frequently progress-monitoring data are collected and examined. And of critical importance, all involved must be able to identify exactly what a student needs to demonstrate to be exited from the intervention.<br><br>When these components are not clear and not consistently followed, intervention becomes a remediation or a placement and ceases to be an intervention. | |

References and Resources

Buffum, A., Mattos, M., & Weber, C. (2012). *Simplifying response to intervention: Four essential guiding principles*. Solution Tree Press.

DuFour, R., & Marzano, R. J. (2011). *Leaders of learning: How district, school, and classroom leaders improve student achievement*. Solution Tree Press.

Hattie, J. (2023). *Visible learning: The sequel—A synthesis of over 2,100 meta-analyses relating to achievement*. Routledge.

President's Commission on Excellence in Special Education. (2002, July). *A new era: Revitalizing special education for children and their families*. U.S. Department of Education Office of Special Education and Rehabilitative Services. Accessed at https://files.eric.ed.gov/fulltext/ED473830.pdf on November 26, 2024.

# Collaborative Activity: Design a One-Page RTI Process Guide or Flowchart

**Objective:** In small groups, participants collaborate to design a one-page visual representation of the RTI process, clearly outlining each tier, roles, data use, and key decision points.

**Time:** 60 minutes

**Materials:**

- *Large poster paper or chart paper (or digital whiteboard, if virtual)*
- *Markers, colored pencils, sticky notes, and so on*
- *Optional: Printed templates or examples of RTI process visuals (without detailed research)*

Use the following steps to complete this activity.

1. **Form groups (3 minutes):** Divide participants into small groups of about three to five people each.
2. **Set the goal (2 minutes):** Explain that each group's goal is to create a clear, one-page visual guide to the school's RTI process. This guide will provide an overview of what RTI looks like in practice.
3. **Engage in group discussion (10 minutes):** Have groups start by discussing what they already know about RTI and how they can best represent the following.
   → *Tier descriptions*—A simple summary of Tier 1, Tier 2, and Tier 3, focusing on the type of support provided at each level
   → *Student movement*—How students move between tiers (based on progress-monitoring results, for example)
   → *Roles*—Who is involved in providing support (teachers, interventionists, and so on)
   → *Decision-making process*—When and how decisions are made regarding movement in the tiers
4. **Design the flowchart (15 minutes):** Using their discussion notes, groups design a flowchart that:
   → *Shows the flow of* students through the RTI tiers, from Tier 1 (universal support) to Tier 3 (intensive reinforcement)
   → *Includes decision points* between each tier, where it's decided whether a student moves up, stays, or moves down in tiered support
   → *Uses symbols or colors* to represent each tier and make the chart visually clear and engaging
   → *Identifies the roles* of the people involved in each part of the flowchart
5. **Present the flowcharts (15 minutes):** Each group presents its flowchart, explaining the flow of students, the decision points, and the roles of staff members at each level. Encourage the participants to ask questions or give constructive feedback to clarify any steps in the process.
6. **Reflect and synthesize (15 minutes):** After all groups have presented, facilitate a discussion to identify the strongest elements from each group's flowchart. Consider combining the best elements into one chart that can serve as a reference for everyone. Identify where there is a lack of clarity, and identify next steps in addressing areas for improvement.

# PART 3

# Leading *Yes We Can!*

# CHAPTER 7
# *BELIEVE* IS A VERB

**Envision What's Possible**

| Picture a school where . . . | . . . The culture reflects a commitment to believing in ourselves, our colleagues, and our students |
|---|---|
| At the end of this chapter, you will have the opportunity to further reflect on this vision by considering your role in its achievement, potential challenges along the way, ways to address those challenges, and the positive impact achieving this vision will have on students. ||

Part 3 of this book is deliberately called *"Leading Yes We Can!"* This chapter purposefully puts extra emphasis on the idea that *leading* is an action by *any* member of a school—not just title- or role-identified leaders—grounded in the power of belief.

We suggest it is important to identify what we believe, who we believe in, and how we will act on those beliefs before we shift the focus to leading the work. Carlos Wallace (2013) speaks of the fact that beliefs determine actions, and actions determine results. Given this, a focus on our beliefs naturally precedes the discussion of leading the *Yes We Can!* way. Additionally, the word *lead* can often imply leaders in the formal or titled sense of the word. This can be interpreted to mean those in formal leadership roles, like school and district administrators. Certainly, these adults in a system do lead, but we'd like all our readers to consider themselves leaders, too. *Leaders*, in our *Yes We Can!* context, refers to anyone doing the work and trying to work better for all the learners in the system.

So, let's begin with the word *believe*. When you think about what you believe in, what comes to mind? While responses to this question will surely vary from person to person, the things people think of first tend to be what they value most. For many people, this list would include faith, family, politics, habits and passions, pedagogy, mindset, and so on. In the context of this work, we are asking you to think about three specific beliefs and the actions we take that are aligned with them.

Choosing to focus on belief can help us all truly reflect on *what* we are believing in each day, *who* we are working with and believing in, and—perhaps most importantly—*how* we are choosing to act based on our beliefs. As educators, we are challenged now more than ever to make decisions quickly, respond to situations we could have never imagined, and, in the midst of all of this, continue to ensure all students learn at high levels. So, we ask, What do you believe?

## What Do You Believe About Yourself?

We are all innately our own toughest critics. For most of us, when given the opportunity, we are harder on ourselves than anyone around us. It's human nature to focus on our shortcomings instead of our strengths, and staying in that habit can keep us stuck in a pattern of worry and anxiety. What would happen if we purposely focused on our positives, if we chose to believe in the very best in *ourselves*?

For many, believing the best about ourselves starts in our own heads. We have to decide to speak to ourselves using positive messages. For example, when you may be worrying about a decision you have to make, how you will be perceived, or the likely outcomes of a situation, you have a choice to make. You can decide to think about all the negative possibilities—thoughts like "I'll get it wrong," "This will really make people upset," or "Here are all the problems that will probably result from this." When we choose to focus on the negative what ifs, not only do we propel ourselves into a negative thought spiral, but we also increase the chances of all those negatives actually happening. Such negative inner self-talk is any inner dialogue you have that may be limiting your ability to believe in yourself and your own abilities and to reach your potential. It is any thought that diminishes your ability to make positive changes or choices in your life or your confidence in yourself to do so (Scott, 2023). One study on athletes compares four types of self-talk (instructional, motivational, positive, and negative), finding that positive self-talk is the greatest predictor of success (Tod, Hardy, & Oliver, 2011).

When our actions become reactive and stress based, they inevitably lead to less-than-positive results. What if, instead, we shifted the inner monologue? What if we embraced Brené Brown's (2010) findings, which encourage us to speak to ourselves in the same way we would speak to someone we love? What if our mental messages sounded more like, "I've done my research and have heard others' perspectives, and this is a great way to move forward," "I'm excited to share this idea with other people to see what they think," or "Here are all the possibilities this could create."

We are not suggesting that we approach the world in blind naivete; rather, we challenge us all to purposefully choose to seek the best possible outcomes, focus on them in our thought patterns, and then align our efforts to reach for our best hopes. What if we look in the mirror and say to ourselves, "Yes, I can!" instead of saying, "I won't. I can't. I'm not good enough"? While this certainly doesn't guarantee success, it does increase our chances of decreasing stress and anxiety while we navigate life, and it likely will lead to more positive outcomes because we are purposefully choosing to focus on the possibilities rather than obstacles.

How can we strategically believe and therefore act with belief in ourselves? Here are two tips for success.

1. On the first day of each month, create a top-ten list of things you appreciate about yourself. Yes, it's hard and very awkward. No, you don't have to force yourself to come up with all-new list items each time. However, don't let yourself look back at the old lists until you've written the new one. After the update is complete, you may or may not go back and look at the past lists. Keep these lists in a plain notebook that "me, myself, and I" are the only people to see. For example, one recent list of ours included the following in response to the prompt "I appreciate . . ."

    a. My sense of humor
    b. My work ethic
    c. My growing ability to have hard conversations
    d. My attempts to show empathy for others
    e. My workouts
    f. My relationship with my husband and kids
    g. My commitment to my job
    h. My excitement for the upcoming holiday season
    i. My ability to organize things
    j. My opportunities to share learning with others

2. Dig into the concept of educator wellness, as described in Timothy D. Kanold and Tina H. Boogren's (2022) *Educator Wellness*. This work is truly as revolutionary to our field as that of other long-known and well-respected researchers. The dimensions of educator wellness (illustrated in figure 7.1, page 170) and the aligned tools, strategies, and frameworks lay out a road map to become the best versions of ourselves, which, in turn, allows us to believe more strongly in ourselves. We absolutely suggest that every educator investigate these dimensions using any tool they may find, but specifically those tools found in Tim and Tina's book.

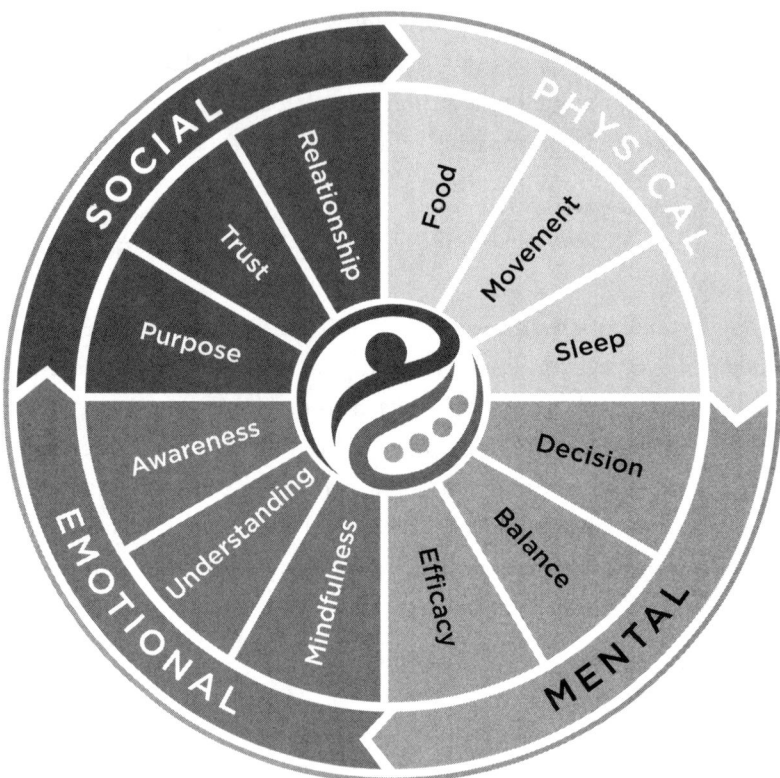

*Source: Kanold & Boogren, 2022, p. 3.*
**Figure 7.1:** Wellness Solutions for Educators framework graphic model.

## What Are You Believing About Your Colleagues?

Believing isn't just about how you view yourself, although that is a key place to start. As educators, we are all leaders, collaborators, learners, and facilitators, regardless of title or position. By choosing to work in our field, we also choose to work with others. So, it's fair to focus on how we choose to look at others.

Here's the thing: We are all different. We have different experiences, habits, aspirations, and values. If we really engage in meaningful conversations and work together, we will, at times, agree and, at other times, disagree. In good times and bad, we make a choice in what we then believe about those around us. It's easy when everyone is getting along, and there's no conflict or significant change facing us. But let's be real—that is almost *never* the case in our field, and it's certainly not our current reality.

So, it becomes all about how we see a situation and then how we believe and act. When we are in a place of seeing things differently, we choose to view that as an opportunity or a conflict. When we disagree, we can view that as a chance to seek to understand and be understood or as a reason to get angry or bitter or to retreat or disengage.

In a PLC, the second big idea is a collaborative culture focused on making sure *all* students learn (DuFour et al., 2024). This does not mean that everyone gets along merrily all the time. In fact, if that is the case, it may be important to ask if you're actually tackling the hard topics of learning for *all*—equity, guaranteed and viable curriculum, and resource allocation—or simply going through the motions in the name of keeping the peace rather than risking stirring the pot to change the system.

Rather, in a true collaborative culture, each person brings their assets and opportunities, their wisdom, and their weaknesses to the table to share and seek to improve. In doing so, differences will arise, and that's both predictable and challenging. How we believe in each other directly impacts the response to this. If we believe that conflict must be avoided, any perceived differences shut down growth. If we believe that "getting it done" is more important than working through it together, then we likely aren't believing very positively about our colleagues or about collaboration. Conversely, if we believe that everyone has something to offer, others' perspectives—when shared—create opportunities for each of us to grow. Differences of opinion really can help us find a shared and best plan of action, and we are all geniuses in our own way (while no one is an expert in everything). We create the conditions for growth, connection, and improvement.

When we believe in each other, are willing to be vulnerable, and seek to see others' strengths rather than focusing on their struggles or differences from us, we open the door to true collaboration and, therefore, create the opportunity for shared greatness, seeking the highest levels of learning for the students we serve.

How can we strategically believe and therefore act with belief in our colleagues? Here are two tips for success.

1. Choose to believe that each person is doing the best they can in that moment. Oh, this can be a hard one, for sure. It is very, very easy to assume the worst in others, just as we do about ourselves. What if we challenged ourselves to assume the *best* in others, to be curious about their perspective, experiences, and decisions, and to find common ground rather than great divides? A structure for this could look like the following questions.

    a. Who am I working with?

    b. What are they great at doing or contributing?

    c. How are we different from each other?

    d. If I assume this person is bringing the best version of themselves to this situation, what does that mean? What does that look like?

    e. What unites us or helps us complement each other?

    f. How can I listen and hear from this person, believing that they are bringing their best forward?

2. Compliment others! Tell colleagues what you value about them. It's far easier to do this for others than for ourselves, but it can still be awkward. This can be as simple as expressing gratitude for another's work or contribution. It can be a statement of appreciation for what another person does to lighten your load. It can be taking the time to give someone a special treat for helping you out. For most of us, it is the little but meaningful actions that have the most impact. Many of us keep the thoughtful notes and cards we receive, and we likely also have a folder for our emails that "fill our buckets" or serve as an emotional reserve for us to access when needed. We can look back to these things to help remind us of times others have helped us see the best in ourselves, so be sure that you are a person who sends those messages. It's also key to dig into the sorts of language and actions that mean the most to people; we find that the book *The Five Languages of Appreciation in the Workplace* (Chapman & White, 2011) is an excellent resource to help with this.

## What Are You Believing About Your Students?

Be honest. When asked a question like, "Do you believe that all students can learn at high levels?," what's your response? Is it an emphatic "Yes, and here's how . . ."? Is it "Yes," but perhaps with a bit of a shaky voice? Is it "Yes, but . . . ," where you seek to explain why some students can't or won't excel? Is it a flat-out "Nope"? Here's the thing: What you believe about your students and their abilities directly impacts how they actually perform.

Please know we are not saying that simply believing all students will learn at high levels will actually make it happen. Striving to help each and every learner reach proficiency, close existing learning gaps, or learn functional skills when significantly impaired is tough work. It takes rich collaboration, clarity in learning standards, shared understanding of proficiency, use of instructional best practices, assessments used formatively to drive instruction, open sharing of data, responsive intervention and extension, and a deep commitment to doing whatever it takes to reach each and every learner. It requires us to seek to continually learn and improve.

In other words, we have to commit to becoming a high-performing PLC that adheres to all the other core concepts and strategies referenced in this book, as well as those of many others. Underlying all these actions is a shared belief that each and every student—with appropriate support, time, and resources—can and will learn. Each and every one, regardless of background, ability or disability, race, gender, religion, family, income level, or any other factor that makes them the wonderful person they are, can and will learn.

What we will say, however, is that when we create reasons to justify why some students don't learn or why some students can't learn, we all but guarantee they won't learn. Our belief, or lack of belief, in our students can and often does negatively impact them and creates the conditions where they don't learn at the highest levels, where they learn to also believe that they can't or won't learn, or where they themselves lose faith in school being a place that sees their potential and all they can be and achieve.

So, what do you believe about your students? How do you talk about them? Do you talk about their greatness, what they can do, what they can't *yet* do, and the hopes you have for them? If not, we ask you to carefully consider how you're thinking and talking about your students. Your thoughts and words have a powerful way of translating into their reality. Are you choosing to believe in the potential of your students? Are you willing to confront others whose language or beliefs are perpetuating a "they can't" mindset? As educators, we have the gift and responsibility to be our students' biggest fans, strongest advocates, and most trusted resources. Think carefully about what you believe about the students you serve; they are directly impacted by your thoughts and aligned actions.

How can we strategically believe and, therefore, act with belief in our students? Here are two tips for success.

1. Strive to use asset-based language when speaking about students. When we focus on a student's assets, we speak positivity into them and others around them. When we do this, others, including the students, hear it, and it matters. In an article for *NEA Today*, Tim Walker (2017) writes:

   **If we pay attention to *how we talk* when we label students, discuss their outcomes, describe their "intelligence" or their communities, or describe their progress, their lives, and the opportunities they have and need, we have a powerful lever for constant equity effort in school.**

   Table 7.1 offers some purposeful shifts in language to consider.

**Table 7.1:** Language Shifts for Talking About Students

| Instead of this . . . | Try this . . . |
|---|---|
| "Subgroups" | "Student groups" |
| | "The group of students who . . ." |
| "SpEd kids" | "Students with IEPs" |
| | "Students who qualify for special education services" |
| "My kids" or "my caseload" | "Our students" |
| "Low performers" | "Students who need additional time and support" |
| "The low kids" | |
| "Sweet and lows" | |
| "Regular education" | "General education" |
| "Normal education" | "Inclusive education" |
| | "Your classroom" |
| "Tier 3 kids" | "Students who need Tier 3 support" |

*continued →*

| "Autistic student" | "Student who has autism" |
| | "High- or low-support autism" |
| "English learners" or "ELs" | "Emerging bilingual students" |
| | "Students halfway to bilingual" |
| | "Multilingual learners" |

2. Build your understanding of trauma-informed instruction. As educators, we have always tried to be aware of the impact of challenging home lives on students. However, our reality now is that the impact of the COVID-19 pandemic on *every* student remains, and the shifts still resonate for all of us and, most importantly, for our students. Research and resources help us be better able to support students facing challenges of all kinds, and a model to consider would be that of exploring how a student functions in their "upstairs brain" versus their "downstairs brain." Specifically, the writings of Daniel J. Siegel and Tina Payne Bryson (2011) in *The Whole-Brain Child* provide a framework for helping us understand and manage emotions, behavior, and relationships.

   Put simply, the upstairs brain is able to function when our systems are regulated, allowing any of us to access higher thinking and logic. Conversely, when under stress, we close up and access only our downstairs brain, where emotions and impulses drive our actions.

   When we become better informed of these naturally occurring responses, we can then better support students in navigating between them, helping learners then strive to stay in the upstairs brain. Kristin Souers's (2016, 2019) books *Fostering Resilient Learners* and *Relationship, Responsibility, and Regulation* are outstanding resources to build any educator's skill set in this realm.

## Summary

Let's be real. We all have days when it's harder to seek and believe the positives. Daily, we navigate the roller coaster that is education. The message isn't to live blissfully unaware or not give ourselves the grace to sometimes get down, feel frustrated or anxious, or flat-out feel rotten. However, it *is* our choice to decide to focus on positive perspectives and believe in ourselves, our colleagues, and our students. It is our choice to use our time to plan for purposeful instruction, examine our results, celebrate our successes, view our struggles as opportunities, and focus on solutions rather than admire our problems. It is our choice to see the best in those around us, both our colleagues and our students, and strive to support them and help them see the best in themselves. Finally, it is our choice to look at ourselves and look for all that we *can* do, set goals to get even better, and celebrate our successes. It is our choice to believe in the best, seek it out, and see it in ourselves. Now more than ever, believing may just be the one thing that helps us keep going and strive for the greatness that is within each and every one of us. Use the reflection tool in figure 7.2 to begin taking your next steps.

| Picture a school where . . . | . . . The culture reflects a commitment to believing in ourselves, our colleagues, and our students |
|---|---|
| Consider your role in making this vision a reality in your context. How would you contribute? | |
| Identify some challenges you may face in achieving this possibility. | |
| Consider ways to overcome these challenges (over, around, and through). | |
| Anticipate the impact on students. How would bringing this possibility to life impact students academically and personally? | |

**Figure 7.2:** Envision What's Possible reflection tool for understanding *believe* is a verb.

*Visit **go.SolutionTree.com/PLCbooks** for a free reproducible version of this figure.*

# CHAPTER 8
# LEADING THE WAY

**Envision What's Possible**

| Picture a school where . . . | . . . Everyone collaborates in and advocates for the work of *Yes We Can!*, and leadership is not by title but represents collective ownership |
|---|---|
| At the end of this chapter, you will have the opportunity to further reflect on this vision by considering your role in its achievement, potential challenges along the way, ways to address those challenges, and the positive impact achieving this vision will have on students. ||

As we start this final chapter, we would like to ensure we approach it with one shared sentiment: We are *all* leaders. As John C. Maxwell (2018) writes, "Everyone is a leader because everyone influences someone." No matter what role you play in your context, you are a leader of the work. With leadership typically comes needing the skills to navigate change and colleagues being less than thrilled about the shifts coming their way. It's important to remember that resistance to change is a very natural and predictable reaction. When we understand and acknowledge this in advance, we create an opportunity to prevent this outcome. Put another way, because we know that what can be predicted can be prevented, we are called, as leaders, to be ready to maneuver through the change process.

Given that, we also know that one strategy with which educators typically feel comfortable is an acronym, letters that create a message in short form. Therefore, this chapter ends with a call to action through the lens of the letters in LEAD. It's our hope that this acronym simplifies complex ideas and gives you a framework to approach leading the way, embedding your approach to change with supporting tools and strategies.

We will dig into each letter, but to summarize, we consider *LEAD* through the following key actions.

- **Learn about the change process:** When we better understand a process, we are better able to prepare for it.
- **Embrace hard conversations:** With change will always come opportunities for challenging conversations, so we will look at strategies to plan for and respond during difficult conversations.
- **Actively celebrate successes and attempts to make change:** A focus on celebrating not just the wins but the attempts helps establish a culture built less on fear and more on the power of possibilities.
- **Design systems and tools to do the work:** Change remains fear-inducing until we start actually doing the work. It can still be difficult, but what's far more intimidating than doing something and even floundering with it is the fear of waiting for something to happen to us.

Let's dig into each letter and consider strategies that may be used to help build your skill set in managing change, inspiring excellence, and leading the way! To best do so, consider a change you or your system is managing. Then, apply the strategies that fit within your context. This will help you personalize the tools and find a way to apply them immediately!

## Learn About the Change Process

There are *a lot* of books and resources to inform us about the change process. However, when thinking about the one resource we use most often to understand and navigate change, we consistently return to the Concerns Based Adoption Model (CBAM), which was developed by Gene E. Hall and Shirley M. Hord (2020) to help anyone better understand the change process through the lens of stakeholder perspectives and then help themselves and others move through the stages of concern any systemic change brings. They identify the seven stages of concern detailed in figure 8.1 as common responses to change, around which we developed the strategic ways shown to help ourselves and others move through the stages to a more open mindset related to change.

You can use figure 8.1 as a tool to help anyone better understand the change process, how it impacts people with different perspectives, and how to help yourself and others move from one target to another.

| Stage of Concern | Common Responses to Change | Ways to Create an Open Mindset About Change |
|---|---|---|
| 0. **Awareness:** Aware that an innovation is being introduced but not really interested or concerned with it | "I am not concerned about this innovation." <br><br> "I don't really know what this innovation involves." | • If possible, involve teachers in the discussions and decisions about the innovation and its implementation. <br> • Share enough information to arouse interest but not so much it overwhelms. <br> • Acknowledge that a lack of awareness is expected and reasonable and that there are no foolish questions. |
| 1. **Informational:** Interested in some information about the change | "I want to know more about this innovation." <br><br> "There is a lot I don't know about this, but I'm reading and asking questions." | • Provide clear and accurate information about the innovation. <br> • Use several ways to share information—verbally, in writing, and through available media. Communicate with large and small groups and individuals. <br> • Help teachers see how the innovation relates to their current practice—the similarities and the differences. |
| 2. **Personal:** Wants to know the personal impact of the change | "How is this going to affect me?" <br><br> "I'm concerned about whether I can do this." <br><br> "How much control will I have over the way I use this?" | • Legitimize the existence and expression of personal concerns. <br> • Use personal notes and conversations to provide encouragement and reinforce personal adequacy. <br> • Connect these teachers with others whose personal concerns have diminished and who will be supportive. |
| 3. **Management:** Concerned about how the change will be managed in practice | "I seem to be spending all of my time getting materials ready." <br><br> "I'm concerned that we'll be spending more time in meetings." <br><br> "Where will I find the time to plan my lessons or take care of the recordkeeping required to do this well?" | • Clarify the steps and components of the innovation. <br> • Provide answers that address the small, specific how-to issues. <br> • Demonstrate exact and practical solutions to the logistic problems that contribute to these concerns. |
| 4. **Consequence:** Interested in the impact on students or the school | "How is using this going to affect students?" <br><br> "I'm concerned about whether I can change this in order to ensure students will learn better as a result of introducing this idea." | • Provide individuals with opportunities to visit other settings where the innovation is in use and to attend conferences on this topic. <br> • Make sure these teachers are not overlooked. Give positive feedback and needed support. <br> • Find opportunities for these teachers to share their skills with others. |
| 5. **Collaboration:** Interested in working with colleagues to make the change effective | "I'm concerned about relating what I'm doing to what other instructors are doing." <br><br> "I want to see more cooperation among teachers as we work with this innovation." | • Provide opportunities to develop skills for working collaboratively. <br> • Bring together, from inside and outside the school, those who are interested in working collaboratively. <br> • Use these teachers to assist others. |

*Source: Adapted from Hall & Hord, 2020.*

**Figure 8.1:** CBAM model to identify the seven stages of concern about change.

continued →

| | | |
|---|---|---|
| 6. Refocusing: Begins refining the innovation to improve student learning results | "I have some ideas about something that would work even better than this." | • Respect and encourage the interest these individuals have for finding a better way.<br>• Help these teachers channel their ideas and energies productively.<br>• Help these teachers access the resources they need to refine their ideas and put them into practice. |

Visit **go.SolutionTree.com/PLCbooks** *for a free reproducible version of this figure.*

## Embrace Hard Conversations

In *Women Who Lead* (Keating & Kullar, 2022), Heather posited three common statements that you have likely heard or even said yourself:

- **"I can't stand conflict."**
- **"Confrontation makes me so uncomfortable."**
- **"Talking won't change anything. I'm just going to deal with it." (p. 111)**

The problem is that conflict, like change, will always happen in environments where human beings collaborate. Period. On the upside of this, conflict and confrontation do not always have to end in dispute or nastiness.

So, *how* do you have this kind of hard conversation? Brown (2018) uses the term *rumble* to describe a difficult conversation:

> **A rumble is a discussion, conversation, or meeting defined by a commitment to lean into vulnerability, to stay curious and generous, to stick with the messy middle of problem identification and solving, to take a break and circle back when necessary, to be fearless in owning our parts and . . . to listen with the same passion with which we want to be heard. (p. 10)**

In the book *Crucial Conversations* (Patterson, Grenny, McMillan, & Switzler, 2012), the authors define a crucial conversation as "a discussion between two or more people where (1) stakes are high, (2) opinions vary, and (3) emotions run strong" (p. 3). We wish we could say that there's an easy recipe, but there's not. These conversations *are* difficult. While there's no linear approach to the process, in reviewing the research and reflecting on our own past successes with brave conversation, there are a few essential strategies we suggest that will help you along the way.

We regularly refer to *Crucial Conversations* (Patterson et al., 2012) to revisit the ins and outs of brave conversations. Another go-to resource is *Learning by Doing* (DuFour et al., 2024), as its chapter on addressing conflict in a PLC provides tips and tools. The following list provides strategies derived from these two texts, along with insights from our own key learnings along the way, which Heather first put to page in *Women Who Lead* (Keating & Kullar, 2022).

1. **Make a plan:** A surefire way to make the mess even bigger is to react in the moment or jump into it without thinking it through. Reflect on any strategies you plan to use. Play the situation out in your head and even practice the words you plan to say. We like to make a bulleted list of my key points, not to use as a note card while talking but because writing things down helps us process and remember them. You may even want to role-play the conversation with a trusted friend to build your comfort and confidence.

2. **Reflect:** Remember that you have a part in this situation, too. The conversation can't be all about what *you* want *from* the other person. It also has to have a component that speaks to what you are willing to do or commit to in order to improve things.

3. **Seek clarity:** Go into the conversation with a clear understanding of what you want and do not want to come from the discussion before you launch it. This means knowing specifically what you want for yourself, for and from the other person, and for your relationship moving forward. This is no time for a lack of clarity. If you can't be clear, then you should not have the conversation until you are.

4. **Make the conversation as safe as possible:** Schedule a time to talk with the person and let them know what you want to talk about. Meet with them on their "turf." Go to their office, sit with them, and meet at a time that works for their schedule. Use a virtual meeting if that's their preference. This is a place to give a little in order to put the other person in a more comfortable position and, hopefully, a place where they are more likely to engage and not become defensive or feel attacked.

5. **Launch strategically:** Please tell the person that you appreciate their time. Acknowledge that this is a little awkward, but it's important. We typically start a brave conversation by saying, "I'd really appreciate it if you would allow me to share my perspective fully without interrupting." If the other person tries to jump in while you are talking, simply state, "Please let me finish. I promise I'll get quiet and hear your perspective when I've shared mine."

6. **Be concise:** To launch the dialogue effectively, you need to be concise in presenting what you've planned to discuss. You should then be able to clearly and articulately express your perspective and your desired outcomes. This is no time to ramble. It makes you seem less confident, and it can make the other person unclear and uncomfortable as they try to figure out exactly what you are saying and requesting.

7. **Listen:** This can be hard because you have created a plan. By stopping to listen and really understand the other person's perspective, you give up control of the conversation. You have to be willing to hear that person's view on the situation, and it may contain information that you may not be thrilled to hear. However, remember that a conversation is two-directional. If it were just you talking, it would be a speech or a presentation. You have to open the floor and get quiet to let the other person respond. You may also have to be willing to push pause on the discussion, as the other person may need or want time to process what you have said before responding. All of this is part of the process, but it can certainly make seconds seem like hours when it is happening. No matter when the other party shares perspective, you have to remain calm and watch your nonverbal reactions. This is no place for eye rolls, big sighs, or jumping into the conversation.

8. **Find mutual purpose or shared perspectives:** After sharing your perspective and hearing from the other person, there will almost certainly be common ground. Also, you likely will have learned more about what has been happening to be more informed on how to move things forward. Use techniques like paraphrasing to restate what you heard and affirm that you really were listening. We like to use the phrasing, "What I think I heard you say was . . . ." Seek out and state places where you are in agreement and build on those. If you are unclear, ask questions to understand. Both of these strategies help you gain perspective on the other person's lens and also signal to that person that you really do care to hear where they are coming from to help create an improved reality.

9. **Find common ground on disagreements:** When there are points where you continue to disagree or have differing perspectives, talk together to try to find compromise points. Perhaps your colleague isn't able to meet all the expectations you hoped for, and maybe you aren't able to meet the ones they have presented to you. The essential focus becomes finding the place where you both feel that you can act and move forward. Where can you meet in the middle to start moving forward?

10. **Conclude with clarity:** Once you've identified your points of agreement, be sure to end the conversation with clarity to summarize each person's accountability points. This ensures you are both ending with the same understanding, which dramatically increases the chances that what you just discussed will actually happen. We often also send a follow-up email to reiterate how much we appreciate our colleague's time and to restate our shared agreements. Not only does this clarify the discussion, but it also creates a history of it, should you ever need it. While we always hope for the best, we've learned to also document, document, document along the way.

Using the "Preparing for a Difficult Conversation" tool (page 186), you can pull all of these steps together to create a planning template to help you prepare for a difficult conversation. Before launching into the tool's specific steps, it is important to frame the conversation by clarifying the following.

- **What's the conflict?** It is critical to identify exactly what the breakdown is and where the disagreement lies. Without this, it is far too easy for anyone to lump lots of issues or feelings together. When we focus on the actual conflict, it makes it far easier to solve it.

- **Who do you need to talk with to try to improve the situation?** It is very easy to talk to anyone *but* the people who are, or the person who is, central to any issue. However, when we can identify the people at the center of the conflict and with whom we need to speak to move forward, we increase the chances of actually doing so!

- **What does "better" look like?** Focusing on a specific desired outcome allows us to move from a state of venting or complaining to strategizing for consensus, collaboration, or compromise.

These kinds of conversations are not easy. They are uncomfortable and anxiety provoking. However, these are signs that they are also important. If they didn't matter, they would be as easy to have as a discussion over a recent movie, a topic on which there's either already shared agreement or where everyone is happy to walk away from it agreeing to disagree. The fact that they are hard, that they push us out of our comfort zones, and that they require planning and strategy indicates that they are essential work.

## Actively Celebrate Successes and Attempts to Make Change

While there are certainly wins in celebrating when we achieve the result for which we aspire, it can be just as, if not even more, purposeful to celebrate the meaningful attempt to make progress, innovate, or change. As the writer of the New Leaders (2023) blog states:

> **Most of the time, we celebrate when we're at the end of an initiative or long process—not at the points along the way. But it's keeping track of our wins throughout the work that reaps the benefits. According to behavioral scientist B.J. Fogg [as cited in Johnson, 2022], celebrating small wins stimulates dopamine release in the brain, a feel-good chemical that reinforces our learning experiences and strengthens the sense of connection not only to the work but also to those we do the work with.**

Not only does celebration help people in a system feel appreciated, but it can also be even more impactful when people are striving to try new things, struggling but still persevering. Imagine being celebrated for trying and *not* necessarily achieving something! Most of us feel compelled to keep going if we know that the true effort to improve, not just the achievement, is celebrated.

A method we've found to be helpful to celebrate wins and opportunities is the *glow and grow*. Using this method, feedback is given related to the positives, observed as *glows*, and the opportunities to continue, identified as *grows*. This language in and of itself conveys support and encouragement. When paired with a meaningful conversation, coaching, feedback, and support, the glows are likely to continue, and the grows are likely to be considered an opportunity to get better at the craft with positivity, intention, and commitment.

## Design Systems and Tools to Do the Work

The purpose of this book is to provide readers with tools throughout to lead the way on ensuring education for *all*. An additional opportunity to lead the work is the development of student IEPs. While many books, including *The Collaborative IEP* (Bordonaro & Clarke, 2025), expand on this topic, we would be remiss if we did not share a tool we have found to help teams move from working as islands to truly collaborating when creating students' IEPs.

The "SCOOPS IEP Planning Tool" (page 188) is a tool we specifically created to pull all the pieces of LEAD together. The SCOOPS protocol (*strength, challenges, observations, outcomes, progression*, and *success criteria*) is one we suggest you try using to pull all players together—general education, special education, related services, and administrators—to plan for a student's IEP. It is designed to be a collaborative tool to plan for an IEP meeting, whether it be a reevaluation meeting or an annual review. It allows the team to plan together for the IEP so that the meeting allows the team to tell the story of the student. This is *not* a predetermination of anything; rather, it allows all team members to have a voice in the plan from their perspective so that the IEP reflects the entire school team and, therefore, every team member has a sense of commitment to and ownership of the plan.

When starting to use this tool, the conversation will likely feel awkward and take a bit of time. However, as this becomes part of the IEP planning process, teams will likely find that the entire dialogue can be completed in under ten minutes and will most certainly be a very valuable use of time to plan forward for student progress.

## Summary

It is our hope that, throughout this book, you have found a myriad of tools to use in your context. After all, it's easy to read and learn about the work, but it is an entirely new thing to actually implement a strategy to do the work. Leading the work requires a virtual toolbelt of resources, and our hope is that the book in total, and particularly this last chapter, provides clear starting points as you continue the journey to living the *Yes We Can!* way!

Through the lens of a school where *all* staff are committed to the change process, use figure 8.2 to reflect on your role, potential challenges, ways to overcome these challenges, and the impact on students both academically and personally.

| Picture a school where . . . | . . . Everyone collaborates in and advocates for the work of *Yes We Can!*, and leadership is not by title but represents collective ownership |
|---|---|
| Consider your role in making this vision a reality in your context. How would you contribute? | |
| Identify some challenges you may face in achieving this possibility. | |
| Consider ways to overcome these challenges (over, around, and through). | |
| Anticipate the impact on students. How would bringing this possibility to life impact students academically and personally? | |

**Figure 8.2:** Envision What's Possible reflection tool for leveraging *Yes We Can!*

*Visit **go.SolutionTree.com/PLCbooks** for a free reproducible version of this figure.*

Use the following aligned activities included at the end of this chapter to support your work around this chapter's core concept.

- **"Preparing for a Difficult Conversation" (page 186):** Use this reproducible tool to create your own scaffold for a difficult conversation to help you feel more prepared to navigate conflict.
- **"SCOOPS IEP Planning Tool" (page 188):** Use this reproducible tool to help collaborative teams develop the content of and shared ownership for students' IEPs.

# Preparing for a Difficult Conversation

**Objective:** Use this tool to prepare for a difficult conversation. As you prepare using the following steps, frame the conversation using the questions: (1) What is the actual conflict? (2) To whom do you need to talk to try to improve the situation? and (3) What does "better" look like?

| Pre-Planning Questions |
| --- |
| What's the conflict? |
| To whom do you need to talk to try to improve the situation? |
| What does "better" look like? |

| Key Steps | Key for Me |
| --- | --- |
| **Make a plan.**<br>• What are you hoping results from the conversation?<br>• Practice the conversation. Consider role-playing it with a trusted friend or colleague.<br>• Make a bulleted list of key points. | |
| **Reflect.**<br>• What's your role in the conflict? Be honest!<br>• What are your boundaries related to moving forward? | |
| **Make the conversation as safe as possible.**<br>• Schedule the time with the other person in advance.<br>• Meet in the other person's space or use a virtual platform if that's preferred. | |

page 1 of 2

**All Means All** © 2025 Solution Tree Press • SolutionTree.com
Visit **go.SolutionTree.com/PLCbooks** to download this free reproducible.

| | |
|---|---|
| **Launch the dialogue strategically.**<br>• Express appreciation for the other person's time.<br>• Acknowledge that the conversation may be awkward but is important.<br>• Use a starter stem like, "It would be great if I could share my thinking without being interrupted, then I'll do the same for you." | |
| **Be concise.**<br>• Get to the point and don't ramble. Practicing ahead helps!<br>• State your perspective briefly and in a neutral tone.<br>• Use I-statements.<br>• End by expressing your desired outcomes. | |
| **Listen.**<br>• Be quiet when the other person responds.<br>• Be willing to pause the conversation to allow the other person space to process the information and their emotions.<br>• Remain calm and monitor your nonverbal reactions.<br>• Apply active listening strategies. | |
| **Attempt to find mutual purpose or shared perspectives.**<br>• Use paraphrasing.<br>• Ask questions to understand.<br>• Seek out and state points where you agree or have common ground. | |
| **Find common ground on disagreements.**<br>• Try to find compromise points.<br>• Find a place where you can both agree to move forward. | |
| **Conclude with clarity.**<br>• Summarize each person's accountability points or next steps. This may include setting a follow-up time to come back together.<br>• Consider sending a follow-up note or email to show gratitude for the time and to clearly restate your shared agreements for moving forward. | |

*Source: Adapted from Keating, J., & Kullar, J. K. (Eds.). (2022). Women who lead: Insights, inspiration, and guidance to grow as an educator (pp. 121–123). Solution Tree Press.*

# SCOOPS IEP Planning Tool

**Objective:** The SCOOPS protocol refers to **s**trength, **c**hallenges, **o**bservations, **o**utcomes, **p**rogression, and **s**uccess criteria, which are vital aspects of an IEP. Use this tool to plan for an IEP meeting and pull all the pieces of LEAD together: (1) **l**earn about the change process, (2) **e**mbrace hard conversations, (3) **a**ctively celebrate successes and attempts to make change, and (4) **d**esign systems and tools to do the work.

### Strength

What are the goals, objectives, standards, or behaviors of strength for this student?

| Goal or Objective | Proficiency |
|---|---|
|  |  |
|  |  |
|  |  |
|  |  |
|  |  |

### Challenges

What are the goals, objectives, standards, or behaviors that represent challenges for this student?

| Goal or Objective | Proficiency |
|---|---|
|  |  |
|  |  |
|  |  |
|  |  |
|  |  |

### Observations

What accommodations does this student need? What, if any, modifications are needed? What are the contributing factors to this student's success or struggle?

_____
_____
_____
_____
_____
_____
_____
_____
_____

## Outcomes

What will we do to address student needs as a team? Who will do what? What is the timeline?

| What is the need? | What strategy will support the desired outcomes for this need? | Who will provide support for the student for this need? When? For how long? What data will be collected? |
|---|---|---|
|  |  |  |
|  |  |  |
|  |  |  |
|  |  |  |
|  |  |  |

## Progression

How will we, as a team, take steps to make sure the plan is achieved? What is a skill progression that makes sense for the student when considering all the needs?

_____
_____
_____
_____
_____
_____
_____
_____
_____
_____

## Success Criteria

| What is needed for the student to move to a less restrictive setting? | What are the criteria by which this student would exit IEP eligibility? |
|---|---|
|  |  |

# Epilogue

As we bring a close to this book, our last recommendation for systems for change is a simple one: Focus on the first next steps and stops. The change process, especially when adults have passion and increased knowledge about how to help even more students, can become overwhelming when we try to take on too much at the same time. Being strategic means doing a few things well, learning from them, and adjusting when and if shifts need to be made.

The point of this book is *not* for you to walk away with a long list of things to do. Rather, we see this book's guidance as a call to action that anyone using this book can identify. Specifically, we ask that you consider and act on the following two questions.

1. What are our first next *starts*? Where will we begin to do the work, learn together, study the impact, and problem-solve when needed?

2. What are our first next *stops*? What will we stop doing because we know more and can do better?

We firmly believe that, by embracing the simplicity of this priority process and then taking action, you and your system will truly be able to say *Yes We Can!* for all students and for each other!

# References and Resources

Advocate. (n.d.). In *Merriam-Webster's online dictionary.* Accessed at www.merriam-webster.com/dictionary/advocating on December 4, 2024.

Alhossyan, F. (2023). Collaboration between special and general education teachers: A systematic review. *Information Sciences Letters, 12*(4), 1021–1029.

Allen, R. (2012, August 1). Support struggling students with academic rigor. *Educational Leadership, 54*(8). Accessed at https://ascd.org/el/articles/support-struggling-students-with-academic-rigor on January 17, 2025.

AllThingsPLC. (n.d.). *About.* Accessed at https://allthingsplc.info/about on February 24, 2025.

Andersen, E. (2013, May 31). *21 quotes from Henry Ford on business, leadership and life.* Forbes. Accessed at www.forbes.com/sites/erikaandersen/2013/05/31/21-quotes-from-henry-ford-on-business-leadership-and-life on January 17, 2025.

Argyris, C. (1990). *Overcoming organizational defenses: Facilitating organizational learning.* Allyn and Bacon.

Artiles, A. J., & Kozleski, E. B. (2007). Beyond convictions: Interrogating culture, history, and power in inclusive education. *Language Arts, 84*(4), 357–364.

Bailey, K., & Jakicic, C. (2023). *Common formative assessment: A toolkit for Professional Learning Communities at Work* (2nd ed.). Solution Tree Press.

Bailey, K., Jakicic, C., & Spiller, J. (2014). *Collaborating for success with the Common Core: A toolkit for Professional Learning Communities at Work.* Solution Tree Press.

Berliner, W., & Eyre, D. (2018). *Great minds and how to grow them: High performance learning.* Routledge.

Blackburn, B. (2018, December 13). *Productive struggle is a learner's sweet spot.* Accessed at www.ascd.org/ascd-express/vol14/num11/productive-struggle-is-a-learners-sweet-spot.aspx on December 4, 2024.

Blanchard, K. (2007). *Leading at a higher level: Blanchard on leadership and creating high performing organizations.* Prentice Hall.

Boogren, T. H., Kanold, T. D., & Kullar, J. K. (2023). *The educator wellness plan book and journal: Continuous growth for each season of your professional life.* Solution Tree Press.

Bordonaro, K. M., & Clarke, M. (2025). *The collaborative IEP: Working together for life-changing special education.* Solution Tree Press.

Brown, B. (2010). *The gifts of imperfection: Let go of who you think you're supposed to be and embrace who you are.* Hazelden.

Brown, B. (2018). *Dare to lead: Brave work, tough conversations, whole hearts.* Random House.

Bryant, A. (2014, January 4). Management be nimble. *The New York Times.* Accessed at www.nytimes.com/2014/01/05/business/management-be-nimble.html?_r=0 on June 17, 2024.

Buffum, A., Mattos, M., & Malone, J. (2018). *Taking action: A handbook for RTI at Work.* Solution Tree Press.

Carroll, T. (2009). The next generation of learning teams. *Phi Delta Kappan, 91*(2), 8–13.

CAST. (2024). *Universal Design for Learning guidelines version 3.0.* Accessed at http://udlguidelines.cast.org on January 17, 2025.

Centers for Disease Control and Prevention. (2025a, April 15). *Autism and Developmental Disabilities Monitoring (ADDM) Network.* Accessed at www.cdc.gov/autism/addm-network on February 24, 2025.

Centers for Disease Control and Prevention. (2025b, April 15). Data and statistics on Autism Spectrum Disorder. Accessed at www.cdc.gov/autism/data-research on May 16, 2024.

Center for Leadership and Educational Equity. (n.d.). *Compass points: North, south, east, and west—An exercise in understanding preferences in group work.* Accessed at www.clee.org/resources/compass-points-north-south-east-and-west-an-exercise-in-understanding-preferences-in-group-work on November 11, 2024.

Chapman, G. D., & White, P. E. (2011). *The five languages of appreciation in the workplace: Empowering organizations by encouraging people.* Northfield.

Chenoweth, K. (2009). It can be done, it's being done, and here's how. *Phi Delta Kappan, 91*(1), 38–43.

Code of Federal Regulations, Title 34, § 300.8 (2022).

Collaborate. (n.d.). In *Merriam-Webster's online dictionary.* Accessed at www.merriam-webster.com/dictionary/collaboration on January 3, 2025.

Collaboration. (n.d.). In *Oxford English Dictionary's online dictionary.* Accessed at www.oed.com/dictionary/collaboration_n?tab=meaning_and_use on January 3, 2025.

Cortiella, C., & Horowitz, S. H. (2014). *The state of learning disabilities: Facts, trends and emerging issues* (3rd ed.). National Center for Learning Disabilities. Accessed at www.advocacyinstitute.org/resources/2014StateofLD.pdf on February 25, 2025.

Costello, J., & Crowell, M. (2023). *Improving special education: District management group's framework and approach.* District Management Group. Accessed at https://cdn2.assets-servd.host/dm-group/production/documents/DMJ33_Spotlight.pdf on January 17, 2025.

Curley, B. (2024, May 25). *Top autism statistics in 2024.* Accessed at www.motivity.net/autism-facts on February 24, 2025.

Cushman, K. (2003). *Fires in the bathroom: Advice for teachers from high school students.* New Press.

Danielson, C. (2013). *The Framework for Teaching Evaluation Instrument.* Danielson Group.

Darling-Hammond, L. (2000). Teacher quality and student achievement: A review of state policy evidence. *Educational Policy Analysis Archives, 8*(1).

Darling-Hammond, L. (2010). *The flat world and education: How America's commitment to equity will determine our future.* Teachers College Press.

de Boer, H., Bosker, R. J., & van der Werf, M. P. C. (2010). Sustainability of teacher expectation bias effects on long-term student performance. *Journal of Educational Psychology, 102*(1), 168–179. https://doi.org/10.1037/a0017289

Doidge, N. (2007). *The brain that changes itself: Stories of personal triumph from the frontiers of brain science*. Viking.

Druskat, V. U., & Wolff, S. B. (2001). Group emotional intelligence and its influence on group effectiveness. In C. Cherniss & D. Goleman (Eds.), *The emotionally intelligent workplace: How to select for, measure, and improve emotional intelligence in individuals, groups, and organizations* (pp. 132–156). Jossey-Bass.

Duckworth, A. (2016). *Grit: The power of passion and perseverance*. Scribner.

Duckworth, A., Peterson, C., Matthews, M. D., & Kelly, D. R. (2007). Grit: Perseverance and passion for long-term goals. *Journal of Personality and Social Psychology, 92*(6), 1087–1101.

DuFour, R., DuFour, R., Eaker, R., Many, T. W., & Mattos, M. (2016). *Learning by doing: A handbook for Professional Learning Communities at Work* (3rd ed.). Solution Tree Press.

DuFour, R., DuFour, R., Eaker, R., Many, T. W., Mattos, M., & Muhammad, A. (2024). *Learning by doing: A handbook for Professional Learning Communities at Work* (4th ed.). Solution Tree Press.

DuFour, R., DuFour, R., Eaker, R., Mattos, M., & Muhammad, A. (2021). *Revisiting Professional Learning Communities at Work: Proven insights for sustained, substantive school improvement* (2nd ed.). Solution Tree Press.

DuFour, R., & Eaker, R. (1998). *Professional Learning Communities at Work: Best practices for enhancing student achievement*. Solution Tree Press.

Duhigg, C. (2016, February 25). What Google learned from its quest to build the perfect team. *The New York Times Magazine*. Accessed at www.nytimes.com/2016/02/28/magazine/what-google-learned-from-its-quest-to-build-the-perfect-team.html on January 14, 2025.

Dweck, C. S. (2006). *Mindset: The new psychology of success*. Random House.

Dweck, C. S. (2010, September). Even geniuses work hard. *Educational Leadership, 68*(1), 16–20.

Dweck, C. S. (2016). *Mindset: The new psychology of success* (Updated ed.). Random House.

Dynamic Learning Maps. (n.d.). *What is a learning map model?* Accessed at https://dynamiclearningmaps.org/model on January 3, 2025.

Eastwood, K. W., & Louis, K. S. (1992). Restructuring that lasts: Managing the performance dip. *Journal of School Leadership, 2*(2), 212–224.

Every Student Succeeds Act, 20 U.S.C. § 6301 (2015).

Family Educational Rights and Privacy Act, 20 U.S.C. § 1232g (1974).

Farbman, D. A., Goldberg, D. J., & Miller, T. D. (2014, January). *Redesigning and expanding school time to support Common Core implementation*. Center for American Progress. Accessed at https://cdn.americanprogress.org/wp-content/uploads/2014/01/CommonCore-reprint.pdf on January 14, 2025.

Ferriter, W. M., Mattos, M., & Meyer, R. J. (2025). *The big book of tools for RTI at Work*. Solution Tree Press.

Fisher, D., & Frey, N. (2021). *Better learning through structured teaching: A framework for the gradual release of responsibility* (3rd ed.). ASCD.

Florida Policy Institute. (n.d.). *Special education funding in Florida: An overview*. Accessed at www.floridapolicy.org/tags/education on February 24, 2025.

Foundation. (n.d.). *In Merriam-Webster's online dictionary.* Accessed at www.merriam-webster.com/dictionary/foundation on October 30, 2024.

Francis, E. M. (2022). *Deconstructing depth of knowledge: A method and model for deeper teaching and learning.* Solution Tree Press.

Friziellie, H. (2021, Spring). First thing: What are you believing? *AllThingsPLC Magazine.*

Friziellie, H., Schmidt, J. A., & Spiller, J. (2016). *Yes we can! General and special educators collaborating in a professional learning community.* Solution Tree Press.

Fuchs, D., & Fuchs, L. S. (2006). Introduction to response to intervention: What, why, and how valid is it? *Reading Research Quarterly, 41*(1), 93–99.

Fuchs, D., Fuchs, L. S., Mathes, P. G., Lipsey, M. W., & Roberts, P. H. (2001, August 27–28). *Is "learning disabilities" just a fancy term for low achievement? A meta-analysis of reading differences between low achievers with and without the label* [Paper presentation]. Learning Disabilities Summit: Building a Foundation for the Future, Washington, DC, United States.

Fulton, K., Yoon, I., & Lee, C. (2005, August). *Induction into learning communities.* National Commission on Teaching and America's Future. Accessed at https://files.eric.ed.gov/fulltext/ED494581.pdf on January 23, 2024.

Goleman, D., Boyatzis, R., & McKee, A. (2004). *Primal leadership: Learning to lead with emotional intelligence.* Harvard Business School Press.

Gordon, D. (Ed.). (2024). *Universal Design for Learning: Principles, framework, and practice.* CAST Professional.

Gordon, R., & Gordon, M. (2006). *The turned-off child: Learned helplessness and school failure.* Millennial Mind.

Grant, D. (2023, May 12). Collaboration, relationships and partnerships—The heart of effective service-centered organizations. *Forbes.* Accessed at www.forbes.com/councils/forbestechcouncil/2023/05/12/collaboration-relationships-and-partnerships-the-heart-of-effective-service-centered-organizations on December 5, 2024.

Hall, E. T. (1976). *Beyond culture.* Anchor Press.

Hall, G. E., & Hord, S. M. (2020). *Implementing change: Patterns, principles, and potholes* (5th ed.). Pearson.

Hall-Mills, S. (2021). Shifting prevalence patterns for special educational needs in the era of response-to-intervention policy. *Frontiers in Education, 6,* Article 676646. https://doi.org/10.3389/feduc.2021.676646

Hall, T. E., Meyer, A., & Rose, D. H. (2012). *Universal design for learning in the classroom: Practical applications.* Guilford Press.

Hannigan, J., Hannigan, J. D., Mattos, M., & Buffum, A. (2020). *Behavior solutions: Teaching academic and social skills through RTI at Work.* Solution Tree Press.

Hannigan, J. D., & Hannigan, J. (2024). *Behavior academies: Targeted interventions that work!* Solution Tree Press.

Hattie, J. (2009). *Visible learning: A synthesis of over 800 meta-analyses relating to achievement.* Routledge.

Hattie, J. (2012). *Visible learning for teachers: Maximizing impact on learning.* Routledge.

Hattie, J. (2015, June). *What doesn't work in education: The politics of distraction.* Pearson. Accessed at http://visible-learning.org/wp-content/uploads/2015/06/John-Hattie-Visible-Learning-creative-commons-book-free-PDF-download-What-doesn-t-work-in-education_the-politics-of-distraction-pearson-2015.pdf on January 14, 2025.

Hattie, J. (2023a, March 30). *John Hattie on the factors that influence learning in schools.* Accessed at www.socialsciencespace.com/2023/03/john-hattie-on-the-factors-that-influence-learning-in-schools on November 26, 2024.

Hattie, J. (2023b). *Visible learning: The sequel—A synthesis of over 2,100 meta-analyses relating to achievement.* Routledge.

Illinois State Board of Education. (n.d.). *Special education reimbursement.* Accessed at www.isbe.net/Pages/Special-Education-Approval-and-Reimbursement.aspx on February 24, 2025.

Individuals With Disabilities Education Act, 20 U.S.C. § 1400 (2004).

Jackson, R. R. (2011). *How to motivate reluctant learners.* ASCD.

Jackson, R. R., & Lambert, C. (2010). *How to support struggling students.* ASCD.

Johnson, W. (2022, January 26). Celebrate to win. *Harvard Business Review.* Accessed at https://hbr.org/2022/01/celebrate-to-win on December 12, 2024.

Johnston, W. R., & Berglund, T. (2018). *The prevalence of collaboration among American teachers: National findings from the American Teacher Panel.* RAND Corporation. Accessed at www.rand.org/pubs/research_reports/RR2217.html on December 5, 2024.

Kanold, T. D., & Boogren, T. H. (2022). *Educator wellness: A guide for sustaining physical, mental, emotional, and social well-being.* Solution Tree Press.

Kaput, K., & O'Neal Schiess, J. (2024, October). *Who pays for special education? An analysis of federal, state, and local spending by states and districts.* Accessed at https://bellwether.org/publications/who-pays-for-special-education/?activeTab=4 on January 29, 2025.

Katzenbach, J. R., & Smith, D. K. (1993). *The wisdom of teams: Creating the high-performance organization.* Harvard Business School Press.

Keating, J., & Kullar, J. K. (Eds.). (2022). *Women who lead: Insights, inspiration, and guidance to grow as an educator.* Solution Tree Press.

Kegan, R., & Lahey, L. L. (2001). *How the way we talk can change the way we work: Seven languages for transformation.* Jossey-Bass.

Kildeer Countryside Community Consolidated School District 96. (2021). *About KCSD 96.* Accessed at www.kcsd96.org/about on January 14, 2025.

Kissflow. (2025, February 24). *The importance of collaboration in the workplace.* Accessed at https://kissflow.com/digital-workplace/collaboration/importance-of-collaboration-in-the-workplace on December 5, 2024.

Ladson-Billings, G. (1995). Toward a theory of culturally relevant pedagogy. *American Educational Research Journal, 32*(3), 465–491.

Ladson-Billings, G. (2006). From the achievement gap to the education debt: Understanding achievement in U.S. schools. *Educational Researcher, 35*(7), 3–12.

Lencioni, P. (2005). *Overcoming the five dysfunctions of a team: A field guide for leaders, managers, and facilitators.* Jossey-Bass.

Mann, H. (1849). *The twelfth annual report of the board of education, 1849: Together with the twelfth annual report of the secretary of the board.* Commonwealth of Massachusetts.

Many, T. W., & Sparks-Many, S. K. (2015). *Leverage: Using PLCs to promote lasting improvement in schools.* Corwin Press.

Marzano, R. J. (2003). *What works in schools: Translating research into action.* ASCD.

Marzano, R. J. (2007). *The art and science of teaching: A comprehensive framework for effective instruction.* ASCD.

Marzano, R. J. (2017). *The new art and science of teaching.* Solution Tree Press.

Marzano, R. J., & Hardy, P. B. (2023). *Leading a competency-based secondary school: The Marzano Academies model.* Marzano Resources.

Marzano, R. J., & Pickering, D. J. (2011). *The highly engaged classroom.* Marzano Resources.

Marzano, R. J., Pickering, D. J., & Pollock, J. E. (2001). *Classroom instruction that works: Research-based strategies for increasing student achievement.* ASCD.

Marzano, R. J., & Toth, M. D. (2014, March). *Teaching for rigor: A call for a critical instructional shift.* Learning Sciences International. Accessed at https://eohighschool.com/wp-content/uploads/MC05-01-Teaching-for-Rigor-Paper-05-20-14-Digital-1-1.pdf on April 21, 2025.

Marzano, R. J., Warrick, P., & Simms, J. A. (2014). *A handbook for High Reliability Schools: The next step in school reform.* Marzano Resources.

Mason Crest Elementary School. (n.d.). *Mission, vision, goals, and collective commitments.* Accessed at https://masoncrestes.fcps.edu/about/mission-vision-and-goals on January 14, 2025.

Mattos, M., Buffum, A., Malone, J., Cruz, L. F., Dimich, N., & Schuhl, S. (2025). *Taking action: A handbook for RTI at Work* (2nd ed.). Solution Tree Press.

Maxwell, J. C. (2018). *Developing the leader within you 2.0* (25th anniversary ed.). HarperCollins Leadership.

McLaughlin, M. W., & Talbert, J. E. (2006). *Building school-based teacher learning communities: Professional strategies to improve student achievement.* Teachers College Press.

Meyer, A., Rose, D. H., & Gordon, D. (2014). *Universal Design for Learning: Theory and practice.* CAST Professional.

Nation's Report Card. (2022a). *NAEP report card: 2022 NAEP reading assessment.* Accessed at www.nationsreportcard.gov/highlights/reading/2022 on January 17, 2025.

Nation's Report Card. (2022b). *NAEP report card: Mathematics.* Accessed at www.nationsreportcard.gov/mathematics/?grade=4 on November 26, 2024.

National Center for Learning Disabilities. (2020). *Significant disproportionality in special education: Current trends and actions for impact.* Author. Accessed at https://ncld.org/wp-content/uploads/2023/07/2020-NCLD-Disproportionality_Trends-and-Actions-for-Impact_FINAL-1.pdf on April 8, 2025.

National Center on Intensive Intervention. (2013, March). *Data-based individualization: A framework for intensive intervention.* Office of Special Education Programs, U.S. Department of Education. Accessed at https://intensiveintervention.org/sites/default/files/DBI_Framework.pdf on December 9, 2024.

National Center on Response to Intervention. (2010, April). *Essential components of RTI: A closer look at response to intervention*. U.S. Department of Education, Office of Special Education Programs, National Center on Response to Intervention. Accessed at https://mtss4success.org/sites/default /files/2020-07/rtiessentialcomponents_042710.pdf on December 9, 2024.

National Commission on Teaching and America's Future. (2003, January). *No dream denied: A pledge to America's children*. Author.

National Education Association. (2021, January 26). *IDEA funding gap*. Author. Accessed at www.nea .org/sites/default/files/2021-01/IDEA%20Funding%20Gap%20by%20State%20FY%202020.pdf on January 9, 2025.

National Governors Association Center for Best Practices & Council of Chief State School Officers. (2010a). *Common Core State Standards for English language arts and literacy in history/social studies, science, and technical subjects*. Authors. Accessed at https://corestandards.org/wp-content /uploads/2023/09/ELA_Standards1.pdf on December 12, 2024.

National Governors Association Center for Best Practices & Council of Chief State School Officers. (2010b). *Common Core State Standards for mathematics*. Authors. Accessed at https://corestandards .org/wp-content/uploads/2023/09/Math_Standards1.pdf on December 12, 2024.

New Leaders. (2023, June 13). *How celebrating your school's wins leads to more wins* [Blog post]. Accessed at www.newleaders.org/blog/how-celebrating-your-schools-wins-leads-to-more-wins on December 12, 2024.

New Teacher Project. (2018). *The opportunity myth: What students can show us about how school is letting them down—and how to fix it*. Accessed at https://tntp.org/publications/the-opportunity-myth on November 26, 2024.

Newberg, A., & Waldman, M. R. (2012). *Words can change your brain: 12 conversation strategies to build trust, resolve conflict, and increase intimacy*. Hudson Street Press.

Newmann, F. M., & Wehlage, G. G. (1995). *Successful school restructuring: A report to the public and educators by the Center on Organization and Restructuring of Schools*. Center on Organization and Restructuring of Schools.

Noguera, P. A. (2003). The trouble with Black boys: The role and influence of environmental and cultural factors on the academic performance of African American males. *Urban Education, 38*(4), 431–459.

Oakes, J. (1985). *Keeping track: How schools structure inequality*. Yale University Press.

Office for Civil Rights, U.S. Department of Education. (n.d.). *Data on equal access to education*. Accessed at https://ocrdata.ed.gov on February 19, 2025.

OpenAI. (2024). *ChatGPT* (Nov 1 version) [Large language model]. https://chat.openai.com/chat

Patterson, K., Grenny, J., McMillan, R., & Switzler, A. (2012). *Crucial conversations: Tools for talking when stakes are high* (2nd ed.). McGraw-Hill.

Popham, W. J. (2007, April). All about accountability: The lowdown on learning progressions. *Educational Leadership, 64*(7), 83–84.

President's Commission on Excellence in Special Education. (2002, July). *A new era: Revitalizing special education for children and their families*. U.S. Department of Education. Accessed at https://files.eric .ed.gov/fulltext/ED473830.pdf on November 26, 2024.

Project IDEA. (2024). *Strategies for effective collaboration between general and special education teachers.* Accessed at https://project-idea.org/strategies-for-effective-collaboration-between-general-and-special-education-teachers on December 5, 2024.

Reeves, D. B. (2002). *The leader's guide to standards: A blueprint for educational equity and excellence.* Jossey-Bass.

Rehabilitation Act of 1973, 29 U.S.C. § 794 (1973).

Rojewski, J. W., Lee, I. H., & Gregg, N. (2015). Causal effects of inclusion on postsecondary education outcomes of individuals with high-incidence disabilities. *Journal of Disability Policy Studies, 25*(4), 210–219. https://doi.org/10.1177/1044207313505648

Rutherford, P. (2008). *Instruction for all students* (2nd ed.). Just ASK.

Schlechty, P. C. (2009). *Leading for learning: How to transform schools into learning organizations.* Jossey-Bass.

Schmidt, J. (2022). First thing: Your PLC as an iceberg. *AllThingsPLC Magazine, 7*(1).

Schmoker, M. (2018). *Focus: Elevating the essentials to radically improve student learning* (2nd ed.). ASCD.

Scott, E. (2023, November 22). The toxic effects of negative self-talk. Accessed at www.verywellmind.com/negative-self-talk-and-how-it-affects-us-4161304 on January 3, 2025.

Sempeles, E., & Cui, J. (2024, September). *Parent and family involvement in education: 2023* (NCES 2024-113). National Center for Education Statistics. Accessed at https://nces.ed.gov/pubsearch/pubsinfo.asp?pubid=2024113 on February 24, 2025.

Senge, P. M. (1990). *The fifth discipline: The art and practice of the learning organization.* Doubleday/Currency.

Shinn, M. R., Good, R. H., III, & Stein, S. (1989). Summarizing trend in student achievement: A comparison of methods. *School Psychology Review, 18*(3), 356–370.

Shinn, M. R., & Walker, H. M. (2010). *Interventions for achievement and behavior problems in a three-tier model including RTI.* NASP.

Siegel, D. J., & Bryson, T. P. (2011). *The whole-brain child: 12 revolutionary strategies to nurture your child's developing mind.* Delacorte Press.

Skiba, R. J., Simmons, A. B., Ritter, S., Gibb, A. C., Rausch, M. K., Cuadrado, J., et al. (2008). Achieving equity in special education: History, status, and current challenges. *Exceptional Children, 74*(3), 264–288.

Sonju, B., Powers, M., & Miller, S. (2023). *Simplifying the journey: Six steps to schoolwide collaboration, consistency, and clarity in a PLC at Work.* Solution Tree Press.

Souers, K. (2016). *Fostering resilient learners: Strategies for creating a trauma-sensitive classroom.* ASCD.

Souers, K. (2019). *Relationship, responsibility, and regulation: Trauma-invested practices for fostering resilient learners.* ASCD.

Spiller, J. (2020, January 29). *Does 'all' mean 'all'? Labels, be gone!* [Blog post]. Accessed at www.allthingsplc.info/blog/view/409/does-all-mean-all-labels-be-gone on December 4, 2024.

Stewart, R. F., & Lipp, J. E. (1962). *Development planning at Lockheed Aircraft Corporation.* Lockheed Aircraft Corporation.

ThoughtFarmer. (n.d.). *What collaboration really means* [Blog post]. Accessed at www.thoughtfarmer.com/blog/what-collaboration-really-means on January 3, 2025.

Tod, D., Hardy, J., & Oliver, E. (2011). Effects of self-talk: A systematic review. *Journal of Sport and Exercise Psychology, 33*(5), 666–687. https://doi.org/10.1123/jsep.33.5.666

U.S. Department of Education, Office of Special Education and Rehabilitative Services, & Office of Special Education Programs. (2021, January). *42nd annual report to Congress on the implementation of the Individuals with Disabilities Education Act, 2020*. Authors. Accessed at https://files.eric.ed.gov/fulltext/ED612645.pdf on January 17, 2025.

U.S. Department of Education, Office of Special Education Programs. (2021, August 9). *OSEP fast facts: Race and ethnicity of children with disabilities served under IDEA part B*. Accessed at https://sites.ed.gov/idea/osep-fast-facts-race-and-ethnicity-of-children-with-disabilities-served-under-idea-part-b on January 17, 2025.

Visible Learning. (2018). *Collective teacher efficacy (CTE) according to John Hattie*. Accessed at https://visible-learning.org/2018/03/collective-teacher-efficacy-hattie on January 3, 2025.

Walker, T. (2017, March 23). Words matter: The repercussions of what we say—and don't say—about students. *NEA Today*. Accessed at www.nea.org/nea-today/all-news-articles/words-matter-repercussions-what-we-say-and-dont-say-about-students on December 10, 2024.

Wallace, C. (2013). *Life is not complicated—you are: Turning your biggest disappointments into your greatest blessings*. iUniverse.

Walling, M. D., & Martinek, T. J. (1995). Learned helplessness: A case study of a middle school student. *Journal of Teaching in Physical Education, 14*(4), 454–466.

Webb, N. (2025). *What is Depth of Knowledge (DOK)?* Accessed at www.webbalign.org/dok-primer on December 12, 2024.

WestEd. (2000). *Teachers who learn, kids who achieve: A look at schools with model professional development*. Author.

White River School District. (n.d.). *Strategic plan: The White River promise*. Accessed at www.whiteriver.wednet.edu/apps/pages/index.jsp?uREC_ID=1473103&type=d&pREC_ID=1625707 on January 14, 2025.

Wiliam, D. (2018). *Embedded formative assessment* (2nd ed.). Solution Tree Press.

Williams, K. C., & Hierck, T. (2015). *Starting a movement: Building culture from the inside out in professional learning communities*. Solution Tree Press.

# Index

## A

accommodations.
*See also* modifications
    collaborating on, 96
    and differentiated assessments, 95, 96
    and Dynamic Learning Maps, 69
    and grading students with IEPs in a general education context, 93–94
    and STAGES planning process, 116
    use of, 43

accountability, importance of, 17

action and expression in UDL, 119

advocacy and productive struggle, role of, 51–52. *See also* productive struggle

agendas, example of, 151

aligning beliefs and behaviors.
*See also* believe is a verb
    about, 39–41
    core concepts, 1–2
    culture as an iceberg, 49–50
    envision what's possible, 39, 53
    impact of language and labels, 51
    our beliefs: foundation, 44–49
    reflection rubric for, 52–53
    reproducibles for, 55–60
    role of advocacy and productive struggle, 51–52
    summary, 52–54
    what *all means all* means, 41–44
    what we have learned, 41

all students, what *all means all*, 41–44

appreciation of self, 169

artificial intelligence (AI), use of, 89–90

assessments
    diagnostic assessments, 145, 154
    differentiated assessments with the same standards, 95–96
    fitting assessment, instruction, and monitoring together, 148
    formative assessments, 84, 95–96
    learning progression assessment information, use of, 90–91
    learning progressions and, 84, 86–90
    priority standards and, 78, 79
    screening tools, 149
    STAGES planning process and, 116
    standards-based grading to clarify expectations, 95

asset-based language, 173

attitudes and challenge, 123

autism spectrum disorders (ASDs), 11, 12, 13

avoidance, 121

## B

Bailey, K., 81

behavior, separating academic achievement from effort and, 97.
See also aligning beliefs and behaviors

believe is a verb.
See also aligning beliefs and behaviors
- about, 167–168
- beliefs about colleagues, 170–172
- beliefs about self, 168–169
- beliefs about students, 172–174
- envision what's possible, 167, 175
- summary, 174–175

Brown, B., 39, 180

Bryant, A., 47

## C

celebrations
- actively celebrating successes and attempts to make changes, 178, 183–184
- celebrating effort, 122, 123
- persistence and, 121
- process monitoring and record keeping and, 151

change
- actively celebrating successes and attempts to make, 183–184
- CBAM model to identify the seven stages of concern about, 179–180
- learning about the change process (LEAD), 178–180

clarity
- hard conversations and, 181, 182
- standards-based grading and, 95

collaboration
- about, 61–62
- barriers to, 64–65
- conditions for effective, 65–66
- core concepts, 2
- definition of, 61
- envision what's possible, 61, 72–73
- inclusive grading culture through, 99
- interdependency, ways to strengthen, 66–71
- learning progressions and, 86
- priority standards and, 78, 79–80
- reasons for/why should we collaborate, 62–63
- reflection rubric for assessing collaborative practices, 72
- reproducibles for, 74–76
- research on, 62–64
- RTI, common mistakes, 153–154
- summary, 72–73

collaborative culture, 40, 44, 171

collaborative learning, 117.
See also gradual release of responsibility (GRR)

collaborative teams
- and critical questions of a PLC, 43–44
- and effective collaboration, 65
- and inclusive grading culture, 99
- interdependency, strengthening, 66–71
- and learning progression assessment information, 90–91
- paraprofessionals, 68
- and planning processes, 113, 114
- and priority standards, 79–80, 81
- reasons for/why should we collaborate, 63
- and supporting students who have low-incidence learning challenges, 69

colleagues, beliefs about, 170–172

collective teacher efficacy, definition of, 62

common ground, finding, 182

communication
- and common RTI mistakes, 153–154
- with families, 97–98

hard conversations, 180–183

Compass Points preference tool, 67

compliments and gratitude, 172

concerns about grading and self-esteem, 94–98. *See also* grading

Concerns Based Adoption Model (CBAM), 178, 179–180

confidence, 93

conflict and hard conversations, 180–183

crucial conversations, 180. *See also* communication

*Crucial Conversations* (Patterson, Grenny, McMillan, and Switzler), 180

culture as an iceberg, 49–50

curriculum

    and grade-level alignment for students with disabilities, 93

    guaranteed and viable curriculum, 77–78, 99–100

    learning progressions and curriculum alignment, 85–86

## D

*Dare to Lead* (Brown), 39

data

    decision making, 116, 144

    effective collaboration and, 65–66

    goals and, 47, 49

    statistical trends and realities and, 10–11

    tiers of intervention and, 149, 150, 154

deafness, 12, 13

decision making, 46, 116, 144, 149–150

destructive struggle. *See also* productive struggle

    fixed mindsets and, 123

    persistence and, 120

    productive and destructive struggle characteristics and taking action, 120

    versus productive struggle, 52, 121–122

    struggle and, 119

developmental delays, 12, 13

diagnostic assessments, 145, 154. *See also* assessments

differentiation

    differentiated assessments with the same standards, 95–96. *See also* assessments

    and grading students with IEPs in a general education context, 93–94

    and learning progressions, 84

    and STAGES planning process, 116

disproportionality in special education, 14–17

DuFour, R., 50

DuFour, R., 41–42, 50

Dynamic Learning Maps (DLMs), 69

dyscalculia, 12

dyslexia, 12

## E

Eaker, R., 50

early identification and intervention, importance of, 17

educator wellness, 169, 170

effort

    separating academic achievement from effort and behavior, 97

    strategic effort versus reliance on ineffective or random approaches, 121–122

emotional disturbances (EDs), 12, 13

engagement

    active engagement versus passivity or avoidance, 121

    need for deep engagement, 20

    Universal Design for Learning and, 119

English language arts common challenges, strategies, and resources, 132, 133, 134

equity and inclusivity, grading for, 93. *See also* grading

Essential Elements within the Dynamic Learning Map (DLM) assessment, 69

expectations
- beliefs about students, 172–174
- grade-level alignment for students with disabilities and, 92–93
- grading students with IEPs in a general education context and, 93–94
- lowering of, 110
- need for high expectations, 20
- priority standards and, 80
- rigorous grade-level expectations, 112–113
- standards-based grading to clarify expectations, 95
- urgency and, 19–20

# F

feedback
- differentiated assessments and, 95–96
- grading students with IEPs in a general education context and, 94
- learning progressions and, 84
- separating academic achievement from effort and behavior, 97
- supporting growth with, 98

fixed mindsets, 123. *See also* growth mindsets

focus on learning, 40, 44

focused instruction, 78, 84, 117. *See also* instruction

Ford, H., 152

formative assessments, 84, 95–96. *See also* assessments

funding structures, 18

# G

general education classrooms
- access to, 147
- disproportionality in special education and, 16
- grading practices and, 92
- scaffolding and, 131
- Tier 1 instruction and, 145

goals
- about, 47, 49
- example of an aligned goal-setting process, 48
- grade-level alignment for students with disabilities and, 93
- IEP goal planning and monitoring progress, 2, 3
- learning progressions and, 83–84
- pillars of a PLC, 40

grade-appropriate assignments, 20

grade-level alignment for students with disabilities, 92–93

grading
- academic achievement, effort, and behavior, 97
- accommodations and modifications and, 96
- communication with families and, 97–98
- concerns about grading and self-esteem, 94–99
- differentiated assessments with the same standards and, 95–96
- feedback to support growth and, 98
- grade-level alignment for students with disabilities, importance of, 92–93
- grading students with IEPs in a general education context, challenge of, 93–94
- inclusive grading culture and team collaboration, 99
- principle that students with IEPs are general education students first, 92
- standards-based grading to clarify expectations, 95
- strengths-based grading, 94

gradual release of responsibility (GRR), 115, 117–118

Grant, D., 66

Great Eight, 79–81, 102

Grenny, J., 180

growth mindsets, 93, 111, 120, 121, 122

guaranteed and viable curriculum (GVC), 77–78, 99–100

guided instruction, 117.
See also instruction

## H

hard conversations, embracing, 180–183.
See also communication

hearing impairments, 12, 13

*How to Support Struggling Students* (Jackson and Lambert), 112

## I

identification and disproportionality, 15

inclusive grading, 94, 99.
See also grading

independent practice, 117–118.
See also gradual release of responsibility (GRR)

individualized education plans (IEPs)
    accommodations and modifications and, 96
    communication with families and, 97–98
    design systems and tools for, 184
    grade-level alignment for students with disabilities, importance of, 93
    grading and self-esteem, concerns about, 94–99
    grading students with IEPs in a general education context, challenge of, 93–94
    IEP goal planning and monitoring progress, 2, 3
    learning progressions and, 85
    principle that students with are general education students first, 92

Individuals with Disabilities Education Act (IDEA)
    disability categories recognized by, 12–13
    disproportionality and, 15, 16
    history of, 9
    legal and policy compliance and, 93
    resources for, 14
    response to intervention and, 17, 143, 152, 154

instruction
    fitting assessment, instruction, and monitoring together, 148
    focused instruction, 78, 84, 117
    guided instruction, 117
    need for strong instruction, 20
    specialized instruction, 10, 131, 152
    specially designed instruction, 94, 96
    targeted instruction, 70, 84, 85, 100
    unit cycles of, 146

intellectual disabilities (IDs), 12, 13

interdependency, ways to strengthen, 66–71

interventions.
See also response to intervention (RTI)
    early intervention services, 17
    learning progressions and, 84
    priority standards and, 80
    progress monitoring, 150
    summary of intervention tiers, 152
    time for, 147

introduction
    about this book, 3–5
    core concepts, 1–3

## J

Jackson, R., 112

Jakicic, C., 81

## K

Keating, J., 180
Kullar, J., 180

## L

labeling students, 20, 51
language shifts for talking about students, 173–174
leaders in context, 167
leading the way
    about, 177–178
    actively celebrating successes and attempts to make change, 183–184
    designing systems and tools to do the work, 184
    embracing hard conversations, 180–183
    envision what's possible, 177, 185
    learning about the change process, 178–180
    reproducibles for, 186–189
    summary, 184–185
learned helplessness, 110–111
*Learning by Doing* (DuFour, DuFour, Eaker, Many, and Mattos), 50
learning pathways, 83–84
learning progressions
    about, 83
    connecting to instruction and assessment, 86, 89–90
    and curriculum alignment, 85–86
    example protocol for connecting learning progression to assessment, 87–89
    and grade-level expectations, 112
    learning progression assessment information, use of, 90–91
    power of for students who struggle, 83–85
    and standards identification, 116
learning targets, 81, 83, 85, 90, 91
least restrictive environments (LREs), 138, 156
legal and policy compliance, 93
listening and hard conversations, 181–182

## M

"Management Be Nimble" (Bryant), 47
Many, T., 50
master schedules, 62, 69, 70, 71
mastery
    learning progressions and, 84–85
    standards-based grading to clarify expectations and, 95
mathematics common challenges, strategies, and resources, 135, 136, 137
Mattos, M., 50
Maxwell, J., 177
McMillan, R., 180
mission, 40, 44–45, 50
modifications, 43, 80, 93, 96, 116. *See also* accommodations
motivation and learning progressions, 84
multiple disabilities, 12, 13
multitiered system of supports (MTSS), 3, 10, 11, 144

## N

neuroplasticity, 109–110
New Leaders, 183
norms, 63, 67

## O

orthopedic impairments, 12, 13
other health impairments (OHIs), 12, 13
ownership and learning progressions, 84

## P

paraprofessionals, 68, 69, 155
parent involvement, importance of, 18–19
passivity, 121

Patterson, K., 180

persistence in problem solving, 120–121

placement and disproportionality, 15

planning.
*See also* STAGES planning process
- hard conversations and, 181
- IEP goal planning and monitoring progress, 2, 3

priority standards
- development of, 81–82
- as the focus of teaching and learning, 78–82
- Great Eight, 79–81
- importance of, 78
- standards-based grading to clarify expectations and, 95

processing disorders, 12

productive struggle.
*See also* destructive struggle
- advocacy and productive struggle, role of, 51–52
- attitude and, 123
- engagement and, 121
- expectations and, 112
- importance of, 110
- persistence, 120
- productive and destructive struggle characteristics and taking action, 120
- risk taking and, 122
- role of advocacy and, 51–52
- struggle and, 119

professional development, 18, 99, 114

professional learning communities (PLCs)
- collaboration in, 61
- critical questions of, 65
- pillars, big ideas, and critical questions of, 40, 44

progress monitoring
- clear processes and criteria, 150
- fitting assessment, instruction, and monitoring together, 148
- learning progressions and, 86
- priority standards and, 78
- process monitoring and record keeping, 150–151

purpose and shared perspective, 182

# R

re-examining the past, present, and future
- about, 9
- envision what's possible, 9, 22–23
- findings from 2002 versus our current realities, 17–19
- reflection rubric for raising collective awareness about who our students with disabilities are, 21–22
- reproducibles for, 24–36
- sense of urgency, 19–21
- statistical trends and realities, 10–17
- summary, 21–23

reflection
- feedback to support growth and, 98
- hard conversations and, 181
- learning progressions and, 85

relationships and interdependency, 66–71

representation and UDL, 118–119

reproducibles for
- asset analysis protocol, 74
- beliefs: mix, pair, share, 57
- class list reflection, 58
- collaborative activity: analyzing common RTI mistakes, 158
- collaborative activity: defining advocacy for students, 59–60
- collaborative activity: design a one-page RTI process guide or flow chart, 163
- common RTI mistakes, 159–162

conversations and activities for low-incidence teams, 75

disability profiles, 31–32

engaging in understanding and addressing disproportionality in our school, 26–27

examination of alignment: discussion and planning tool, 55–56

great eight priority standard checklist, 102

preparing for a difficult conversation, 186–187

profiles in perspective: understanding and supporting students with disabilities, 24–25

protocol for connecting the learning progression to assessment, 106–107

rigor audit template, 33–36

SCOOPS IEP planning tool, 188–189

simple as 1, 2, 3: the prioritizing process, 103–104

STAGES lesson planning template, 140–141

SWOT analysis for the master schedule, 76

team rigor audit process, 28–30

unpacking document, 105

resource allocation, 78

responding when students haven't yet learned

about, 143–145

clear processes and criteria, 148–151

common RTI mistakes, 151–155

core concepts, 2

envision what's possible, 143, 156–157

importance of Tier 1, 145–147

reflection rubric for, 156

reproducibles for, 158–163

role of Tier 2 and Tier 3, 147–148

summary, 155, 157

response to intervention (RTI)

common mistakes of, 151–155

flexibility and fluidity of, 155

IDEA and, 17, 143, 152

resources for, 144

responding when students haven't yet learned and, 3

RTI at Work pyramid, 145

statistical trends and realities and, 10, 11

Tier 1, importance of, 145–147

Tier 2 and Tier 3, roles of, 147–148

results orientation, 40, 44

*Revisiting Professional Learning Communities at Work* (DuFour), 41–42

risk-taking and resilience versus reluctance to take risks and fear of mistakes, 122

rumble, 180

## S

scaffolding

about, 131

gradual release of responsibility and, 115

learning progressions and, 84, 86

productive struggle and, 52, 110

tailoring the STAGES process with, 131–137

school culture, components of, 50

scientifically based instruction, implementation of, 17–18

SCOOPS protocol (strength, challenges, observations, outcomes, progression, and success criteria), 184

screening tools, 149

self, beliefs about, 168–169

self-advocacy, 93

self-esteem, concerns about grading and, 94–98. *See also* grading

self-talk, power of, 168

skill-development and learning progressions, 84–85

special education

disproportionality, 14–17

distribution of special education students by category, 13

eligibility for, 10–11

who our students with disabilities are, 11–14

specialized instruction, 10, 131, 152. *See also* instruction

specially designed instruction (SDI), 94, 96. *See also* instruction

specific learning disabilities (SLDs), 10–11, 12, 13

speech or language impairments (SLPs), 12, 13

STAGES planning process

about, 113–115

activity design, 117

common challenges, strategies, and resources at the elementary level, 132–133, 134–135

common challenges, strategies, and resources at the middle and high school levels, 134, 136–137

elementary STAGES example, 123–125

elements of universal design, 118–119

gradual release of responsibility, 117–118

high school STAGES example, 128–130

middle school STAGES example, 125–128

standards identification, 115–116

struggle, 119–123

tailoring the STAGES process with scaffolding supports, 131–137

thinking through assessment, 116

standards-focused planning, instruction, assessment, and grading for all

about, 77–78

core concepts, 2

envision what's possible, 77, 100–101

grading and reporting student learning for students with IEPs, 92–99

learning progressions, use of to plan the journey to mastery, 83–91

priority standards as the focus of teaching and learning, 78–82

reproducibles for, 102–107

summary, 99–101

strategic effort versus reliance on ineffective or random approaches, 121–122

strengths-based grading, 94. *See also* grading

students

beliefs about students, 172–174

labeling students, 20, 51

language shifts for talking about students, 173–174

principle that students with IEPs are general education students first, 92

what *all means all* means, 41–44

who our students with disabilities are, 11–14

support

feedback to support growth and, 98

learned helplessness and, 111

supporting students who have low-incidence learning challenges, 69

tailoring the STAGES process and, 131–137

Switzler, A., 180

SWOT analysis, 71

# T

tailoring instruction

about, 109–112

core concepts, 2

envision what's possible, 109, 139

reflection rubric for, 137–138

reproducibles for, 140–141

rigorous grade-level expectations, 112–113

STAGES planning process, 113–130

summary, 137–139

tailoring the STAGES process with scaffolding supports, 131–137

targeted instruction, 70, 84, 85, 100.
*See also* instruction

teacher quality and professional development, 18

teams.
*See* collaborative teams

Tier 1.
*See also* response to intervention (RTI)
importance of, 145–147
rigorous grade-level expectations, 113
summary of intervention tiers, 152

Tier 2.
*See also* response to intervention (RTI)
clear processes and criteria, 148–151
role of Tier 2 and Tier 3, 147–148
summary of intervention tiers, 152
Tier 1 and, 145–147

Tier 3.
*See also* response to intervention (RTI)
clear processes and criteria, 148–151
role of Tier 2 and Tier 3, 147–148
summary of intervention tiers, 152
Tier 1 and, 145–147

time and barriers to collaboration, 64, 65

trauma-informed instruction, 174

traumatic brain injury, 13

## U

unit cycles of instruction, 146.
*See also* instruction

Universal Design for Learning (UDL)
expectations and, 138
inclusive and accessible curriculum, 93
STAGES planning process and, 115, 118–119

unpacking the standard, 81, 82

upstairs brain, 174

## V

values, 40, 46–47, 50

vision/vision statements, 40, 45–46

visual impairments, 13

## W

Walker, T., 173

wellness/educator wellness, 169, 170

"what to fail" model, 143

*Women Who Lead* (Keating and Kullar), 180

### Yes We Can!
*Heather Friziellie, Julie A. Schmidt, and Jeanne Spiller*
Utilizing PLC practices, general and special educators must develop collaborative partnerships to close the achievement gap and maximize learning for all.
**BKF653**

### The Collaborative IEP
*Kristen M. Bordonaro and Megan Clarke*
Geared toward a collaborative approach, this book equips educators to write effective individualized education plans (IEPs). The authors break down IEPs to provide a practical working knowledge of how collaborative teams can create stronger IEPs, leading to more robust instruction and learning.
**BKG122**

### Co-Teaching Evolved
*Matthew Rhoads and Belinda Dunnick Karge*
As co-teaching becomes more commonplace, there is a need for change. This book walks educators through building relationships and creating an accord between co-teachers. Using a blend of research-based co-teaching strategies and cutting-edge instructional practices, teachers can learn to prepare their students to be lifelong learners in a dynamic world.
**BKG202**

### The ADMIRE Framework for Inclusion
*Toby J. Karten*
Cultivate an environment that creates successful inclusion classrooms. Use this framework to help strengthen self-efficacy and accommodate students with diverse abilities. Dive into evidence-based practices and strategies to assess, delineate, model, instruct, reflect, and engage the skill sets of all learners.
**BKG174**

# Solution Tree | Press

a division of
Solution Tree

Visit SolutionTree.com or call 800.733.6786 to order.

# Global PD teams
**Collaborative Learning for School Improvement**

# Quality team learning **from authors you trust**

Global PD Teams is the first-ever **online professional development resource designed to support your entire faculty on your learning journey.** This convenient tool offers daily access to videos, mini-courses, eBooks, articles, and more packed with insights and research-backed strategies you can use immediately.

**GET STARTED**
SolutionTree.com/**GlobalPDTeams**
800.733.6786